SCAMMED

Learn from the Biggest Consumer and Money Frauds How Not to Be a Victim

Gini Graham Scott, PhD

ALLWORTH PRESS
NEW YORK

Allworth Press books may be purchased in bulk at special discounts for sales promotion, corporate gifts, fund-raising, or educational purposes. Special editions can also be created to specifications. For details, contact the Special Sales Department, Allworth Press, 307 West 36th Street, 11th Floor, New York, NY 10018 or info@skyhorsepublishing.com.

19 18 17 16 15   5 4 3 2 1

Published by Allworth Press, an imprint of Skyhorse Publishing, Inc.
307 West 36th Street, 11th Floor, New York, NY 10018

Allworth Press® is a registered trademark of Skyhorse Publishing, Inc.®, a Delaware corporation.

www.allworth.com

Cover design by Mary Belibasakis

Library of Congress Cataloging-in-Publication Data in available on file.

Print ISBN: 978-1-62153-503-4
Ebook ISBN: 978-1-62153-504-1

Printed in the United States of America

TABLE OF CONTENTS

CHAPTER 1

RECOGNIZING AND UNDERSTANDING THE DYNAMICS OF A SCAM

Scams have a long history, rooted in the use of lying and deception to achieve an aim—skills that go back to the beginnings of human history and are even found among animals and plants. Such skills are used for survival and are based on basic human drives to achieve power, status, prestige, and love. Individuals use deception to win political office, gain military success, find a job, win a love interest from a rival, escape a threat, or for countless other reasons—strategies I described at length in several books on lying: *Playing the Lying Game*, *The Truth About Lying*, and *Lies and Liars: Why Sociopaths Lie and How to Deal with Them*.

While a scam employs lying and deception, it is usually a more elaborate scheme that involves a fraudulent business scheme or swindle[1] that is used to cheat someone out of something, as in a confidence game.[2] One classic example of a scam is the Trojan horse scheme in which the Greeks constructed a wooden horse filled with soldiers to gain access to the city of Troy during the Trojan War in the twelfth or thirteenth century BC. In today's high-tech age, this scheme has been updated to refer to a malware program containing a malicious code. When executed, this code carries out actions determined by the hidden Trojan and is typically meant to cause the loss or theft of data and sometimes to harm a computer or whole system. Like the Greek Trojan horse, this modern malware acts as a backdoor enabling the perpetrator to gain unauthorized access to the affected computer.[3]

In the United States, major scams have occurred throughout history, from the Boston Tea Party to trick the British and help the United States gain independence; to the 1921 to 1924 Teapot Dome Scandal, in which President Harding's Secretary of the Interior Albert G. Hall leased navy petroleum reserves at low rates to private oil companies without competitive bidding in return for bribes from the companies; to Bernard Madoff's notorious scheme to rip off investors with the largest Ponzi investment scheme in US history, defrauding investors of billions. And worldwide every day, scams affect millions of individuals, from counterfeit products and unneeded and overcharged auto repair and home repair scams to tricks at gaming tables and many more.

In turn, dozens of websites have sprung up where individuals can report all manner of scams, such as Ripoff Report (www.ripoffreport.com), ScamOrg (www.scamorg.com), Scam Book (www.scambook.com), Complaints Board (www.complaintsboard.com), Complaints List (www.complaintslist .com), ScamGuard (www.scamguard.com), and Scam Adviser (www.scam adviser.com). Still others are Hoaxbusters (www.hoaxbusters.org), specializing in Internet hoaxes; Truth or Fiction (www.truthorfiction.com), which includes the truth about scams, rumors, hoaxes; urban legends, and false stories spread by the Internet; and Snopes (www.snopes.com), which provides the truth about misleading information and has a page devoted to frauds and scams (www.snopes.com/fraud/fraud.asp).

As new technologies have transformed all aspects of our lives, scams have become more sophisticated, taking advantage of these technologies to create all manner of new scams, costing the victims and the economy ever more money. However, the basic dynamics remain the same—to trick someone by appealing to the basic motivators, such as the promise of money, fame, success, power, beauty, and youth, to get that person to take some action that benefits the scammer. Only later does the victim discover that he or she has been duped.

The costs of these scams are in the many billions of dollars. The National Center for Victims of Crimes estimates the annual total cost of financial fraud at $40 to $50 billion a year,[4] while phone scams cost approximately $8.6 billion a year and defraud 17.6 million Americans, according to a 2014 Truecaller/Harris survey.[5] Even earlier studies have estimated that scams cost the United States alone over $100 billion a year, with much of this due to the spread of the Internet globally.[6] In fact, the US Office of Consumer Affairs has estimated that "85% of all consumers have been deceived, defrauded, or cheated in some manner." Sometimes this deception comes from fraudulent emails, referred to as "phishing," which masquerade as communications from established companies such as eBay, PayPal, and national banks. In one survey, Gartner Inc. estimated that 24.4 million Americans had clicked on phishing emails in 2006, and 3.5 million of them provided the scammers with sensitive information, while the financial losses for phishing were estimated at nearly $3 billion.[7]

Presumably, the costs today are even higher, and the daily news regularly brings reports of even more sophisticated scams, such as phony IRS phone calls and emails advising individuals to quickly send a payment via Western Union to an "IRS" address to avoid potential imprisonment. Another popular con is the Nigerian email, which offers victims a high commission to help transfer money out of the country, though they first have to send a small amount for transfer or good faith fees. Or sometimes these emails ask the victim to send money to help a relative or friend who is in trouble in another country.

Unfortunately, the real costs of all these scams are hard to estimate, since according to a 2012 Financial Industry Regulatory Authority survey, more than 75 percent of the victims don't come forward. And still other studies, such as from the Canadian Anti-Fraud Centre, indicate that the $60 million a year in losses from personal fraud represents only 1 to 5 percent of the total, since 95 percent or more of the victims don't report the crimes.[8]

In some cases, particular groups are targeted for a fraud, such as the elderly, people seeking a roommate, job seekers, and others. A common scam involves sending an individual an email, purportedly from a family member, friend, or business associate, in which the con artist sends what appears to be a certified check and asks the victim to return an overpayment or refund via Western Union. The reasons for sending the money vary, but the check proves to be worthless and any money sent by Western Union ends up funding the scammer.

For example, in one scheme, speech therapists received an email asking for a price quote for helping a person in need of a speech treatment. If the therapist responded, he or she got a second email saying the person previously sent a certified cashier's check to another professional who is charging more, and so they want to forward the check to the therapist to prepay for the treatment, and the therapist should then return the difference. The scam is that the certified check looks legitimate but isn't, so when the check is returned, the therapist is out that money plus any charges for depositing a bad check, while any money sent to the scammer is gone. In another variation of the scheme, the scammer sends a phony check and subsequently sends an email describing a serious family situation requiring them to cancel a planned treatment, so now they would like the therapist to return their money immediately via a Western Union payment.[9] But here, too, the check is worthless and the money sent via Western Union is lost. More recent variations on this scheme offer phony roommates or jobs and require payments to refund money from a check sent to pay for a room or job.

Unfortunately, law enforcement attempts to stop the scams seem to be whack-a-mole efforts. Some of the most notorious scammers are arrested and prosecuted by law enforcement in the hopes of dissuading other bad actors, but this is without much noticeable effect; other scammers continue to operate and still other new ones pop up. An example of this difficulty is the major crackdown by the National Association of Attorneys General (NAAG) on telemarketing swindlers in 1998, with a special emphasis on targeting scams victimizing the elderly, funded by a $700,000 federal grant. The plan was to put 250 prosecutors and investigators into this fight using various antifraud activities, such as setting up reverse boiler rooms to call consumers to alert them of possible scams, tightening state laws to go after scammers, employing more stings—including having a repeat victim's phone ring in the attorney general's office—and using more forfeiture and fine penalties.[10]

Yet nearly twenty years later, telephone scams are as prevalent as ever, especially those against the elderly, though the particular natures of the scams differ. For example, recent news alerts have described a new round of IRS scams, directed especially against the elderly and recent immigrants, in which victims are scared by a phone call into quickly sending Western Union or preloaded debit card payments to an "IRS" address to avoid an imminent arrest, deportation, jail time, or suspension of a business or driver's license. Besides using fake names and spoofing the IRS toll-free number, some scammers even have an IRS badge number and can recite the last four digits of a victim's Social Security number to seem legit.[11]

Making it even harder to distinguish what is real and what is fake, some of these scam operators use sophisticated call centers that are run much like a call center selling or taking orders for legitimate products. For example, long-time journalist Shirley Streshinsky investigated such a scam after a neighbor received a call from a scammer posing as an attorney who asked for her help in getting her grandson out of jail after a bomb-threat hoax at a courtroom. Now the "lawyer" said he needed $1,950 sent immediately, and after she sent that, he said he needed another $1,950 due to court delays. After Streshinsky began investigating, she discovered that Montreal, Canada, has become something of a center for phone scams, including the grandparent scam, much like Nigeria has been linked to email fraud. She also learned of the Centre of Operations Linked to Telemarketing Fraud (COLT), which joins Canadian and US agencies in trying crack down on illegal telemarketing by shutting down the call center "boiler rooms" at the center of the scammers' operations. However, these are hard to stop because Montreal has twenty to thirty scam organizations that move around from apartment to commercial office space and back again every six months or so to evade the law. Then, after the scammer persuades the victim to send off a wire transfer, the funds go to different countries around the world, such as Spain, Ecuador, Mexico, and the Dominican Republic, where they are moved untraceably through MoneyGrams, Western Union orders, and MoneyPaks from Walmart. Eventually the balanceless commissions go back to Montreal.

As for finding the victims, scammers easily obtain them by buying lead sheets with lists of names and phone numbers from legitimate businesses, which provide data for company acquisition to clients like

Time and FedEx. Such companies are easily found through the phone book or online searching.

The scams work because the callers get people unnerved and worried, so they don't think rationally. They feel they must respond quickly to deal with what appears to be a problem, such as a grandchild in serious trouble who needs them to send money to save them from a terrible fate. In the grandparent scam, typically the victims spend between $1,500 and $3,000. Some have spent much more, even as much as $30,000, which one Seal Beach woman spent to help her grandchild. Scammers typically earn about $2,000 to $5,000 in an average week, $10,000 in a good week, and occasionally as much as $20,000.[12]

Another big problem has been fraudulent and deceptive ads and the glut of information in cyberspace, making it difficult to determine what is real and legitimate and what is not. Moreover, there is a lack of sufficient policing and punishment for offenders, while online giants like Google, Yahoo, and Microsoft provide scammers with an easy-to-use platform for carrying out their deceptions. For example, in 2011, in response to an FTC request, a federal court stopped Internet serial scammer Jesse Willms, freezing his assets after he allegedly obtained over $400 million from US and Canadian consumers. He duped them into responding to "free" or "risk-free" offers and then charged them for products without their agreement to buy them. But though Willms was stopped from selling fake diet products, he switched to selling information services, such as driving records and vehicle-history reports. He was able to resume operations, because scammers can easily use online commerce due to the lack of a law enforcement presence. As Crain observes, citing a January 2014 *Atlantic* story:

> Jesse Willms . . . provides us with a perfect symbol of the savage landscape of online commerce. If the internet is still in many ways a Wild West, seemingly ungovernable in its vastness, then people like Willms may well be its canny snake-oil salesmen, talking fast and hustling unsuspecting consumers in the digital equivalent of broad daylight . . .
>
> The internet continues to be "astoundingly under policed." Regulatory authorities like the FTC are undermanned; courts seem

reluctant to punish offenders, "and worse yet, even, the sheriffs we believe are imposing order online—Google, Yahoo, Microsoft—often end up providing scammers with a platform for deception."[13]

So why do victims keep falling for these scams? Stopping the victims from doing so would seem to be the first line of defense. However, there are so many different scams that law enforcement is overwhelmed and cannot do much more than pick off the biggest scammers. It is the equivalent of putting up some walls here and there to hold off a vast ocean. The obstacle of educating and dissuading the victims is that the swindlers use "visceral influences" of persuasion so victims respond emotionally instead of rationally. One reason that victims do so is the proximity of the reward in time and space and the vividness of the appeal. For example, some ads use well-known or easily imagined illustrations or show a person who is similar to the victim in occupation, age, lifestyle, or other characteristics who has benefited from the offered opportunity. Another reason is that certain personality traits make people more vulnerable to the appeal, such as social isolation, gullibility, and cognitive impairment, while other qualities make people less vulnerable, such as interpersonal information, skepticism, and scam knowledge.[14]

As Langenderfer and Shimp explain, a visceral appeal overrides the ability to reason and persuades the vulnerable victim to act quickly to gain the opportunity. Once the potential victim, or so-called mark, is located and targeted directly by phone or email or answers an ad, this prequalifies him or her as having the potential to be scammed. Then, as Langenderfer and Shimp describe, the deception begins by the con artist gaining the mark's confidence and garnering trust through "slick salesmanship that focuses attention on the promised benefits or rewards of the particular scam . . . Most commonly, swindlers appeal to the lowest common denominator of human motivations, with offers of money, prizes or wealth, and less commonly, miracle cures or sex. In any event, once the mark's confidence is gained, they must be enticed to participate and pay"; generally, the victim has to pay money in advance before receiving any prize, goods, or services.[15]

The victims are willing to pay because as Langenderfer and Shimp note:

> The skill of the con artist lies in justifying the procedure and convincing the mark to fork over their money. This is often accomplished by focusing the mark's attention on the reward being offered, while overcoming any concerns the mark may have about parting with their money before the reward is received.
>
> The scam operator must also justify the reason such an extraordinary deal is available in the first place. . . . Thus, a reasonably credible tale must be told that explains why a deal that is ostensibly something for nothing is truly something for something. This deception is at the heart of a successful swindle.[16]

However, while some individuals may be more or less vulnerable to these appeals, the power of the language used in these scam appeals can be particularly compelling. These same words can also be a warning of a potential scam to avoid, as Deborah Schaffer illustrates in analyzing Nigerian fraud emails; her findings can also be applied to other email and advertising appeals. For example, she points out that some common persuasive strategies involve "apologies, flattery, attempts to intrigue recipients, and appeals to greed, altruism, trust, and religious feelings," while writing patterns include using "attention-inducing buzz words like 'urgent' and 'secret' in both subject headings and in the letters."[17] Other appeals include subject headings such as "Confidential—mutual benefit" or "Very urgent business proposal," and key words such as "urgent," "business," "please," "assist," "help," "proposal," or "proposition."[18]. The scammers also benefit from using free, anonymous email accounts they can easily and cheaply access through cybercafe computers.[19]

Yet, while law enforcement has made little headway in controlling and getting rid of the scammers, the social media and search platforms have also done little to alert potential victims or stop scammers from promoting and advertising their scams, even though they have the ability to create barriers. For example, Google has begun to lower the rankings of piracy sites in their search engines or has taken them out of their search engine database entirely.[20] And most recently, the company has begun to take action to prevent terrorists from using their platforms to mobilize recruits and launch terrorist attacks, such as by disabling several hundred ISIS sites.

Likewise, these platforms could aid the victims of scams or reject the ads that scam them. For example, potential victims could use these search functions or check profiles on Google, LinkedIn, Facebook, or other social media platforms to learn who the advertisers are or what others are saying about them. Similarly, while D. Armano discusses how these tools can be used to check up on purported social media experts who really aren't,[21] these same tools can be used to investigate potential offers before making a financial commitment. For instance, by putting the name of a new product or company in a search engine or combining it with the word *complaint*, one can quickly discover if there are complaints or negative reviews about a company, which might undercut the appeal of a seemingly attractive offer.

Likewise, these sites that use a combination of algorithms and human moderators to distinguish fraudulent from genuine reviews could use these tools to distinguish fraudulent from genuine advertisers. While M. Learmonth discusses how sites such as TripAdvisor, Google+ Local, and Yelp use these tools to weed out the fraudulent reviews that companies use to build their businesses,[22] the same approach might be used to rate a company based on the number of complaints received about its advertising, much like the Better Business Bureau grades businesses from A to F in response to customer feedback. Just as Yelp has been especially aggressive in trying to catch fraudsters and doesn't display 20 percent of the reviews submitted, a similar approach might be used against scammers using online websites and advertising, so they are less able to appeal to vulnerable individuals who become their victims.

Notes

1. *American Heritage Dictionary* (1985). Boston: Houghton Mifflin Company.
2. Webster's New College Dictionary (2007). Cleveland, Ohio: Wiley Publishing, Inc.
3. Landwehr, C. E., Bull, A. R., McDermott, J. P., and Choi, W. S. "A taxonomy of computer program security flaws with examples" (1993). *DTC Document*.

4. Brenoff, A. "Study finds elderly scams cost twelve times more than previously thought" (2015). *Huffington Post, Ann Brennoff's On the Fly.* 2, 5.
5. van Cleve, Kris. "Phone scams cost Americans $8.6 billion last year—here's how to protect yourself" (2014). *ABC 7 News/WJLA.com, 8* (27).
6. Langenderfer, J., and Shimp, T. A. (2001). *Psychology & Marketing 18* (7), 763-783.
7. BCR Access. "Phishing in troubled waters" (2007). *Business Communications Review. 1,* 6.
8. Streshinsky, S. "Grandpa, I'm in trouble" (2014). *Pacific Standard 10,* 49-55.
9. Kuster, J. M. "Scammers and spammers" (2007). *The Asha Leader, 9,* 4.
10. BCR Access. "Targeting phone scams" (1998). *Business Communications Review. 1,* 8.
11. IRS. "IRS warns of pervasive telephone scam" (2013). *IRS 10,* 31.
12. Streshinsky, S. "Grandpa, I'm in trouble" (2014). *Pacific Standard 10,* 49–55.
13. Crain, R. "In digital-data frontier, scammers and hackers find pickings all too easy" (2014). *Advertising Age 85* (4), 1–3.
14. Langenderfer, J., and Shimp, T. A. (2001). *Psychology & Marketing 18* (7), 763-783.
15. Ibid.
16. Ibid.
17. Schaffer, D. "The language of scam spams: linguistic features of 'Nigerian Fraud' e-mails" (2012). *ETC 4,* p. 157.
18. Ibid, pp. 161, 164.
19. Ibid, p. 171.
20. Scott, G. G. *Lies and Liars: How and Why Sociopaths Lie and How to Detect and Deal with Them* (2015). New York, New York: Skyhorse Publishing.
21. Armano, D. "Separating the social-media snake oil from the vinegar" (2009). *Advertising Age 80* (31), 1–2.
22. Learmonth, M. "As fake reviews rise, Yelp, others crack down on fraudsters" (2012). *Advertising Age 83* (35), 1–3.

CHAPTER 2

STUDYING THE BEAU DERMA–REVITA EYE SCAM

The serious damage due to scams and the way scammers operate to successfully appeal to victims led me to look more closely at the dynamics of an especially effective scam. Through its ads, it appears to have the endorsement and backing of major celebrities and experts, along with supporting research, and these ads convince hundreds—if not thousands—of victims to sign up for what seems to be a no-risk, no-obligation "free trial." But in fact the ad enables the scammer to obtain the victim's credit card information and put through unauthorized charges, under the cover of a purported legal agreement that the victim unknowingly accepts upon placing a trial order for only a small shipping fee. Later, the victim discovers the true charges, which are the result of the victim unknowingly agreeing to receive and pay for a membership and monthly automatic shipment of each product that continues until cancelled.

I chose to study this scam and use my experience along with the complaints of dozens of victims as a case study. This scam—the Beau Derma and Revita Eye Scam—is one that initially drew me in as a victim. I was able to get back most of my money, apart from shipping fees, after spending about two hours going back and forth between the company, credit card company, and my bank. However, hundreds of other victims have lost hundreds of dollars, and for some, this loss resulted in devastating consequences because they were unemployed or living on very little income. These numbers are only for the very few victims who have registered complaints on the major spam report sites. Thus, it is important to look at this scam as a case study of how a scam works. In this way, we can help victims avoid being scammed and show potential victims what they can do to minimize and overcome the results of being scammed.

To guide this research, I used a pragmatic framework focused on the outcome of the research and finding out "what works" as a solution to problems, as noted by M. Q. Patton, cited by J. W. Creswell.[1, 2] Rather than using a particular method, what is most important in this research "is the problem being studied and the questions asked about this problem".[3] This pragmatic approach lends itself to choosing the methods, techniques, and procedures best suited to the researcher's goals, so that researchers can use multiple sources of data collection and focus on the practical implications of the research, as in conducting a case study. Among the main theorists contributing to this pragmatic approach are G. K. Rossman and B. L. Wilson, C. H. Cherryholmes, T. Murphy, L. Luck et al, and R. K. Yin.[4, 5, 6, 7, 8]

To gather data for this case study, I used the instrumental case method, whereby a case study is designed to understand a specific issue, problem, or concern[9]—in this case, the problem of victims being lured in and harmed by the company or companies advertising free trials of Beau Derma and Revita Eye. To conduct the study, I used my own case as well as the reports of several dozen victims on Ripoff Report who claimed to have suffered credit card fraud from these companies. While victims posted many of the same or similar reports on other complaint sites, the Ripoff Report had the largest and most comprehensive number of complaints. Since the complaints were similar, I chose to review a sampling of the several hundred complaints posted—about thirty-five complaints from the six-week period of January 1, 2015, to February 15, 2015.

In keeping with this method, I assumed that the individuals who described their experience were honestly describing what happened. Though there was some variation in the total amount lost, their conversations with customer service representatives, and the effects the fraud had on them, each reported a common pattern. Then I examined these accounts and my own for common patterns in the nature of the scam, the effect on the victim, and the victim's response after discovering the unauthorized charges on their credit card.

This chapter describes this case study of the Beau Derma and Revita Eye Scam.

How the Beau Derma and Revita Eye Scam Snares Its Victims

The Beau Derma and Revita Eye Companies have snared hundreds of victims nationally, and perhaps even internationally, and many of these victims have filed complaints in multiple places. Many of these victims have filed their complaints with the Better Business Bureau in Santa Ana, where the companies are based—or at least where they have a mail drop in the UPS Store, as the companies are not listed as having a physical presence at that address on Google Maps. The Better Business Bureau has given both an F rating, due to twenty-six complaints filed against Beau Derma and nineteen complaints filed against Revita Eye. There have been dozens of complaints against these companies on ScamOrg.com. Additionally, there have been 215 complaints against Beau Derma and thirty-one complaints against Revita Eye on RipoffReport.com.

These complaints are typically made jointly; even though they have different phone numbers for customer service, the two companies share the same address, follow almost exactly the same procedures, and have the same terms-of-service contracts. Given the large number of complaints, all charging credit card fraud and some additionally reporting damages due to the products themselves, it is surprising the owners of these companies are not under arrest, in jail, or at least under investigation. It would appear that this same scam exists for other products and has been operated by the present owners under other product names and addresses, including the following:

- Pristine DermaCare Anti-Aging Serum and Vitalita DermaCare Eye Serum with multiple addresses, including Hollywood, Florida; Savannah, Georgia; and East Sussex in the United Kingdom
- Revival Eye and Face Products in St. Petersburg, Florida, and Greenville, South Carolina
- Lifecell from South Beach Skin Care in Miami Beach and Hollywood, Florida
- CelloPlex Anti-Aging Cream and JuvaLift Eye Serum, and LifeCell All-in-One Anti-Aging Treatment, with a disguised website registration that doesn't list its true location and lacks reviews on scam sites since it is new

The basic scam involves advertising a health or beauty product online—in this case for an anti-aging product—Beau Derma—that produces smoother, younger-looking skin, and a recommended companion product—Revita Eye—that removes wrinkles around the eyes. These products' advertising claims that well-known celebrities have praised and endorsed the product, and there are pictures of celebrities and others before and after using the product. The primary market for both products is largely women thirty and older, since women looking much younger after using the products are featured in its ads. One of the expert endorsers is supposedly Dr. Oz, who allegedly recommended the products on his show.

I got involved, as other victims do, by seeing an ad, in this case on a Yahoo News feed, which featured some before-and-after photos of a woman who used the product. The ad copy highlighted the great benefits of the product, suggested that well-known celebrities used it, and claimed it was endorsed by major health and medical professionals, most notably by Dr. Oz.

The company also offered a "FREE" fourteen-day trial, which made trying this product sound like a "no lose" proposition. One's only cost was supposedly for the shipping—$4.95 for one product, $5.95 for the other—and the sign-up form recommended that one order both products, because they worked most effectively together. Supposedly a customer could cancel at the end of the trial period if he or she didn't like the product, with no further obligation. So, on its face, this offer seemed like an attractive one: at most the buyer would pay about $10 for shipping if he or she didn't like the product; if the buyer liked it, he or she could order additional supplies.

Thus, like other victims, I clicked a button online to place my order on January 11, 2015, to start the trial, and filled in the requested information that seemed quite standard—name, delivery address, city, state, zip, email, phone number, and credit card information. Then, to finalize the order, I was asked to click a button indicating that I accepted the terms of the sale—again a common practice by many companies online. So I didn't think anything of clicking this button. Nor did I see any link for reading these terms of agreement. When I later found the agreement on the bottom of the company website and read it, it was a ten-page, single-spaced document, and it seemed unlikely that anyone would find it or, if they did, would take the time to read it.

About a week later, two packages arrived as USPS-tracked shipments, which meant, as I later learned, that the "FREE" trial had only seven more days to go, since the trial period was counted from the day the order was placed, not from when it arrived. However, since I was busy with other things, I didn't open the package until about six days later, with one more day of the "FREE" trial left to go. The Beau Derma product came in a small, white jar with only the words "Beau Derma" on the side, while the Revita Eye product came in a small, thin, lavender bottle with ultra-tiny lettering on it—perhaps two- to three-point type, making it unreadable to the human eye. On opening the packages, I saw there were no instructions in either that explained to how the product should be used; one would normally expect such information with a medical or health product, such as guidelines on how much should be applied, where, how often, what results to expect, and any warnings about potential side effects.

But I never did get around to trying either product, because that night I discovered this "FREE" trial offer was a scam. Once I did a little Internet research, I discovered the same bait-and-charge tactics were used on at least several hundred other victims, and very likely more who didn't file complaints about what happened to them.

The realization that this could be a scam began when I checked my bank statement. I discovered that there were two payments—one for $85.95 for Revita Eye and the other for $89.95 for Beau Derma—on my debit card, posted on January 26, exactly fourteen days after my shipping charge payments were posted. I immediately called the companies, beginning with Beau Derma, to complain that I had never authorized this charge.

This call was the beginning of an extended debate with the customer service rep, who claimed I owed the money, and I began to realize how the scam worked. Among other things, she said I had received a thirty-day supply of both products, and I didn't cancel my subscription before the end of the trial period. So I owed the money for the product that was already sent to me, and if the subscription wasn't cancelled, I would get another shipment for the same amount in thirty days. At least she told me how to call back and cancel.

When I said I wanted to simply return the product, she said I couldn't, because it was after the fourteen-day trial period so my card was already charged, and I could only return it if I was given an RMA with an authorized return number. But because it was after the fourteen-day trial period she couldn't give me that number.

However, if I wanted to keep the product, she said she was authorized to give me a 15 percent discount. When I said that was unacceptable, she increased the discount to 33 percent and finally to 50 percent, which she said she could refund because I had had the product for more than fourteen days.

When I said that a 50 percent discount still wasn't acceptable, and that I wanted to return the product, which I hadn't even tried, she fell back to claiming I couldn't return it because it was after the trial period. When I told her that I would file a complaint with my bank and credit card company to reverse the charge, she insisted that I couldn't do that and that the company would win, because I had an iron-clad agreement with them.

"What agreement?" I asked. That's when she told me about the Terms of Service Agreement that was available on the company's website. When I said it was unclear on the advertisement about these terms, she said it was my responsibility to read this, and since I hadn't, I was bound by those rules. When I argued that these terms weren't made clear in the advertisement, she fell back on offering me a 50 percent discount to keep the product, since I was "a good customer," to which I said that offer still wasn't acceptable, that I wasn't a good customer, and that I would complain to my credit card company and bank. Ultimately, after about a half hour of arguing back and forth, she relented and said she would issue me an RMA, but I would have to return the product within fourteen days for it to be effective. I assured her I would return it the next day, and later I found an email confirming the RMA number she had given me.

But there was still a second product return to deal with, since the company made it more difficult for anyone to complain by having customers deal separately with two customer service reps at different phone numbers, even though the product was shipped from the same Santa Ana address.

Meanwhile, I became curious about these products and the company's very obstinate customer service person. I put "Beau Derma" in Google and later did the same for "Revita Eye." What I discovered was eye-opening. It showed the vast extent of this scam, as I read complaint after complaint with variations on my experience—first on RipoffReport.com, where there were more than 200 complaints about Beau Derma and more than fifty for Revita Eye. There were also several dozen listings on ScamOrg.com. Other complaints were on Yahoo and Yelp. And the Better Business Bureau in Santa Ana gave both companies an F because of the large number of complaints—twenty-six for Beau Derma, nineteen for Revita Eye.

The gist of these complaints was much the same as mine—the consumers suddenly found two purchases for nearly $90 each charged to their cards, and when they called to complain, the customer service rep gave them multiple offers of discounts to keep the product or told them they weren't allowed to return it because the fourteen-day trial period was over. In some cases, the victims had two or three charges on their card before they were able to cancel their orders and stop the charges. In many cases, people had given up trying to get a refund and complained of losing nearly $200 to $550 to the company. And many who tried the product reported that it had made their skin and eyes even worse by causing burning, peeling, and flaking, so they felt doubly victimized.

With that information, I called the customer rep at Revita Eye, who was even more difficult to work with and repeatedly yelled at me. Aside from giving me the standard line that the trial period had ended so I couldn't return anything, and that I was obligated for another shipment since I hadn't cancelled my subscription, she insisted I had a completely legal contract with the company to get these shipments. When I said I hadn't seen this contract, she informed me that was my responsibility, and when I told her about the 200-plus people who had complained about getting their card charged without authorization, she said they hadn't read the agreement either. When I said I hadn't even had a chance to try the products, she said that was my fault, too. Even my statements that I would complain to my bank and credit card companies and cancel my card had no impact, since she firmly asserted that I had agreed to the terms and conditions by indicating my approval online. Even my statements that I planned to contact the police and FBI about this big scam had no effect. She claimed that having a customer service person answer these calls indicated that this was a legitimate company. It was as if she had been well trained in what to say in response to every argument for a refund.

Ultimately, after about a half hour of arguing back and forth, I hung up frustrated. The next day when I called back and spoke to another Revita Eye customer rep to ask for the name of the person I had spoken to before, she asked me why. When I explained I wanted to know because the woman wouldn't give me an RMA and I planned to make a complaint to the police and FBI about what had happened, she did give me an RMA number.

Even so, since I had read many complaints by people who had gotten RMAs and still couldn't get their refund even though they had returned the product, I stopped further payments on my card and cancelled it. The next day, on Monday, January 26, I went to my bank to file an affidavit that the charges were unauthorized, and the next day I was refunded the $89.95 and $85.95 payments. However, in reading the complaints, I learned that the vast majority of complainants weren't so fortunate; they felt helpless and lost their money.

Upon doing further research, I discovered the Terms of Service contracts on both of their websites, and both contracts turned out to be the same ten-page, single-spaced "Terms and Conditions: Member User Agreement." Not only was it difficult to find these agreements on their websites in the first place—the link was in small type at the very bottom of the home page—but it was unlikely that any potential customer would read this agreement or even understand how this agreement, which might actually be unenforceable, made it clear that this was not really a "FREE" trial. Among other things, the agreement stated the following:

> By using, visiting, or browsing the Website, as well as placing an order with Beau Derma (or RevitaEye) through the Website, You accept, without limitation or qualification, these Terms of Use and agree, without limitation, to the terms of Our Privacy Statement. If You do not agree to be bound by these Terms of Use and Privacy Statement, You should exit the Website immediately. By accessing, using or ordering products through the Website, You affirm that You have read this Agreement and understand, agree, and consent to all Terms contained herein.

But what if someone doesn't see this agreement or read it? How can they be bound by these terms—and what legitimate sales company would expect a customer seeking a free trial of a product to read a ten-page, single-spaced document? The agreement goes on to bind the person to its terms anyway. As it continues:

> You manifest Your agreement to the Terms in this document by any act demonstrating Your assent thereto, including clicking any button containing the words "I Agree"; "Rush My Order"; "Submit" or similar syntax, or by merely accessing the Website, whether You have read these terms or not.

Following that is a Product Disclaimer that contradicts the claims made in the ads and on the website. The implication in the ad copy and photos is that the product will improve a person's skin as an anti-aging product, but the Disclaimer seems to be included to relieve the company of any responsibility for any problems caused by the product's use or by the company's failure to include any instructions for proper use with either product. As the disclaimer states:

> I understand the statements regarding these products have not been evaluated by the Food and Drug Administration. This product is not intended to diagnose, treat, cure or prevent any disease. . . . I understand

the information on this Website or in emails is designed for educational purposes only and is not intended to be a substitute for informed medical advice or care. I understand I should not use this information to diagnose or treat any health problems or illnesses without consulting my doctor. I also understand that Beau Derma is not intended to be used to treat any type of medical condition.

But in contradiction to this, the advertisement for the product promotes it as providing skin care and revitalization.

The refund policy also contradicts this being a "FREE" trial, since, among other things, the agreement states that the company will only "credit one returned unopened product per customer if the received package is postmarked within thirty days of the original order date and included with a RMA number obtained from customer service." But if this is a "FREE" trial, how can one try the product without opening the package, which makes it impossible to return anything once it is tried. And if the customer service people are trained to deny an RMA, this is another reason one can't get a refund.

Moreover, the contract makes it difficult to keep the trial from turning into a recurring monthly subscription, with monthly charges of $89.95 for Beau Derma and $85.95 for Revita Eye, because it is not clear until one gets hit with these charges that the fourteen-day trial membership begins on the day of the application and not when one actually gets the product. As the agreement states:

> You agree that if you do not send us notice of cancellation of your trial membership from the expiration of your trial membership terms, we shall automatically and without further notice: convert your trial membership to a standard RECURRING MONTHLY SUBSCRIPTION to Beau Derma Services, at the standard one month membership rate; renew your monthly membership to the Beau Derma Services for successive periods of one month each at the then current standard one-month membership rate, which on our auto-shipment program will have a new 30-day supply sent to you every month . . . .
> TO CANCEL AUTOMATIC RENEWAL AT THE END OF THE PAID TRIAL MEMBERSHIP PERIOD, YOU MUST NOTIFY

Beau Derma PRIOR TO THE END OF THE PAID TRIAL PERIOD, BY CONTACTING Beau Derma BY TELEPHONE.

But supposedly in the ad, it is a "FREE" trial period, and since people who place orders are unlikely to realize that the fourteen-day "FREE" trial begins when they place their order, not when they get their product, they are unlikely to discover they have a charge for these products on their credit card account or bank statement until *after* the fourteen-day period.

The contract then goes on authorizing Beau Derma to charge one's credit card using the information entered on the sign-up page, and unless one notifies Beau Derma of a cancellation, the company can continue charging one's card. In fact, there is even a clause stating that if someone fraudulently reports a lost or stolen credit card to obtain goods or services from the site or fraudulently reports an unauthorized charge on their credit card, that makes them liable to Beau Derma for "liquidated damages of $25,000." And further, this liquidated-damages liability doesn't limit "any other liability you may have for breaches(es) of any other terms, conditions, promises and warranties set forth in this Agreement."

Should someone actually read the agreement and want to protest the unexpected, unauthorized charges, this statement that one could incur a huge liability by simply claiming the charge was unauthorized might scare one away from making such a claim. Or it could give the company the basis for fraudulently seeking even more money from someone in court or as a settlement to avoid fighting a case in court.

Still other terms provide for the complete indemnity of "Beau Derma, its affiliates, officers, directors, shareholders, employees, independent contractors, telecommunications providers, and agents from any and all claims, actions, loss, liabilities, expense, costs, or demands, including, but not limited to, reasonable legal and accounting fees, which are not limited to Florida's Statewide Uniform Guidelines for Taxation of Costs in Civil Actions, for all damages directly, indirectly, and/or consequently resulting or allegedly resulting from Your use, misuse, or inability to use the Website, or Your breach of any of these terms and conditions of this agreement."

It was not clear at the time why Florida's law should apply, since the company is based in Santa Ana, California. However, I later discovered several similar "free trial" promotions for anti-aging products from companies based in South Beach, Hollywood, Boca Raton, and Miami Beach, Florida. But wherever the company or companies are actually located, it would seem that this provision is intended to protect the company and its owners from any claims of its being a scam. Moreover, there are even provisions that individuals agree not to "pursue arbitration on a consolidated or classwide basis," presumably to protect the company from the many individuals who have been scammed joining together in a class action against it.

Moreover, the company claims that it can change any provisions in this agreement at any time and that anyone agrees to review these terms and conditions each time they visit the website. Otherwise, "Your continued use of the Website following the posting of any changes to these terms and conditions constitutes Your acceptance of such changes." Moreover, in this agreement, Beau Derma (and Revita Eye in virtually the same agreement) states that it has no obligation to provide users with a notice of any change to this document.

In short, this is a contract that seems to be designed to enable the company to carry out its scam and protect itself legally from complaints that it is scamming consumers. But the huge number of complaints suggests that this is clearly a scam, and this agreement is merely a legal cover to further the scam and dissuade victims from pursuing any redress. Though I was able to get the charges reversed by my bank, and I was able to persuade two customer service people to give me RMA numbers to return the unopened products, the vast number of complaints by people who have lost money suggests that most people are taken in by the scam and are unable to get back their money, in many cases because they give up. And in some cases people experience dire consequences due to the money they lose, such as having trouble paying for food and rent.

It is also significant that there is nothing up front about the cost of a subscription to get these products each month after the "FREE" trial period. That information only comes after one discovers the charges on one's credit card and if one actually reads the Terms of Agreement. The victim simply discovers he or she is supposedly bound by a contract he or she hasn't seen or read in advance and then is presumably held to its terms. In fact, the contract specifically states the individual is bound just by clicking a button on the Website, regardless of whether he or she has read the agreement.

However, it seems questionable that this should be a legal contract. How can one be bound by a contract one hasn't read, when clicking the button doesn't provide the person with a clear explanation of what this offer of a "FREE" trial really means? I would imagine an opposing lawyer, prosecutor, or judge could see through this claimed contract and recognize that this agreement is being used to conduct a scam to charge victims almost $180 a month for two products, which come with no instructions for use and in some cases damage the skin rather than improving it as advertised. Surely this is misrepresentation as well as a massive fraud on hundreds of unsuspecting consumers.

I was able to get my money back after extended conversations of about an hour with customer service reps for the two different products, per-haps because I repeatedly insisted that if I didn't get an RMA to return the products, I would be filing complaints with my credit card company, my bank, and with the local police and FBI. Then I cancelled my debit card and obtained a new one, so my card couldn't be charged again. But other victims weren't as fortunate. In fact, most of those filing complaints described losing the money—sometimes as much as $500 to $600, when their cards were repeatedly charged. Some even reported bad reactions from the product, which came without instructions for use.

Despite all of these complaints on many scam reporting sites and negative reports from the Better Business Bureau, the misleading ads on the Internet have continued to persuade people to order a "free trial" of these products that are supported by expert research, celebrity endorse-ments, and before-and-after examples of past clients successfully using the products. Two months after my own experience, it does not appear that law enforcement has done anything to stop the scam, so the victims continue to accumulate.

So what makes these many victims respond to the inducement that leads them to become victims and give up their credit card information, enabling each company to charge them hundreds of dollars for a trial that obviously isn't free? And what enables the company to keep these funds from its victims, as well as elude a crackdown by authorities despite hun-dreds of complaints, including reports to the attorneys general and other

law enforcement officials in a number of states? Following are examples
of these victims' reports, to illustrate their common experiences and difficulty in getting back their money.

The Common Experiences of the Many Beau Derma–Revita Eye Victims

The basic experience of hundreds of victims who reported being ripped off
are described on numerous report-your-scam sites—most commonly on
Ripoff Report (www.ripoffreport.com), but also on ScamOrg (www.scamorg.
com), Yelp (www.yelp.com), Complaints Board (www.complaintsboard.com/
complaints/beau-derma-scam-c741861.html), the Better Business Bureau
of Santa Ana, California (www.bbb.org/sdoc/business-reviews/skin-car/
beau-derma-in-santa-ana-ca-17200923), and other sites.

The victims describe how they saw the ad for a no-risk fourteen-day
free trial of Beau Derma and Revita Eye, which were promoted as working well together, and they responded by providing their credit card information to pay for the shipping and handling—$4.95 or $5.95 respectively
for each of the products. There was nothing in the advertising to suggest
that there would be any further charges after this "free" trial, because
the website implied that if people liked the product, they would have the
option of buying more products after they had a chance to try it. But
otherwise there is no further obligation, especially if the language of the
offer states that this is a "no risk" free trial.

However, after getting the product about a week later, fourteen days
after placing their order, the victims discovered unexpected charges for
$89.95 for Beau Derma, $85.95 for Revita Eye, or both on their credit
card statements. These charges were not only for the products they had
already received: because they hadn't yet cancelled, they were also now
enrolled in an automatic membership in which they would get the products shipped to them every month, and the recurring monthly payments
would be charged on their card. The victims had no idea they would be
agreeing to an automatic membership and continued monthly charges.
Those who regularly monitored their credit card might discover this the

day the charges appeared; others might not know until they got their statement a few weeks later.

When the victims called about the unexpected charges, they were told that the free trial period had passed, often by a customer service rep who didn't speak English very well, and they would be told they had to pay. Some who protested were given various options, such as paying for half and getting the balance refunded if they returned the product, since they had already used a fourteen-day supply. Some victims were offered a discount of 15 percent, 33 percent, or even 50 percent if they protested enough. Some also obtained a phone number they could call to cancel their membership and future shipments; however, when they called, many were told they were too late to cancel the next shipment, so they would be or had been charged for another month.

As if set up to create more barriers to returning the product or getting a refund, victims had to separately call a customer service number for each product and speak to a different service rep. They also had to call another number to cancel future orders, even though both companies were at the same Santa Ana address (which actually appears to be a box at a UPS store according to Google Maps) and the products were advertised together. Moreover, the requirement to get an RMA for the return of the product placed another barrier to getting a refund, since the customer service reps made it difficult to get one on the grounds that the victim had called after the fourteen-day trial period. This barrier seemed effective, and most of the victims reported that they gave in after being told they couldn't get an RMA or after being offered a partial refund.

While some victims threatened to go to their credit card company or bank to get their money refunded (although one of the customer service reps I spoke to told me that if I filed a dispute, the company would win since I had agreed to a contract), it seems that most victims were not successful. Instead, after being persuaded to accept the customer service rep's definition of the situation, they simply conceded to being a victim and complained about what happened on one of the scam complaint sites.

Those who complained probably make up a small percentage of the actual victims, since it is likely that most people did nothing, given the careful set-up of the scam to seem legal based on acceptance of the contract by clicking an "agree to terms" button without reading the ten-page, single-spaced document—which gives the company a right to charge their card after a fourteen-day period for the products they receive, requires an RMA for any returns, and signs the individual up for a continuing membership with monthly charges unless cancelled. Normally people did not read or even look for a contract to read, since the advertisement seemed so credible and compelling in promising a no-risk free trial, and seemingly backed up by celebrity and expert endorsements, along with scientific research. A few people reported reading the agreement after they got scammed and were told they had entered into this agreement. They didn't realize they had agreed to it until after they felt ripped off and scammed by the unexpected charges.

While most victims reported being angry at being duped, whether or not they ultimately prevailed in getting some or all of their money back, many were also angry and frustrated by the hassle of dealing with the company. One of the many problems encountered was that it was difficult to call the number, either because no one answered or victims had to speak with someone who had difficulty understanding or speaking English. Also, many victims were frustrated with the long process of making a complaint to their credit card company or bank. And for some, the effects of the scam were even worse. Some who used the product found that it damaged their skin, resulting in burning, scaling, and flaking conditions; and some found that the high amount charged created a financial crisis, since they were unemployed and struggling financially. One victim even reported that these charges caused them to be unable to pay their utility bills. So the scam sucked in many lower-income individuals by the supposed risk-free "free" trial offer, with no knowledge of the high cost they would be expected to pay for the products.

While a few contacted their county district attorney or state attorney general and some wondered why law enforcement did nothing to shut down this scam, most did nothing—and it would appear that there was little law enforcement response, just a report taken and filed.

Some Examples of the Victims' Complaints

Following are some examples of the comments that appeared during a six-week period from January 1 to February 15, 2015, on just one of these complaint sites, the Ripoff Report. These reports come from all over the United States. Given that thirty-five comments appeared during this period, about 250 complaints would appear in a year on just this one site. In turn, these complaining victims are only a sample of a scam that probably ropes in thousands of victims in the United States alone, since these ads are pitched to an international audience.

For example, in the following account, Sue from Manassas, Virginia (January 2, 2015), describes the way the scam works, the company's legal language to make what they are doing appear to be legal, and the difficulty of getting a refund as a result of a lack of response by consumer service reps who seem trained to deflect customer complaints:

> A warning to all women/people who get pulled in by these companies deceptive advertising about their products. . . . What they don't tell you is that you will receive a 1 month's supply of product. . . . If you do not cancel your membership within the 14 days, you will automatically be enrolled in their monthly program and get charged $80 plus and $90 plus on your credit card and receive monthly shipments.
>
> This IS the kicker - you agree to the 14 day trial expecting to pay the mentioned shipping fees, receive your product once, and that's the end. . . . What you don't know is that the company sends you a 1 month's supply of the product to which you are entitled HALF (14 days' worth), which makes you financially responsible for the other half, or 14 day supply. . . . You WILL be charged for this!! . . .
>
> These companies both hook you by sending the 1 month's supply, to which you think is included in the FREE 14 day trial just pay shipping fees ad on the internet. . . . They allready[sic] have your credit card info from the trial payment, and the next thing you know is there's a whopping $80-$90 charge or charges. . . .
>
> They are deceptive!! They use semantics to stay within their legal limits, and so many of us have been scammed by this/these companies big, attractive ads to RUSH you your FREE trial/trials. . . .

I called several times to cancel, as a few of the customer service reps told me "the computers were down and a supervisor would call me back as soon as this issue was fixed and my account info could then be looked up." I guess they hope you forget or get busy and agree to this. I hung up with 2 reps and just continued calling the customer service no. again and again until I reached someone to handle my account. After 2 tries, the third rep took my info and mentioned NOTHING about a computer problem at the company???

Also, you MUST call BOTH different customer service phone numbers to cancel if you paid to try both trials!! Make sure you get 1 RMA for each item!!

They are really the same business, but they will NOT cancel both accounts for you!!

I hope something can be done about these falsely advertised products!! Go back to the websites and read the terms and conditions ALL the way to the END!!!

Others describe the extensive hassles with the company of getting a refund and then spending time getting their charges reversed from their credit card company or bank. In some cases, victims complain of having to cancel their card and get a new one to avoid future charges, such as Bev from Weaverville, North Carolina (January 27, 2015), who described her experience thus, sharing this as a warning to others. She also notes the use of an endorsement from a celebrity doctor who helped to legitimize the offer for her, though it is not clear that this doctor actually endorses it.

Beware of this company's offers.

My complaint about this company, Beau Derma, regards their 'Free Trial'. I am interested in a product that might work when I found this which was a link from a DR. OZ story, who should NOT hold any clout, in my opinion, after this 'Ripoff'. . . .

I was not impressed with the products. . . . I found this RIPOFF REPORT site with all these complaints. I read a few and then immediately called to cancel the product for any future charges. The representative I got had a heavy accent and was difficult to understand. I told her I was not satisfied with the products and wanted to cancel any future charges and cancel the sending of additional products.

She told me I had to pay $89.95. I told her no. She said she would give me a special rate of $23.95. I said no and asked to speak with her supervisor. She told me they were busy with other customers. Yes, with all the other complaints, I thought. I told her I would wait. She told me she would give me the best rate of $14.95.

I asked to speak with her supervisor again. She told me again they were busy with other customers. I told her I wanted the address to return the products which she did give me and told me I had to pay the return postage. I agreed with that (telling her) 'I guess I have no choice,' and she said I have to have the Merchandise Return # and put me on hold while she went to get it. In a minute I was disconnected.

I immediately called my credit card company to see it I had been charged and she informed me that after the charge was made I could then dispute it. . . . My credit card rep suggested I cancel the credit card immediately and then there won't be any way for them to make the charge. That is what I did. I would suggest that you don't order 'a free trial' because it is NOT FREE.

Besides the money they will bill your credit card, (and) no one needs the aggravation trying to deal with this company's customer service. It is unnecessary stress, lost time and money. If they do charge your credit card then call your card company and dispute it. A good credit card company should do this for you.

GOOD LUCK.

Other victims described their extensive haggling and negotiating with the sales reps to get the authorization for a refund, which in some cases ended up with them accepting a partial refund, just to cut their losses. Often they found the customer service rep had a foreign accent or difficulty with English, making it hard to communicate and get a refund. For example, Mrs. Parker from Mckenzie, Tennessee (January 21, 2015), had this to say:

I was just like you, was offered a trial size and BAM! later (I saw) this ridiculous amount charged of $85.95 and was told that the sale was final. I am LIVID!

The customer service rep [for Revita Eye had] a thick foreign accent, [but the] rep for BD . . . did try to appease the situation and offered to charge me only $14.71 for the product which is reasonable—verses 4x's the amount of $89.00. I accepted this offer because customer service goes along way, and he was not rude and nasty as [the] Revita Eye rep.

I sure hope that a lawyer sees this and contacts everyone on this list and files a class action lawsuit against these predators. What a waste of money but I must say, I paid the price for [an] invaluable lesson. Never again will I buy online!!

This is nothing more than an egregious online scam! An egregious online offer and making a lot of money ripping people off.

Sandy from Chattanooga, Tennessee (January 21, 2015), similarly had an extended conversation with the customer service reps before finally getting an agreement for a 50 percent refund. In her case, she realized she had been ripped off after reading about two different products under different names but with exactly the same advertising message. As she described it:

I ordered a "Risk Free Trial" of RevitaEye . . . [and] while waiting to receive the free trial, I was reading a news article online, and in the sidebar popup section was another ad for two totally separate products I had never heard of before, [and] this is where I knew I had been ripped off before ever even receiving my free trial. The other products I was reading about had the EXACT words, about the product, the EXACT same people who gave their reviews in the EXACT same words as the products I had ordered.

So I finally receive my products in the mail, and . . . I decide to call and cancel my free trail before the 14 days is up. The very first recording on the 800 number is 'If you are calling to cancel your free trial press 1' OK, simple enough, I press one, and the next recording say, 'Your order has been canceled, your credit card will be billed 42.95 immediately for canceling.'

Not acceptable to me, so I listen to the entire automated spiel thinking I will be given an option to speak with a live person, wrong! So I know that by pressing zero during any automated call gets you to a live person, so I do, only to be told that it's too bad, I ordered the "Risk Free Trial" at my own risk, and canceled it so they had charged me the $42.95 and that was that.

After a heated debate with said person, she said she would give me a refund of 15 percent, not acceptable, after then being placed on hold, she comes back and says refund of 20 percent. I then threatened a law suit, the BBB, and the Chamber of Commerce, and she asks to please not contact an attorney, now I have to go thru the process of mailing back to her the remaining amount of product from my Risk Free, Free Trial, pay for shipping again, and pay for delivery confirmation, and then I will be refunded the $42.95.

And besides this, I also ordered the Beau Derma, same story, same 15 percent and 20 percent story, and they say the two products are not owned or sold by the same company, but the return address is EXACTLY the same address. . . . I call FRAUD on these people, and I only wish an attorney would bring a law suit against them. I would be the first person in line to sign the papers!

In other cases, the victims simply gave up fighting and ended up paying the full or a half-price amount, though they were able to cancel future orders, block future charges, or cancel their card and get a new one to avoid further charges. Here are some examples of what these victims had to say.

From Helena in California (January 11, 2015):

Saw the advertisement on Yahoo. . .

This is what happened. It took 3 or 4 days for the product to arrive. Before I got the products, they have already charged me 89.95 and 85.95 on both products besides the shipping fee I paid.

This is totally a spam. The company just wants to get your credit card number and charge it. What a fake!

From Dee in Whittier, California (January 12, 2015):

I ordered a free trial of Beau Derma and Revita Eye. I only had to pay for the shipping. Absolutely nothing was printed concerning time limits, membership or automatic future shipping. When I searched the internet to discover what the actual cost of the products might be, I discovered warnings from customers saying that I had, without my permission, been signed up for hefty membership fees and ongoing, automatic shipping. Each product was around $100 dollars.

I called the company and first was told that my 2 weeks had expired. What two weeks? Apparently, the 2 weeks began on the day I ordered the product, and I was 2 days past the two week deadline for returns. Also, they had already shipped my second order, and there would be no refunds for anything.

I was allowed to cancel any future orders, but I still had to pay for the fees and products they were shipping to me. Also, I had to call separate phone numbers to cancel each product, because even though the address was the same for both products, they operated separately.

This scam has to be illegal. Who is initiating a class action law suit against these people?

Jennifer in San Antonio, Texas (January 31, 2015), described how she ended up paying half after being unable to talk to anyone about getting her money back.

Revita Eye and Beau Derma ripped me off. Instead of 4.95, they charged me 89.95. When I cancelled, its automated system cancelled me and supposedly my credit card. [Then], automated said for canceling they would only charge me 42.75. What a scam, can't talk to anyone there to get my money back!

Likewise, Marlene in La Quinta, California (February 4, 2015), ended up paying half and blocking her card to avoid further payments, while feeling fortunate to not lose any more.

This popped up after a link with Dr. Oz telling how Beau Derma used with Revita Eye really works. . . .

Upon receiving products a brochure was included stating if you are not completely satisfied call and cancel your subscription. I thought what subscription? I had not ordered anything but the trial. I called Jan. 31 to cancel and was told to press #1 to cancel. A recording said I would be cancelled but a charge of $38.71 would be added and I could keep the recent product sent to me.

The original order was Jan 23, 2015. The $5.95, $4.95, & $38.71 has been pulled from my bank account thru my credit card. I will call the credit card company to block any further charges. Maybe I am lucky to just have that much. This is the most brazen trial fraud I have encountered. Don't let it happen to you.

An anonymous victim from Edgewater, Florida (February 9, 2015), summed up the situation of getting scammed for half the amount thus:

> Their free trial was not free. They charged my account 38.00 right away. I was angry and cancelled my order without opening it. They refused to give my money back. They finally said they would give me half back. They shouldn't have charged me anything unless I wanted to reorder? 14 day free trial? What a laugh.

While most victims emphasized the fraudulent charges and misleading ads leading them to think they were only getting a free trial, some reported even higher charged amounts before they could stop the charges. And some victims experienced extreme hardships as a result of the high charges, since they were unemployed or did not have enough money to meet basic living expenses. But the customer service reps had no sympathy for their plight. Their goal was to charge as much as they could and keep the victims from taking any action to reverse the charges.

Mike in Atkins, Virginia (February 9, 2015), ended up paying $356 before he could stop the scam. As he described it:

> I was supposed to get free trial creams, just pay postage/shipping only. Received TRIAL packages. Then less than a week later, I have been charged $88.28 for 2 bottles then and $89.73 for two other bottles (trial size). Up to about $356.02 now.
>
> I did not catch the bill because I had ordered several things and paid for them in three payments. So, I thought that this payment was part of that; but it was not. . . . There was nothing on the websites about a free period for these products, just get trial ones.

Low Income in San Diego, California (February 13, 2016), found himself stuck with $561 in charges as a result of the company gaining access to a second card. As he explained:

> DO NOT DEAL WITH THESE COMPANIES, they should be decimated and their people charged with interstate fraud!
>
> I ordered free Beau Derma for $4.95 S&H, they sent me 2 samples and they charged CC #1 on 11/22/14 for $105 and $82 totaling $187 on CC#1.
>
> I called the CC and they reversed the charges and changed the # of my card. I thought that was the end of it but wait! there is more!!
>
> I was bill paying through my bank and noticed that this other CC #2 was still high and I had been trying to pay it (remember a totally different card). I went back in my statements and for sure I found 8 charges 2 on 11/22/14, 2 on 12/4/14, 2 on 1/3/15, 2 on 2/2/15 totaling $561 on CC#2.
>
> Contacted CC #2 and they changed my acc # and hopefully will reverse ALL charges and also they are launching an investigation.
>
> What I don't understand is how did they (the company) get a hold of a second card #????? Maybe Beau Derma linked CC #1 to my bank, (and) therefore (gained) access to all my 6 CC's information??? Really I don't know but, I am going to delete my bill pay from my bank and monitor each card directly with their bank.

Lynda in Dubach, Louisiana (January 5, 2015), on social security and disability, found her card charged almost $400 and found no way to call the company to stop the charges. As she described:

> I ordered Revita Creme, then Beau Derma Trials [for] s/h. . . . Nothing on website about needing to cancel service or anything. . . .
>
> On 1/1/2015 I was charged $88.95 and 88.75 from these first two orders.
>
> On 01/04/15 I was charged the same for the other order of items. All came from CA different city/different addresses.
>
> Now up to almost $400 charged my checking account and only the trials and no one to call to stop this. My Bank is trying to help me get numbers to call them. . . . What a joke. Today I really feel old. . . . I'm on social security and disability and now losing my utilities payments.

Rose in Montebello, California (January 17, 2015), similarly found herself stuck with over $170 in charges that she couldn't afford since she was unemployed, and found she couldn't talk to anyone at the companies to tell them that the charges were unauthorized and that she didn't want the products, which she originally was enticed into buying due to Dr. Oz's endorsement. As she explained, asking others for help:

> Dr. Oz was endorsing the products Beau Derma and Revitalize Eye. A free trial of the creams was offered, with a charge of four dollars and change for shipping. However, there was no mention on the advertisement of an automatic withdrawal of eighty dollars and change for each cream to be taken from my credit card.
>
> I did not authorize over one hundred and seventy dollars to be taken from my credit card. I tried calling the companies to tell them I did not want the products and that I did not authorize them to take out funds from my card but was unable to speak to anyone. They do not have a number where you can talk to a real person. I want my money to be put back into my card.
>
> I cannot afford them since I am unemployed and I do not want the creams. Please advise.

In another case, reported by Kat from Evergreen, Colorado (January 22, 2015), even claims of a dire hardship due to the charges were not enough to persuade a customer service rep to provide any refunds. Moreover, Kat's claim that the product harmed her skin didn't matter. The customer service rep refused to budge on giving her a refund, claiming her fourteen-day trial had expired, so too bad. Here's her story.

> I responded to an advertisement offering free samples of 2 eye creams that are endorsed by Dr. Phil. They said I would receive a 14 day trial and only had to pay $4.95 shipping and handling for each product, "No Commitments."
>
> I received the products (just products thrown in a package that did not look like the pictures I saw, no paperwork) and after 4 days of use, the skin around my eyes became very tight and wrinkly. These products were definitely not for me, so I packaged them up and sent them back to the company with a note proclaiming how terrible these products are.

Today, I checked my account balance and saw an $89.95 charge from "tryskinreplenish.com. . . ." (When I called the number that was displayed next to the withdrawal on my statement . . . I got an automated message saying, 'thank you for calling customer service'. . . . After being on hold for 15 minutes, and still not being addressed by a human, I hung up and redialed. This time, I got a human after being on hold for 8 minutes.

(When I asked) the customer service rep why they withdrew $89.95 from my account . . . the barely English speaking male said my 14 day trial had expired, therefore I was charged for the products.

I explained to him that I had just put the package in the mail for return because I was not satisfied with the products. . . . He went on to say I did not call the company and tell them I was returning the products and receive a verification code. Therefore my return is not valid. I did not see any indication that I needed a verification code to return these products on their website nor was there a package insert of any sort that could indicate this information.

I pleaded with the man and explained how I am a single mother with no money to spare and this $89.95 withdrawal from my account meant no food shopping for me and my child this week. I asked to speak to his supervisor. Here's the response I got. . . . "I am a supervisor, so there is nobody higher than me that you can speak to. We cannot refund your money since you did not return the product properly." I said, "You must have a boss and I want to speak with them." He said, "Yes, I do, but they are not taking phone calls, that is my job." I demanded to speak with someone higher up than him and he denied me, once again.

This has created a huge hardship for myself and my son. This company needs to be exposed for their lack of honesty and misleading information!!!

Not only did the victims experience the same unexpected and unauthorized credit card charges, which they dealt with in various ways—from getting a partial to full refund after extensive haggling with customer reps to filing claims with their credit card companies or banks to getting stuck with several hundred dollars in overcharges—but many had a very bad experience with the product which went beyond being dissatisfied.

Not only did the products arrive with no instructions for use, but some experienced very serious reactions, resulting in their skin looking worse—sometimes much worse—than before. Here are some examples of these descriptions.

From Jill in Sugarland, Texas (January 20, 2015):

> I ordered a free trial of Beau Derma and Revita Eye products. The company does not state the price of the product on the web site or in the package with the free trial.
>
> Within days of using the Revita Eye I started to notice bags under my eyes, then my eyes became itchy and dry. The skin under my eyes started to peel and it felt like I was burnt. I don't have sensitive skin and never had a reaction like this before.
>
> I called the company and explained I don't want the products and what it did to me. I asked if I can return the new shipment of products and get a refund. I was told my account was closed and I can keep the products and they are unable to accept the unused shipment back.
>
> I'm stuck with a trial offer and new shipment of products that isn't worth a penny. I don't know what kind of toxins are in the products this company is selling.

Willie of Houston, Texas (January 22, 2015), reported being able to cancel his order after he said it irritated his skin. He even got a confirmation for cancelling the product and was permitted to return the unused portion. Even so, he was charged the full price and couldn't reach anyone. As he described:

> After cancelling the trial orders . . . my credit card was charged $89.95. Unable to reach customer Service. After receiving and using the products, my skin was irritated, thus I called [the] Customer Service Return Department and cancelled the orders. I received confirmation emails of the cancellations (and an RMA number). The Customer Service Representative also instructed me to return the unused portion within 30 days of the cancellation and I did so. But they still charged me.

For some, besides the difficulty of returning the product or struggling to get a refund, the products' effects were horrendous.

Joyhope of Norristown, Pennsylvania (January 28, 2015), reported these devastating results:

> ... I really want to do a class action to sue the company so that they stop doing this to women. Now I have more winkles since my skin was peeled off and the next day the skin was burnt after I tried (the product) less than a week. ...
>
> [Then] the company ... charged me through my credit cards. When I called, horrible and rude people [wouldn't] pay me back ... [a] true nightmare that you don't want to go through again in your life time.

An anonymous victim in Naperville, Illinois (February 4, 2015), described a similarly horrible outcome:

> Biggest ripoff and my skin was totally destroyed. Bead sized rash on face and burning around eyes ...
>
> I googled [the company] after experiencing the worst skin rash in my 42 years of life and found out a lot of people had gone through this scam. I called immediately just to find out I had to pay $38.71 each to "cancel" the trial I was not even committed to.
>
> $90 out for the worst skin product that might cause permanent skin damage to my face! Had to cancel my credit card. Something needs to be done with this!

In another case, C Ryan of St. Pete, Florida (February 8, 2015), similarly reported a terrible experience with a product that couldn't be returned, because the purchase of the product had activated an unwanted membership. As this unsatified customer reported:

> I fell for an internet advertisement for Revita Eye and Beau Dermas' free trial. What a Scam!!!
>
> My credit card was charged 89.00 for each of these worthless products. Almost 200.00. When I called to complain about the outrageous charges I was told I had had 14 days and I hadn't canceled my trial.
>
> I tried the cream for the Revita Eye last week when I received the product. The skin under my eyes turned red and started itching. Just

awful. Even the trial is bogus. It starts the minute they charge your card so it's impossible to have a 14 day trial and cancel because of the shipping time.

They also refused a return because the 89.00 charges were now considered a membership fee. I wonder if Dr Oz knows this company is using his name to promote such an obvious money grab.

Why can't our government put regulations in place to stop this thievery. If you run into this site close it quick!!!

Dale of Henderson, Nevada (February 14, 2015), too, experienced a bad reaction, and to add insult to injury, he had to pay half the cost of the product, plus shipping charges. As Dale commented:

I fell for the free trial offer. I was willing to pay for the shipping costs, but that was it. I was then charged another $38.00 for the trial eye and face cream. . . .

Plus, after using the eye cream for approx. 5 days, my eyelids became extremely sensitive and began burning and stinging when I applied the cream.

This company is a sham and should be shut down.

Finally, a brief comment by Kelly of Austin, Texas (January 5, 2015), provides a shorthand summary of this scam based on fraudulent charges and often dangerous products:

Total scam! They will charge your credit card even if you cancel within the allotted time of cancellation. The products burn and are horrible. I trashed mine.

The Major Elements of the Scam

As my own experience and the previous examples illustrate, this scam is a powerful one. It includes the major elements of a scam that continue to entrap victims. Many victims overlook these key elements, so they get drawn into the scam, discover the damages after the fact, and commonly engage in a struggle to stop or reduce the damages. Most are drawn by the power of the initial advertising, which claims the support of expert and celebrity endorsements, so victims do not think to question the legitimacy of the scam. Law enforcement has not taken any action to stop the scam, despite months of reports, which enables the scammers to continue scamming. The scammers also benefit from using a number of product and company names and locations, so once one scam generates enough negative blowback, the scammers can easily change the names of the products and the company to continue the same scam under another guise, such as promoting other anti-aging products called Revitol and Dermology, as one victim, GLS from Kent, Washington (January 16, 2015), observed:

> I purchased the trial of BeauDerma and RevitaEye before reading consumer reviews. After reading multiple reviews and your site I became concerned. Investigating, I found that different products; Revitol and Dermology are presented in the same manner. All the products have identical advertising; text, same before-after pictures and the same testimonials. They also have "Dr Oz recommended" and the same "Trial" offer. This appears to be deceptive advertising.
>
> Since I read of the unexpected charges many people incurred, I'm cancelling my order immediately via my credit card company. It looked too good to be true and it was!

The major elements of this scam—which apply to many other scams—are the following:

1) An initial enticing offer, which can take the form of a compelling, powerful ad, to be discussed further in the next section.

2) A claim that the prospect will have a limited or no obligation, such as by offering a "No Risk" or "No Obligation" Free Trial that really isn't free.

3) The exclusion of specific information about the agreement to accept the offer, which might show what the prospect is agreeing to, such as Beau Derma's and Revita Eye's ten-page, single-spaced legal contract, which claims that the customer is opting for a membership with recurring automated charges and not just a free trial.

4) An easy way to sign up, which includes a seemingly innocuous "click" button to agree to the terms of the offer. These are actually specified at length in a hard-to-find agreement that most people don't read, since it has become accepted practice in placing orders on the Internet to click a button to accept the "terms and conditions" of a legitimate site or order for a product, service, or online subscription.

5) A lack of customer awareness of complaints about the product before accepting the offer, because the trial offer for the product appears legitimate due to effective advertising with expert and celebrity endorsements and purported scientific research support.

5) A requirement to provide credit card information, which the company can check by charging a small amount for an initial shipping and handling fee.

6) Barriers to getting a refund, which include these:

    a) A short time limit for cancelling the initial free trial, making it unlikely for victims to meet given the time required to receive the product, plus the stipulation that any use of the product means the victim must pay the total amount for it—or at least make a partial payment.

    b) Difficulty in finding a way to cancel an order or get a refund, such as a website where it is hard to cancel online, a customer service number that may not answer, long delays in reaching a customer service rep, and customer service reps who have trouble speaking English. Other hurdles may be having to call separate phone numbers for different products sold by the same company using different names, customer service reps who are trained to give reasons why they can't give a refund—such as stating that the trial period has ended, even if by a day—and claiming that the victim is obligated by an agreement he or she didn't know existed.

    c) The hassle of seeking a refund through one's credit card company or bank, along with the hassle of having to set up another credit card to avoid future unauthorized charges.

7) A product or service that claims to meet the terms of the agreement but is of low quality, and might even have negative effects, as in the case of Beau Derma or Revita Eye causing serious damage to the users' skin.

8) A lack of involvement by law enforcement to investigate the scam and stop it from victimizing others.

The Power of Advertising to Lure Victims

The secret to the success of the Beau Derma and Revita Scam, and of other products using a very similar approach, is its ads. These present a compelling case for why the product works. However, it is not clear from the ads whether the company advertising these products is actually selling the real product, or whether it is using the real product as a come-on for its credit card scam. Both products are available on Amazon for about half the price charged and without any kind of membership commitment. A search on Amazon shows that the Beau Derma Skin Care Treatment sells for $49.99 plus $4.49 shipping, while Revita Eye Anti-Aging Serum sells for $44.99 plus $4.49 for shipping. It may be that the company perpetrating the scam in Santa Ana and other cities is piggy-backing on a real product that has been used by celebrities and mentioned by Dr. Oz. He does not mention any products by name on his website. Whatever the case, these ads are designed to entice people to provide their credit card to obtain a free trial of the product, which makes them vulnerable to a credit card scam.

The ads are extremely persuasive; they convince individuals who become victims to click on the free trial offer, which looks innocuous enough. It just asks the person to "tell us where to send your trial" by entering a "first name, last name, address, city, zip code, state, phone and email," and if a person tries to leave the page, there is a dialogue box stating, "Do you really want to leave this page?" If a person puts in this contact information, he or she is directed to another page to enter credit card information for the small amount for shipping and click on a box indicating agreement to the company's terms and conditions. Lulled by the convincing nature of the rest of the ad, the individual clicks an acceptance, and so begins the scam.

What is so persuasive about the ad? A copy is included in the Appendix to illustrate. First, a typical ad begins with a series of claims that a well-known celebrity has used the product successfully, that a widely known doctor has testified to the great power of the product, and that this endorsement has been featured in well-known publications and news services. In particular, one of these ads begins with the comment: "You Won't Believe The Secret Wrinkle Mix That Jane Fonda's Been Using To Destroy Her Wrinkles in Seconds. Women Everywhere Are Using It Now!"—Dr. Oz. Then, the names of six well-known media brands are featured below the headline: Yahoo!, *Woman's Day*, *Vanity Fair*, *Time*, *People*, and AOL. Then there is a photo of Jane Fonda, with the image of the Beau Derma product in the background, along with the caption: "Can you believe Jane Fonda is almost 80 years old and without Botox or surgery!"

The copy then points out that other starlets use Jane's "secret wrinkle remedy," which is "excitingly effective, safe, and cheap!" followed by before-and-after photos of aging celebrity clients of Dr. Oz who used his "simple advice." Among them are Sandra Bullock, Katie Couric, Barbara Streisand, Ellen DeGeneres, Goldie Hawn, Demi Moore, and Martha Stewart. Then, the copy alleges that Dr. Oz has mentioned these two products that when combined "literally took 10 to 20 years off women's appearance in just a month. More shockingly it is safe, and costs next to nothing!" The miracle products he mentions? Beau Derma and Revita Eye.

Following this buildup, the ad briefly presents some scientific basis for the products' claims, illustrating them with photos of Dr. Oz discussing before-and-after uses of the products, which allegedly contain the two natural ingredients vitamin C and hyaluronic acid. In the right combination, these "work together to erase wrinkles and fine lines at the cellular level—below the surface of the skin—which is why they're so effective." Why? The ad goes on to explain that "Vitamin C penetrates deep into damaged skin and stimulates new collagen—a protein which makes skin appear plump and firm," which has become "all the rage in beauty circles." Further, the ad states that Dr. Oz claims that Beau Derma is so effective because it is one of the few products on the market "with Vitamin C in the right consistency and dosage." Moreover, the ad claims that Dr. Oz said that when combined properly with vitamin C, hyaluronic acid "literally makes your face look two decades younger in weeks!" How? It works by binding to moisture, since it can "hold up to 1,000 times its weight in water, making it an excellent natural skin plumper." As a result, it helps the skin "repair and regenerate itself after suffering from dryness, environmental stresses, or irritation." Then, the ad notes that Revita Eye is one of the only products—if not the only product—you can buy that has an effective concentration of this acid. The key is to use both products before bed, and besides these two ingredients, these products contain "all sorts of anti-oxidants," including Dermaxyl—"also known as facelift in a jar" and Ester-C—"the active anti-aging compound in Vitamin C."

Supposedly, according to the ad, the company put the products to a fourteen-day test with various subjects and used the story of Brenda's "fourteen Day Cell Revival" to show the great results. Instead of using a highly risky and expensive facelift procedure, she tried Beau Derma and Revita Eye, and the ad features illustrations and comments supposedly from Brenda to show the amazing results.

The Day 1 picture shows the wrinkles around an eye with the comments: "After the first day of using Beau Derma and Revita Eye together, I was surprised at how wonderful they both made my skin feel. It felt like every last pore on my face was being tightened and pulled by a gigantic vacuum cleaner."

The Day 5 picture shows much less wrinkling around the eye and the comments: "The lines, dark spots, and wrinkles—without question—were visibly reduced in size right before my eyes! I was astonished by the results, and literally felt 15 years younger again. It was like watching all my wrinkles and fine lines vanish right off!"

Finally, the Day 14 picture shows all the wrinkles gone, along with the comment: "After 14 days, not only had all my doubts and skepticism absolutely vanished—SO DID MY WRINKLES! The lines on my forehead, the loose, sagging skin on my neck, my crows' feet—even the age spots on my face had COMPLETELY disappeared. I've never felt or seen anything tighten my skin with this kind of force before, no matter how expensive the product!"

After this two-week period, Brenda claims that her skin not only stayed that way, but it continued to improve each day "until it became as beautiful and radiant as it was 20 years ago."

Next, the ad invites readers to try both products for themselves with a fourteen-day free trial, which is still available, followed by links to get the product with the lowest possible shipping price, followed by two more before-and-after photos of two women—one appearing to be in her late thirties or forties, the other appearing to be in her fifties—using the product, resulting in a transformation from a plain, even haggard look to the look of a woman in her twenties or thirties. As one of these women, Amanda Michaels from Sarasota, commented: "I wish I could have watched the Dr. Oz show earlier! The results were so shocking I couldn't believe it's my face. I look twenty years younger and I feel giddy like a school girl."

The ad then announces a special offer ending in a few days with only six trials available, and concludes with comments from a dozen people on Facebook who state they were very happy using the product.

In sum, this ad presents a compelling case for the product, featuring examples of celebrities who presumably used the product, a well-known celebrity doctor who endorsed it, a scientific explanation of why the product works so well, testimonials and before-and-after pictures of people who used it successfully, Facebook testimonials from happy users, and an invitation to respond quickly to be one of a limited number of people able to enjoy a free trial of the product for the fourteen days, which seemingly worked so well for others, like Brenda.

Given all of this convincing buildup in the ad, why would prospects think to question the validity of the offer? And why wouldn't they agreeably enter their personal information in a form, include their credit card information, and click on the acceptance of terms button without thinking more about it? After all, everything about the ad seems so legitimate and convincing given the key elements that provide this validation: the celebrity users, the expert endorsement from a well-regarded authority, the scientific explanation about why the product works, the before-and-after photos, and the testimonials.

One of the ads was certainly enough to convince me, as well as hundreds of others, who soon found they received a product that didn't work as expected, credit card charges they didn't authorize, and a membership for automatic shipments they didn't know they had agreed to by clicking the terms of agreement acceptance button. It was like the wolf in *Little Red Riding Hood* using his wiles to lure Little Red into a trap from which she had to figure out how to escape.

The Lack of Attention by Law Enforcement

Given the extensive number of victims and high cost of losses to these scammers, why hasn't law enforcement done anything to stop the scammers? Many victims even noted that they alerted their local law enforcement, district attorney, or attorney general. But so far there seems to have been no law enforcement response. Why? There would appear to be a number of reasons.

- Law enforcement is overwhelmed by the vast number of Internet consumer fraud cases.
- These consumer fraud cases can be very time consuming and difficult to prosecute given the large number of victims in multiple cities and states, involving multiple jurisdictions.
- There is a relatively small amount of money lost by each individual victim, meaning that for each victim, the fraud would be considered a misdemeanor, since a loss of $950 or more is required in many jurisdictions to turn a monetary loss into a felony grand theft. Altogether, the losses from the scam may be in the millions, but individually the losses are small.
- The company can claim a legal cover in its "Terms and Conditions Agreement" document, which the victim agreed to by clicking an acceptance button, even though the victims normally didn't find or read this document. This legal cover would presumably turn any claim of an unauthorized purchase into a contract matter, making it a civil case, although this cover might be undermined by looking at the totality of the circumstances, the many victims making the same claims, and the huge losses suffered by all of them.
- As is common with small theft and fraud cases, only a small number of victims have reported their cases to law enforcement, even though hundreds have complained on the spam complaint sites.
- On the surface, the ads look very legitimate given the claims of celebrity endorsements, the support of an expert doctor, claims of supporting research, examples of successful treatment with photos and testimonials, and real products that are available on Amazon. But the scam comes at the back end, when customers place their

orders and get products that may not be the real products and find themselves signed up for a membership for automatic payments of about $90 for each product, which they didn't authorize. Then, when victims call the customer service number to complain, the customer service reps make this scam seem like a legitimate business by claiming that the person is responsible for payment because they did not cancel before their trial period ended. Thus, for law enforcement, it might seem complicated and time consuming to prove that this relatively small transaction for any single victim is actually a scam.

- The perpetrators of this scam may be hard to arrest and prosecute, because they may be very elusive. The business address they use may be a temporary one or just a mailing address, and they may move from city to city or country to country. Moreover, it would appear that the same perpetrators are behind similar scams using different names and addresses, so they could easily stop promoting one scam to elude a law enforcement crackdown and promote something else with a different name and location.
- Without fully knowing the extent of this scam based on the true number of victims and the total extent of money lost, law enforcement, including the state officials and the FBI, may give this scam less priority than other scams or other crimes generally.

In sum, despite the extent of this scam with its many victims and losses of millions of dollars, there could be many reasons why it might not be subject to a crackdown by law enforcement. However, it is hoped that this report might provide added information and impetus in order to show law enforcement why it should take some action to go after these scammers. And perhaps this analysis might serve to help others avoid becoming a victim of this or similar consumer scams using other advertising and products as the basis for credit card fraud.

Notes

1. Patton, M. Q. *Qualitative evaluation and research methods* (1990). Newbury Park, CA: Sage.
2. Creswell, J. W. *Qualitative Inquiry & Research Design* (2013). Los Angeles, CA: Sage.

3. Ibid, p. 28.
4. Rossman, G. K., and Wilson, B. L. "Numbers and words: Combining quantitative and qualitative methods in a single large-scale evaluation study" (1985). *Evaluation Review, 9* (5), 627–633.
5. Cherryholmes, C. H. "Notes on pragmatism and scientific realism" (1992). *Educational Researcher, 14*, 13–17.
6. Murphy, T. *Pragmatism: From Peirce to Davidson* (1990). Boulder, CO: Westview.
7. Luck, L., Jackson, D., and Usher, K. "Case study: A bridge across the paradigms" (2016). *Nursing Inquiry, 13*, 103–109.
8. Yin, R. K. *Case study research: Design and method*, 4th ed. (2009). Thousand Oaks, CA: Sage.
9. Creswell, J. W. *Qualitative Inquiry & Research Design* (2013). Los Angeles, CA: Sage.

CHAPTER 3

PHONY CASH-THE-CHECK SCAMS—FROM ROOMMATE SHARE SCAMS TO PHONY JOBS

Another major scam that has become well known to many is the phony cash-the-check scam, in which the victim gets a check that appears perfectly legitimate as payment for something. But the catch is that the check is an overpayment or the recipient has to deduct some payment for expenses and send the money to the scamster—usually as a payment through Western Union or cashier's check from his or her own bank, so the payment is good. The catch is that after the victim sends his or her own money, the phony check is discovered about two to three weeks later by the bank. Then the victim not only has the amount of the check taken out of his bank account or owes that money if there isn't enough in the account but may now owe bad check fees. And sometimes there could be a criminal prosecution for trying to pass a bad check. Thus, the victim can be victimized again, and the scammers can be elusive to catch, since they commonly change emails, addresses, and phone numbers and are out of the country, making any kind of prosecution difficult. This is especially true when many victims only lose a few hundred dollars each, well under the current $950 grand theft threshold, though some lose several thousand in the scam.

While the basic principle is that the scamster sends a bad check and gets cash from the victim, the scam takes many different forms, offering different arrangements to different types of victims. One of the most common of this check scam is the offer of a job, such as becoming a mystery shopper, or a request from a prospective roommate who is coming from another state or country. The scenarios differ, as do the effects on the victim and the damages suffered, but the basic structure of the scam is the same. This chapter describes the different ways the scam has been used, the results, and what to do if you get offered an overpayment check and have to send back money to anyone before you know if the check is really good (which takes about three weeks).

Encountering the Cash-the-Check Scam in a Search for a Roommate

My early experience with the cash-the-check scam occurred in the beginning of July 2009, when I had been commuting for two years between a home I owned in Oakland and Santa Monica to get into the film business. I got a notice that my lease on my apartment wouldn't be renewed when it ended, as I was running a small business there. Also, I felt the monthly rent was too high; the economy had recently crashed, triggering the Great Recession, so times were tight. I figured I could only afford to stay in LA and continue commuting if I could reduce my rent. But rather than look for a much smaller place in a less desirable part of LA, I thought I could manage if I could find a roommate.

So I placed a listing in one of the online roommate services, which is like a Craigslist for roommates, where I described a little about my house and myself. I was very naïve about the potential for a scammer to contact me, much like many people placing these ads, so I didn't think to check any of the information readily available on scams at websites like EasyRoommate.com, which describes common scams such as the one where a "prospective roommate" sends a fake check as a deposit and proffers a reason to reimburse the person seeking a roommate for the overpayment. Initially, the scam is so effective because it seems like you have established a good communication via email or even phone, with the scammer posing as the prospective roommate. You think what the scammer tells you is true, so before sending the phony check and asking for some money back from it, the scammer builds up their appearance of being sincere to gain your trust.

For example, in my case, I opened myself up to becoming a victim of the scam by posting a message to make my room for rent as appealing as possible. It went like this:

> Beautiful 2-story townhouse near beach and downtown in safe, trendy, residential area, near parks. Has 2 bedrooms, large living room, patio, enclosed parking. The available room is the master bedroom with a private bath. Large living room and dining room area, plus a patio. Has contemporary style furniture in the living room, dining room, and kitchen. Amenities include a 36" TV and microwave. I'm open to providing the furniture or not for the master bedroom. Share utilities (ie: gas, electric) not paid by landlord. I'm looking for someone who is a non-smoker and generally likes a nice, neat, quiet environment, since I work as a writer. I'm frequently out of town for about 2 weeks a month, so you'll have the whole place to yourself then. No pets. Female roommate preferred, but a guy is okay, too. I'm open to a month to month lease of 2 months or more, and I have an 18 month lease, so this could become a long-term rental. Available July 1. My cell phone number is . . .

I went on the briefly describe how to reach me in LA and in Oakland, where I was living at the time. A day later, I got a notice that a prospective roommate was interested in meeting me. As the email from support at roomates.com read:

> Subject: You have mail . . .
> Hello changemakers,
> Good news! You have received 1 new message from a potential roommate.

At once I wrote back, sending some photos of my house, along with repeating the description. Soon afterwards, I got back what seemed like a long, chatty, and very personal response. Among other things, the prospective roommate, who called herself "Patricia Swiss," described how she really wanted a nice, private place with a "hygienic environment," so my place sounded perfect, and she described herself as a twenty-nine-year-old single woman who was Caucasian/white, Christian, and a Virgo with a wide range of interests. She even listed her favorite foods, music, and described how she bought African beads in Benin and traveled a lot, since she sold these beads all over Europe and the United States. Now she wanted to come to LA to open her own bead company, and she loved my pictures of the house and hoped I would rent the room to her, though she wouldn't be able to check out the place before she moved in on July 5. But if I could assure her the room was nice and hygienic, that's all the reassurance she would need.

In retrospect, I realized her statement that she was out of the country and couldn't look at the room before she agreed to rent it should have been the first warning sign that things might not be on the up-and-up. But I didn't recognize this, especially since I knew a man who had rented a room to a wanna-be actor from out of state and he didn't meet up before they signed the deal. That arrangement was fine, although ultimately the two didn't get along and the actor left after one month. But such roommate rentals without a meeting beforehand are rare. So this woman's willingness to enter into a sight-unseen agreement should have been a sign to be cautious. But back then I was so trusting, as are many people who get victimized by scams, including these check-overpayment-send-us-the-real-money scams.

So judge for yourself. Patricia's compelling message, which sounded so real to me, appeared in my email like this.

From: Patricia Swiss <patricia.swiss@yahoo.com>
Subject: Re: House for Rent and Photos
To: "Changemakers" <changemakers@pacbell.net>
Date: Thursday, July 2, 2009, 10:46 AM
Hi,
Thanks for your response, I'm really interested in renting your

room and I will be glad to rent your place. . . . I'm such a person who like a clean environment and privacy. I need an hygienic environment as I will like to live in a healthy surroundings. However, as i won't be available to come check the place before my move in date which is 5th of July, if you can assure me of the room been a nice and hygienic one (that'll be fine).

ABOUT ME
Name:Patricia Swiss
Age: 29yrs
Height: 5' 9'
Weight: 118
Body Style: Athletic/Fit
Activity Level: Active
Smoking: No
Drinking: Socially
Marital Status: single
Children: no kid
Zodiac Sign: Virgo
Languages I speak: English
Ethnicity: Caucasian/White
Religion: Christian
Education: MC SA/MC SE I'm a quiet and easy going person to live with. I do not have a pic presently on my system but will try to attach one to my next mail. My favorites are: My favorite cuisines:Barbecue, Chinese/Dim Sum, Deli, Eastern-European, Fast Food/Pizza, French, Greek,Indian, Italian, Japanese/Sushi, Mexican, Seafood, Soul Food, Thai, Vietnamese My favorite music:Dance/Electronic, Disco, Easy Listening, Pop/Top 40, Rap/Hip Hop, Soul/R&B and Soundtracks. . . . My favorite physical activities: Basketball, Working Out, Dancing, Swimming and Hiking/Walking . . .

However, I do sell African beads,i used to buy it in BENIN and send it to Europe and U.S.A for sell and i based in Spain but now want to be selling it to the states there and based there. I am into sales of Beads and i do travel alot and i normally come to BENIN to buy them in large qualities and travel over to Euro and Usa and sell. . . .

Right now i am coming down to open my own private beading company and thats means i will be staying there. . . .

I love the pictures and i hope you rent out these room to me.

I await your response.

Regards,

Your future roommate,
Patricia Swiss

Another warning sign which I didn't pick up on at the time was the use of the English language and spelling, which suggests someone who has learned the language elsewhere and whose use of language does not match the supposed high level of education indicated by the degrees supposedly attained. There was also contradiction between the more correct English in the first few paragraphs and the last few paragraphs, which suggests someone cutting and pasting things together. For example, there are some basic errors, such as the use of "i" instead of "I"; in the incorrect grammar and spellings, such as "if you can assure me of the room been a nice and hygienic one"; and the repeat listings of the favorite cuisines and music, as if they have been copied and pasted twice from somewhere, rather than an actual personal letter of interest. But if I missed these errors as being true signs of a scam, given my background as a writer, it seems like other potential victims would likely not recognize these warning signs either.

And so I responded as if this was a sincere response, and when I interviewed other roommate prospects who stopped by in case my prospective roommate changed her mind, I was less responsive than I might have been, thinking I really had a roommate who was about to move in. I even told one man who was eager to rent that I would have to let him know because I thought I had a roommate, and when I called him a couple of days later after realizing the prospective roommate wasn't for real, the man had found someplace else. When I called back a few other prospective roommates, they had found other places, too.

As it turned out, I didn't have enough money to commute back and forth between LA and Oakland anymore, but the experience with the phony roommate helped me decide to live only in Oakland and break my lease on the townhouse, which resulted in losing my initial deposit. But under other circumstances, this phony roommate scam resulting in my not finding a real roommate could have been financially devastating—as has been the case for many other victims who fall prey to such a scam. They not only lose the money they send to the supposed roommate or an associate, but they may lose the opportunity to get a real roommate—or they may lose several weeks in finding one, resulting in more financial losses. For some people in very difficult financial straits, this could mean ending up on the street.

In any case, after getting "Patricia's" enthusiastic response, I wrote back later that night to tell her that I could wait until she arrived on the 5th before I drove back to Oakland. I also let her know I needed a cashier's check or money order from her before she moved in, though she could bring it with her on the 5th. I also explained that I had "just moved in myself" and that the painters had just finished touching up the apartment so the "room is definitely clean and hygienic." I further explained that there was a new cabinet with long and horizontal drawers which would be "good for storing beads," and that there was a large bookcase she could use if she liked it or move somewhere else. I noted that she could do her cooking in the large kitchen and that the neighborhood was "a great place for hiking and walking." Additionally, I told her that I was involved in "all kinds of business networking activities, which might help you in setting up your business." I invited her to call if she wanted, so we could talk on the phone.

My detailed explanation, in turn, helped to draw me further into the scam, much as someone having an email conversation with someone they think is a real person might feel more and more connected by what they write. It's no wonder that people involved in email exchanges with people who are not who they claim to be can easily be duped into believing who the other party wants them to think they are—and what they hope the person will be—such as a real roommate who would be a good match, in my case.

Patricia's response of July 3 was even more warm and inviting. After a friendly "Hi again," she announced, "Here are my pictures," followed by four pictures in different poses. She was dressed casually in a sweat suit in three of them, and in a halter top and cowboy hat in another, as shown in the photos below. Rather than being suspicious of these photos of a hip, picture-perfect woman in her late twenties, I was instead relieved that she looked like a friendly, attractive person who seemed like she would make a nice roommate. I later discovered that these photos were lifted from the Internet and were the photos of a young, not-yet-discovered actress, which one of my friends in the film business pointed out.

That's one of the problems in these long-distance Internet exchanges, even when people put up websites that presumably indicate who they are. In creating photos, video websites, or anything else online, it is very easy to use them to create a fake persona to represent oneself, as the scammer did here, since people want to trust and believe that people are who they claim to be.

But as sociologist Erving Goffman has written in *The Presentation of Self in Everyday Life*, people create a public persona to represent themselves to others so they can appear as they want others to believe they are, just as others want to believe in this representation. This desire to trust is so strong, because trust is the glue that keeps relationships together. And just as relationships are soldered together by trust, so are communities and larger societies. But people who are good at lying and dissembling can create a false persona, as do sociopaths in creating a mask of charm that conceals the manipulative, guilt-free self that lies within. And on the Internet, people can lie and deceive even more easily.

This is exactly what happened when "Patricia" sent me photographs that showed her as this warm, cheery, friendly person, when in fact "she" was cloaked in the anonymity of the Internet and could be anyone.

Then, besides sending the appealing photos of herself, Patricia helped to seal the deal with her comments about how I would be a great roommate. Then came the details of the scam. After explaining that she was very happy about the rental costs, Patricia advised me that her travel agent would be arranging the travel for her, so I should deduce the excess balance after I deducted the one month rent, deposit, and cost of the airfare.

Plus she needed my full name, contact address, zip code, and phone number to prepare the payment. Making the arrangement sound even more real, she wanted to know the nearest airport so she could give me a call to pick her up. Or as she wrote, with her grammatical errors left in:

> I can see all the qualities I want in a roommates in you, and am happy
> to hear more about you, actually, i ll like to secure the room down before
> my arrival.

Moreover, I am comfortable and happy with your rent amount/ move-in cost, My client to forward you a Certified Cashier Check of $2800 to pay, from which i will like you to deduct 1month rent and deposit, fee for the place, and you will help me send down the excess balance after your deduction of the room fee to the travel agent, for my airfare to the apartment.

I will need your full contact details as follow,

full name

Contact address & Zip code

phone number so as to prepare the Payment

I will like to know the nearest airport to the house, so as to give you a call to pick me up on Also i my arrival at the airport.

Patricia Swiss.

After I responded with my contact information in Santa Monica and Oakland, along with my cell phone, the stage for the scam was set. I just needed to get the check, deposit it, and send her US agent the balance, which would be my own check that would draw the real money from my account in a day.

So, still believing she was actually going to be my roommate, I naïvely wrote back about how to make the payments to me and how to get to the apartment from the airport. I even arranged to stay until Monday before driving back to Oakland to get her settled. Then, with her payment, I believed I could afford to keep the townhouse and continue to commute back and forth between Oakland and LA. Everything seemed so perfect. As I wrote on late Friday, July 3:

Patricia . . .

The banks here close at 6 p.m. today. If you aren't able to make the payment into my bank, can you just bring the checks with you when you arrive. Tomorrow is the big July 4th holiday here, so all the banks are closed on Saturday and Sunday; but I will stay over to Monday, so we can take care of any paperwork then for the lease.

Just give the shuttle service at the airport the address below at 1007 5th Street. It's about a half-hour from the airport to here; a little longer in traffic, which will depend what time you arrive. Please let me know so I can have everything ready for you. I made most of the keys for you today; the rest on Sunday or Monday.

But, of course, "Patricia" never arrived on Monday. Instead, she sent an explanation about how she had to tie up some loose ends in her country before she could leave. But in the meantime, she was having her agent send the check before her arrival to me in Oakland, so she could secure the place. As she wrote:

Hello,
How are you doing? I'm so glad to hear from you. . . . Like i said the client who will be issueing out the payment said he can only send usa money order to you so you can just cash and deduct my rent from it. I m so sorry I have to tiding up something and i will be arriving on Friday but nevertheless you should be receiving the check soonest before my arrival. I need your full name, residential address, zipcode and phone number from you so i can forward it to my client to issue out the check to you.
Regards.

Unfortunately, without a real check from a roommate in hand, I could no longer afford to rent the place. Still thinking I could work something out, I suggested that she might take over my lease. Since the landlord had my last month's payment, her rent would begin as of August 1. Thus, her excuse of why she couldn't arrive worked; she still managed to keep the scam going by maintaining my belief that this was real, since to a victim, her explanation of travel delays sounded reasonable; though in retrospect, if someone suspected a scam, her response would be exactly what one would expect—an explanation to avoid a meeting by giving a seemingly logical reason for why it would not be possible to meet along with a request for contact information to send the check. The victim would cash it and send the real money to a confederate at a specified address. But still believing "Patricia" really did want to become my roommate and I could still come to the place when I traveled to LA here's what I wrote:

Patricia . . .
    Since I didn't hear from you about the 5th, I spoke to the landlord about breaking my lease so I can move back to Oakland, since I can't

afford this place without a roommate. If the landlord approves, you could take over the lease, and then pay me for the shared rental for this month, and I could either leave my furniture for someone else to take over my half or move it back to Oakland when I return. Your lease with them would begin August 1st. You might be able to find someone you know who would like to do this or someone you meet after you arrive here. They could take over the phones, everything I have set up. Or if you want to take over the phones from me, you could do this too.

It is a completely furnished office, with a futon that turns into a bed, furnished living room, and furnished kitchen. Then I wouldn't have to move all my things back to Oakland. I would love to be able to come back here myself when I can afford it . . . maybe in 4-6 months. Possibly we could work things out so I could stay here for a couple of days downstairs every 6 weeks or so instead of my going to a hotel.

I have an 18 month lease which I signed but they would be agreeable to a 1 year lease.

Then I gave Patricia the name and contact information of the real estate agent and indicated I would be in LA until about 2 p.m. if she wanted to call to discuss things.

I even continued to think things might still work out on my drive back to Oakland and wrote back to her with my thoughts around 3 a.m., after I arrived back at my Oakland house. As a result, soon after I got home, I sent Patricia another email, describing how I might leave my furniture there and help her find a roommate. I even suggested she could take over my roommate accounts at various roommate services (WestsideRentals, Roommates.com, EasyRoommate.com, and Craigslist)—though in retrospect, I realize these are the same sites where the scammers troll for potential victims. I concluded by explaining that she would be renting from me through July and then from August 1 directly from the landlord. I restated my hope that I could stay at the place from time to time on my trips to LA and I ended by asking her or her agent to contact me at my Oakland number.

But now, instead of addressing any of these possibilities, "Patricia" came straight to the point—letting me know her agent would be sending me a check from which I would deduct funds for the room and send the rest to the agent. Obviously, as I later realized, they had no concern for any upheaval they were causing in the victim's life. All that mattered was getting the victim to send a check for about $300 to their contact's address. As Patricia wrote:

> Hello,
> How are you doing? Thanks for all that info . . . i will like you deduct the funds for the room and send the remainder to my travellers agent at west Africa and you didn't give me any reply.
> Please get back to me with your full name, residential address and zip-code so the check can be sent to you.
> Thanks.

Again, I replied as if this was real, with my address in Oakland, since now I would be only coming occasionally to LA after July. Also, I reminded her to "call the real estate agent about the credit check, since they will need to approve anyone who takes over my lease." As an afterthought, a few minutes later, I asked in another email: "Patricia . . . Why can't you send me one check and your client the other?"

Meanwhile, as I waited for her reply, for the first time I began questioning the plan to send me a check and for me to deduct funds from it. Why not send us each a check for the correct amount? As a result, I began to finally question the arrangement. Was it real or not? On the morning of July 7, I sent a query to Roommates.com, since my ad there is what got Patricia to reply in the first place. I included a copy of Patricia's last email to me and wrote:

> Does this sound legit to you? She wants to send me a check and then for me to deduct funds to send to her client? Sometimes it can take a bank a couple of weeks to determine the check is no good and then the victim is out the money if they send out of the checks?

Even as I was, for the first time, questioning the legitimacy of Patricia's roommate offer, she had a ready explanation for asking for a single check, as she replied, with all her grammatical mistakes and typos:

Hi Again,

Thanks for your mail and question. Yes you are right about that it's jiust my client who me some amount of funds said he can only pay me back in usa certified checks and that the more reason i watch you and oprah winifred, also i saw you on CNN shows you are a woman with so much integrity.

I will be glad to rent a room from you, thanks a lot and yes the check will be sent to you on the following address . . . Oakland, CA 94611 and its to be issued to Gini Graham Scott.

Let me know if i m right about the details or not.

Thanks again.

Before I could even reply to Patricia, a support rep from Roomates responded indicating that yes, her offer to be my roommate was indeed a scam and they had banned Patricia or whoever she was from the site. As the rep put it:

Thank you for the information. Their account(s) have been removed and they have been banned from the site.

If you have any further questions, please feel free to contact me.

Erica

Roommates.com Support.

I finally realized Patricia had never been a real prospective roommate but rather was part of an elaborate scam to convince me she was, so she could send me a check and I would send the refund to her confederate's address. For a while, the idea that she would be my roommate had seemed too real and hopeful; and then suddenly I realized the truth.

It was for the best that I didn't find a roommate, so I had to close down my LA townhouse and stop commuting back and forth between Oakland and LA. The arrangement had been fine during flush times, but now we were in the midst of the Great Recession. However, many other victims of these checking-cashing "pay me the money" scams using the seeking-a-roommate ploy or other strategies to get payments from phony checks are not so lucky.

Even EasyRoommates.com was aware of these scammers and wrote up an advisory to those renting a room as well as those looking for a rental. Their explanation paralleled what happened to me—the scammer sends you a cashier's check and then you have to send back the overpayment, usually via Western Union, only to find about three weeks later that their cashier's check is fake. And in some cases, the refund sent can be much more than the amount I would have lost had I gone along with the scam, since sometimes a scammer may send a fake cashier's check for a full year of rent. The other problem after the scam is discovered is that you have little recourse, since the scammer is often outside the country. Here is EasyRoommate's warning:

Roommate Finder - 190,000 Roommate ads - Rooms for rent - FREE ...   http://www.easyroommate.com/misc/emailscam.aspx

EasyRoommate

Hi Gini | Logout
☆ You have a **Premium** membership

190,000 roommates and room for rent ads in the US
Roommates & Rooms for rent. Find your new roommate today!

Easyroommate > United States > BEWARE OF SCAMMERS

Stay Safe Online

We are dedicated to making your experience with EasyRoommate as secure as possible. Emails in your account removed by our administrators have been found to be attempting the below scams. Please read the text below carefully and discontinue communications if it matches the examples below.
Scammers behave differently if you have a room for rent or if you are looking for a room.
Click on the category that corresponds to your profile to learn more.

I have a room for rent
I am looking for a room

You have a room for rent

Let's say somebody wants to rent your room. They tell you that they want to send you a cashier check for a year's amount of rent. These checks are FAKE. Why? When you get the check, the amount is for more money than necessary. On the day you receive the checks; the scammer will contact you and request a REFUND for the amount of money that he/she "overpaid."

Or they make your life miserable (incessant calls, scary requests, etc) and the only thing you dream of is to give them their money back!!
The scam is this: THEY GIVE YOU FAKE CHECKS AND THEN WANT YOU TO WIRE TRANSFER "PHANTOM" MONEY BACK TO THEM.
Your bank will call you 3 weeks after they credited your account and tell you the check was counterfeit.

Some other notes about scammers:
- Scammers are usually outside the country and most often use Western Union. NEVER SEND MONEY THROUGH WESTERN UNION, THIS IS ALWAYS A SCAM
- Scammers will not only send you cashiers checks for a year - they will ask you to rent your room for three months. The check is then written for a large sum and the Scammer who sent it asks that the balance is sent back minus the rent and deposit. By the time the money is sent off, the victim finds that the check was counterfeit.

Example of Scam:
"Hi I am a very friendly and cool headed computer scientist from Lagos Nigeria, Looking for a person who is as accommodating as I am to live with for about 6 months. I am coming on my annual leave and intend to acquire some more knowledge while I am there. Please send me a mail and let me know your offer, I don't smoke, I drink occasionally and I'm neat. Mail me please..... Please get back to me as soon as possible. So I can send you a check for ($5,000). As soon as you have it, you deduct your amount and send the rest back to me via Western Union Money Transfer"

Scam Testimonial:
"I have just been scammed by someone calling themselves "Jane Timi". It was quite simple, she answered an ad for a room I had in Calgary, Alberta, and then said she was sending a deposit. However, the deposit didn't come, so she emailed and said her mum was sick but that the deposit was coming by messenger. A check arrived about the same time she told me her Mum had died and that the agent that sent the check had made a mistake and sent me all her money instead of the deposit and could I please send the balance to her so she could pay for the funeral and her plane ticket. I waited 5 days for her check to clear (the bank told me 3 days) then I sent her the balance. After another 5 days the check came back as counterfeit"

Conclusion:
- Never send money back to any body before you make sure that the check you have received is real and the money is in your account (3 WEEKS).

For many, beyond the loss of funds and the time spent in corresponding with an invented persona to carry out the scam, far greater damages can occur due to planning for arrangements that don't happen, losing opportunities from other legitimate roommates, and lacking the income to pay for needed roommates, such as food, utility bills, and rent. Then, too, one can feel the humiliation and loss of self-assurance that comes with realizing one has been duped, even after finding out that many hundreds of others have fallen for the scheme.

So it was for me, though I decided to play along for a little while to see if I got a check, determine that it was false, and report the scheme to the FBI. Patricia did not disappoint. Three days later, on July 13, I heard from her again, when she wrote to confirm that she was sending the money and asked me to send the information printed on the receipt. She closed with a personal note about how she was leaving on the 15th, would arrive on the 16th, wanted me to pick her up at the LA Airport, and would be packing her bags the next day, July 14. Had I not already realized this was all a scam, her friendly message would have sounded so reassuring and would have provided just enough time for the recipient of the check to cash it and send out the money order by Western Union transfer, before discovering that she wasn't going to show up at the LA Airport at the time her flight was supposed to arrive, if ever.

In her follow-up email that day, she reported that the check to me had been delivered at 10:24 a.m. in Oakland via UPS Next Day Air on Saturday the 11th at the front desk where a clerk Guevonia had signed for it. She even gave me the tracking number, so at least that was real. Then, in her final email to me, along with the details about her arrival, packing, and pick-up (which I couldn't make anyway, since I was now in Oakland), she asked me to get her the details after I sent the amount of overpayment to her. As she wrote:

Hello again . . .

I am glad that all is working fine and i will be real reliefed if you get things done as soon as you deposit the funds today. My traveling agent Michael Ade said that i can still get a seat with the Continental Flight 74 and we will change London onto Houston . . . and arrive in Los Angeles at 5:30 a.m. . . . .

After sending the money via western union money transfer get to me with the details below that's upon the receipt.

1. 8 digit reference Number upon the receipt.

2. exact amount sent

3. sender's name and address which is you.

I will be leaving here on Wednesday and arrive on thursday that's why i need to know my seat reservation number before tuesday.

I hope you will be available to come pick me up at the (CA) Los Angeles Intl Airport (LAX) at 4:30 p.m. Kindly send asap cos i will not want to miss that flight. I will start filling up my bags tomorrow. Keep me posted and I hope all is well with you too.

Bye for now and reply,

Patricia Swiss.

Soon after I arrived home in Oakland on Monday, the 13th, I found the check waiting for me—supposedly a cashier's check drawn on the Washington Mutual Bank in Las Vegas, remitted by Michael Miller and sent to me by Patty Allen in Long Beach on July 10, 2009, for $2,850, from which I was supposed to send back $800.

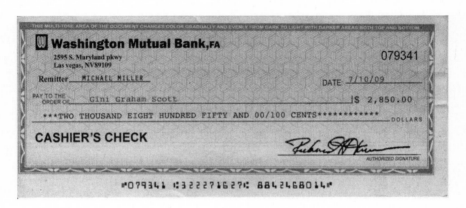

The check might look real enough that some banks might take it, even though the authorized signature was not the same as the remitter, because often tellers are in a rush to process the deposits of many customers and don't look too carefully. But about two to three weeks later, the bank's back office will recognize fraudulent checks. However, in this case, I already was certain the check was a fraud, especially since the Washington Mutual Bank had recently been taken over by the Bank of the West. I went to one of the Bank of the West brokers, who quickly confirmed that this was a fake check. Soon after that I contacted the San Francisco and Oakland Offices of the FBI, who referred me to the Internet Crime Complaint Center, with whom I filed a Complaint Referral form describing the check and the various names that might be involved, including "Patricia Swiss," "Michael Miller," or "Patty Allen," the person to whom I was supposed to send the refund via Western Union, and Patricia's email address, one of the many free ones available in minutes through Yahoo. Though I suggested that "Patricia" might be part of a group that was scamming a lot of different people and indicated I would like to cooperate with the FBI and had kept copies of all my correspondence and a check, since "I would like to help you in pursuing these people who are likely to be preying on others," in the end, I just got a thank-you notice for filing a complaint with the Internet Crime Complaint Center and a copy of the complaint I had filed to review for accuracy. So that was the end of any further action on this complaint or any information to me about what happened, since the IC3 (Internet Crime Complaint Center) is so overwhelmed by complaints they have no way to keep those filing complaints informed. Here is the a form letter sent back to me:

Complaint Referral Form
Internet Crime Complaint Center

Thank you for filing a complaint with the Internet Crime Complaint Center (IC3).

Your complaint has been submitted. Once processed by the IC3, you will be sent an email containing your complaint id and password to be used for future contacts with the IC3. This process can take several hours.

The IC3's mission is to serve as a vehicle to receive, develop, and refer criminal complaints regarding the rapidly expanding arena of cyber crime. The IC3 aims to give the victims of cyber crime a convenient and easy-to-use reporting mechanism. If you have comments or problems related to the IC3 website, please contact us.

Complaint Status

The IC3 receives thousands of complaints each month and does not have the resources to respond to inquiries regarding the status of complaints. It is the IC3's intention to review all complaints and refer them to law enforcement and regulatory agencies having jurisdiction. Ultimately, investigation and prosecution are at the discretion of the receiving agencies.

Evidence

It is important that you maintain any evidence you may have relating to your complaint. Evidence may include canceled checks, credit card receipts, phone bills, mailing envelopes, mail receipts, a printed copy of a website, copies of emails, or similar items. Please keep the items in a safe location, in case you are requested to provide them for investigative purposes.

Unfortunately, there is little a victim can do once scammed to redress any harm except file an affidavit of fraud with their bank to see if they can at least not be held criminally responsible for the bad check. But any money they sent to the scammers via Western Union or other money transfer service is irretrievably gone. And if they suffered any other damages due to their lost income, such as being unable to pay the rent or mortgage, there is little compensation for that either.

Thus, the best way to deal with the phony roommate/phony check scam is to be alert in the first place and avoid corresponding or accepting and cashing a fake check and sending one's own money to the scammer.

So how does this phony rental scam affect others? And how else do the scammers use the check payment scam to get money? The following sections describe what I learned as I later looked into these scams.

The Anatomy of the Phony Roommate Scam

As I discovered after my encounter with the phony roommate scam, it is quite pervasive and it targets individuals advertizing for a roommate on various online sites, such as Craigslist, Roommates.com, and EasyRoomates.com. It also targets an especially vulnerable population, people looking for a roommate, because they are struggling financially and can't afford to pay the full cost of the rent on their own. While some roommate seekers catch on—because they notice red flags in their email correspondence, are warned by a helpful banker about their phony check, or discover one of the roommate scam sites on the Internet—many others fall victim. This large number of victims is reflected in the continuing practice of the scam from at least back to 2007, when I found a complaint from one individual who escaped the scam, as reported on Ripoff Report (www.ripoffreport.com).

The results of the scam on the victims can be devastating. First off, they are struggling financially, which is why they are seeking a roommate. Then they lose the money they send to the scamster or a confederate, ranging from about $300 to $2,000, because the scamster gives them some reason the check sent to them is an overpayment, so they have to send their own money as a refund. Plus they have check charges on their returned check, and in some cases, they may find themselves under investigation for trying to pass a bad check.

To make matters worse, their involvement with a phony roommate means they haven't arranged to rent their room to a real roommate, so not only may this delay them in getting a roommate, but they lose the rent they might have gotten from this roommate. Moreover, they may find that the window for getting a roommate has passed, so they may not be able to find someone, which is what happened to me. Though I didn't actually lose any money, I gave up the possibility of getting a real roommate in time to afford to stay in my place in LA, which could have been a disaster had I had a job or other reason to stay there. In my case, the failure to get a roommate turned out to be an advantage, since it was better I go back to Oakland for good at the time. But for many people, having to leave a place because they can't find a roommate can put them in a serious financial bind and destroy job opportunities. As a result, they can end up having to pay moving expenses they may not be able to afford, quickly find a cheaper, smaller place in a less desirable location, and get rid of furniture and property because they no longer have room for it in their new place. Then, too, they may get stuck with the costs and penalties of breaking a lease, and in some cases, victims can even end up homeless after they are evicted, because they can't pay the rent.

The basic structure of the roommate scam is similar from victim to victim, although the specific details in the scammers' stories differ. This scam also has many parallels with the phony job scam, because the underlying mechanism of the scam involves sending a phony check that includes an overpayment requiring the victim to send in a real payment to the scammer. But otherwise, the type of victim, story, acts the victim must do, and the effects on the victim differ greatly, as described in the next section.

The way the scam works is this: First, the victim places an ad on one of the roommate ad sites describing him or herself, the place for rent, the cost, and other expectations about the roommate (such as age, sex, type of person, etc.). Usually the victim also uploads some pictures to indicate what the apartment or house looks like, and some photos may show the neighborhood, too.

Then the scammer responds with an email expressing interest in the place, and usually this initial email is followed by email exchanges between the renter and prospective roommate in which they share information about each other. In a real prospective roommate situation, the two might talk on the phone. Then, if still interested, the prospective roommate comes over and looks at the place; there is some discussion about what the roommate wants and how this place may satisfy that need, and how the roommates will fit together in terms of their lifestyle.

For example, a typical conversation may bring up interests, concerns about the place being neat and quiet, whether the roommate will be working or spending much time at the place or not, and so on. Then, each party assesses how well the roommate arrangement will work. If the potential for a match seems good and the prospective roommate is comfortable with the financial arrangements, including how to share utilities, the roommate seeker will ask the prospect to fill out an agreement form, and thereafter may check some references. After that, if all systems are go, the prospective roommate will pay a deposit—commonly the first month and last month—get the keys, and move in when he or she is ready, a process that usually takes two or three days.

But with the roommate scam, none of that happens. Instead, the scammer quickly comes to the point of the scam—he or she thinks the place would be ideal, but can't view it personally for some reason—usually because he or she is traveling, lives in a distant location, or is very busy right now, such as for a work assignment. But that inability to see the place now doesn't matter; the prospective roommate feels the photos of the place and your description of it are sufficient to decide that you would be the perfect roommate.

The prospective roommate also provides an extensive bio and description of lifestyle and interests to show why he or she would be a good roommate for you, as well as an explanation of how someone else will be sending the payment to you. In my case, Patricia claimed she was traveling from Benin selling art objects and had a travel agent who was handling the arrangements. In other cases, it is the person's parent who will send the funds, such as in the roommate scams involving someone coming to the United States to attend school—and here the target may be another college student.

Next comes the explanation of why the payment being sent to the victim is too large, so that the victim is asked to send a refund from this much larger check. In some cases, a mistake leads to the overpayment; in other cases, the extra money is to cover the prospective roommate's expenses of shipping furniture or a car overseas. Sometimes the additional payment is for a travel agent or business associate that set up the trip, and there is commonly some urgency about the victim sending the funds right away.

There is additionally some explanation of how the victim should send the money—generally by payment through Western Union, which is untraceable, though sometimes the victim can send a cashier's check from his or her bank, which is what I was requested to do.

Then, even if the victim has not made a decision, the check usually goes out and arrives the next day, often by FedEx, though if the victim notices, he or she will realize that the name on the check is commonly not the same as the name of the prospective roommate or the representative handling the payment. Nor does the check come from the representative's address. For example, a complainant on one of these victim sites reported that he got an envelope from an address in Brooklyn, New York, which had never been mentioned in any correspondence before.

Another characteristic of these emails is they are full of poor grammar, and it appears that there are form letters that the scammers use which they adapt by inserting different countries, jobs or fields of study, and details about where to send the money. In fact, some complainants have even reported getting multiple emails in response to their room listing from different individuals with essentially the same message.

The scammer may also ask the prospective victim to do a favor for them to help them move in, perhaps because this helps to make the relationship with them seem more real. The prospective roommate is creating a real-world connection, even though the meeting will never happen. For example, in my case the scammer asked me if I could meet her at the LA Airport, and even continued to request that after I indicated that I was leaving LA to return to Oakland. In some scams, the request has been to pick up the person's car when it arrives at the airport before the person arrives in the country.

Finally, the last phase of the scam occurs when the victim gets the ersatz check, deposits it, and sends off the payment to the scammer via the scammer's agent—or perhaps to the scammer who is acting alone—after which the scammer is never heard from again. Typically, the check will look like a cashier's check drawn on a legitimate bank, although it will often be printed on regular paper, not the paper with special fibers used in real checks. Often the signature will be a printed copy, not a real one. In some cases, the victim may actually deposit the check, since the teller or banker doesn't pay attention, though sometimes a banker will catch the phony check and notify the victim this is a fraud. In other cases, the victim will be given a reason, such as an unexpected emergency, to explain why he or she needs to send the money to the scammer's contact before even getting the check or depositing it. In any case, the key to the scam is getting the victim to send the money, usually via Western Union, with specific instructions about the recipient and how to do this.

Once the victim deposits the check, it may appear that it is being put into the person's account like a regular check within a day or two of making the deposit, depending on the time of day when the victim deposits it—one day if deposited before 4 p.m., two days if after 4 p.m. However, after the bank initially accepts the check, the bank's back office will catch the phony check after two or three weeks. Then the funds will be withdrawn from the victim's account—sometimes causing an overdraft, at which point the victim realizes he or she has been scammed.

Meanwhile, the scammer may send some explanation of why the trip has been delayed but the victim should hold the room anyway, which is a way to buy time before the victim suspects anything. Alternatively, the scammer simply drops out of sight, doesn't respond to the victim's emails, and can't be reached by phone.

After that, the victim is typically out any money sent to the scammer, plus the returned check and other fees. And usually the victim can do nothing to get back any lost funds, especially when the scammers are in another country. The scammer has the money, and there is little that law enforcement can do to find or prosecute them. And unlike credit card scams, where the credit card companies or banks may refund the money, there is nothing for the bank to refund, since the victim brought in the phony check and may even be suspected of passing bad checks. In effect, if the victim falls for it, this roommate/bad check scam is the perfect scam, as are the variations on it, such as the phony job offer that depends on the victim similarly getting a check as an overpayment and having to pay a refund to the scammer.

Some Examples of How the Roommate Scam Works

Here's one of the earliest examples of the roommate scam—in this case reported on Ripoff Report on June 18, 2007, by Elmira, in Ft. Lauderdale, Florida, who listed her apartment for rent on Rommates.com and Craigslist. A woman in Nigeria, Tonnia Williams, claimed she wanted to rent the room and send the total to her associate, also in Nigeria, Odunlami Raphael. As Elmira reported, Tonnia first wrote on June 6 stating that she was coming to the United States for some seminars, and perhaps to make herself seem more warm and nurturing, she claimed she was involved in a program for children with heart problems. So now she had to make sure she had a place to stay before she arrived. As Tonnia wrote:

> Subject: Am interested!!!!!
>
> Hello
>
> I am interested in your room/apt posting online. I will be having some seminars coming up soon in the USA. Right now I am in Western Part of Africa for a programme on children with heart related problems. My next program/seminars will be in the USA and I will be needing a room to stay for this seminars and I need to secure a room before my arrival to the US. I am having fun here and I can't wait to arrive. Get back to me with the room description and the charges for the first month and the deposit. Awaiting your reply.
>
> Regards

After Elmira responded, thinking that Tonnia would be an ideal roommate, Tonnia shared more information about herself, making herself seem like the perfect roommate, because not only was she involved in humanitarian activities to help children, but she didn't drink or smoke and had no pets or boyfriend because she was very busy. Additionally, she listed a number of positive keywords that someone seeking a roommate might want in their counterpart, such as being "honest, responsible, trustworthy and hardworking." As Tonnia wrote:

Subject: Thanks!!!

Hello,

Thanks for your email. Well my name is Tonnia and I am 27 years old. I am a humanitarian officer involved in projects that includes orphans, orphanages, heart related diseases in children between the ages of 4-10 yrs. I will be staying for a minimum of 12-13 months. I don't drink nor smoke, no pets and no boyfriend because I am a very busy woman. I like honest, responsible, trustworthy and hardworking people while I dislike lazy, messy, uncaring people and I love pets so much. I like the job because it involves traveling which is one of my hobbies. I will be through with my programme soon and will be on study leave in states, i will still be getting paid, so paying my rents on time won't be an issue of discussion, so i want you to get back with me with the full name and the address the payment will be send to with your contact cell number and pics of the room if available. i won't mind if you please tell me about your self in your next mail. i will be expecting to hear from you soon.

Regards

Initially, the claims of characteristics and activities in the letter might make Tonnia seem like the highly desirable, professional woman she is claiming to be. But a red flag that this could be a scam is the disconnect between the first few sentences, which are well written in good English, and the last few sentences, which are full of errors, including spelling "I" as "i." However, the average prospective victim might be likely not to notice, since he or she isn't looking for errors and is just pleased to have found a roommate.

But then the scam kicks in when Tonnia indicates that the payment has been mailed out by her boss with the deposit payment. However, the boss has mistakenly sent too much money, because he sent the money to pay for the shipment of her furniture and car along with the rent payment; so now, as soon as Elmira gets the check, she should send the money for shipping the car and furniture for $1,850, as detailed in the email, to the shipping agent, along with the details of transfer. Elmira kept thinking this was real, and presumably did not pay attention to the even greater number of grammatical errors that should have been a tip-off that this was a scam and that Tonnia described herself as having a professional occupation as a humanitarian officer. As Tonnia wrote in her letter of June 9:

> Subject: Payment sent via usps tck #1747WR190194632026
> Hello.
> Am very happy to inform you that payment has been mailed out by my boss and i just got the confirmation now that he has mailed out my deposit fee to you. Payment is been mailed out via usps with tracking # . . . and it will be deleiver to you soon. Pls keep me posted as soon as payment gets to you Hope to hear from you soon, it will be very nice to be roomie with you, cant wait o meet with you.
> Regards.

So now, presumably, the victim is hooked. Elmira thinks the roommate, who seems ideal from her email description of herself, is actually sending a payment to secure the room, and as requested, she sends Tonnia some pictures of the room. But then comes the scammer's explanation of why she needs the victim to send her money—in this case, the excuse is that the boss made a mistake requiring a $1,850 refund, and here's how to send it. As Tonnia wrote:

> Subject: WAITTING TO READ FROM YOU MAMA!!LOL
> Thanks mama,
> its lovely pics. Just to keep you update that i av book my flight already also to let you know that i got number 6 for the secon right hand sit,flight information as schedule. i will be departing from here by 1:45p.m Nigeria time so i will like you to pls make trasation as soon as you receive this message by sending $1,850 to the shipping agent so he can take my car and furniture in my present and i can hand-over the key for landlord immediately before my departure. Below is the agent information you will sending the cost fee for the shipment to . . .
> NAME . . . ODUNLAMI RAPHAEL
> ADDRESS . . . 24,MARYLAND RD,IKEJA
> STATE . . . LAGOS STATE
> COUNTRY . . . NIGERIA

ZIP-CODE . . . 23401

TEXT QUESTION . . . SAJEEN

ANSWER . . . TONNIA

AMOUNT . . . $1,850

Please after sending the money you will forward the details of transfer to me for reference. . . .

1. NAME/ADDRESS OF SENDER

2. AMOUNT SENT

3. TEXT/QUESTION/ANSWER

4. CONTROL/REFERENCE NUMBER

Please do SEND it through Westernunion money transfer. . . .

Warmest Regards.

At this point, despite all of the mistakes, Elmira planned to send the money once the money order arrived. Meanwhile, Tonnia wrote her several times during the day asking if she had cashed the money order yet, since she needed to leave her apartment within two days and she had packed up all her things and was waiting for the shippers to come. Elmira assured Tonnia she would do so, and during her lunch time the money order finally arrived and she took it to her bank to cash it. But after her bank said they would hold the money order against her account for two days like a normal check, and would only cash it now if she had enough money in her account to cover it, she backed off. As Elmira explained on the Ripoff Report: "I wasn't going to take out my money to help someone I don't know, so I drove off."

Even so, after work, she still sought to cash the check, and took it to a check-cashing store, where a clerk said the store would cash a MoneyGram money order even if it was made out by Walmart. However, as soon as the clerk turned over the check to a cashier, the scam was over. At once, the cashier said the check was a fake, and she demonstrated this by asking Tonnia to hold her hand under the glass and feel a real money order compared to the money order she brought in. While the real one had a texture, the fake one was smooth, like a photocopy. Plus the real one had a security code that turned white when the clerk applied heat, and when she photocopied a real one, the photocopy showed "VOID" on it, so there was no way to duplicate a real cashier's check, though she could make a photocopy of the fake check Tonnia gave her.

So the scam was up, and though Elmira didn't have a roommate, at least she didn't lose any money. After she sent Tonnia a letter about the fake check, Tonnia responded with an excuse about how she couldn't believe her boss had sent one "because her boss is a man of integrity and she cant believe anyone in his office will issue a false check." Tonnia even complained she would have to change her flight, though the day before she had told Elmira she had already shipped off some of her luggage. But regardless of Tonnia's futile attempts to explain away the scam, Elmira had exposed it, and after that, Elmira never heard from Tonnia again.

What is especially amazing about this story is how Tonnia was able to convince Elmira to go along with the scam despite the many errors in her letters. But like many victims, Elmira appeared to be so trusting to believe in Tonnia's false story. She never thought to question anything Tonnia claimed, such as the claim that she would ship all of her furniture and a car to the States for approximately a year. Why not store them in her country and rent a furnished apartment and a car? Yet Elmira was willing to accept this initial unusual request, and she overlooked the change in grammatical usage in the letters, with multiple errors made by a supposedly well-educated woman involved in managing a humanitarian health care program. All of the discrepancies screamed "scam." Yet Elmira ignored them until the very end, just before she was about to send off the money.

That's what happens for others ensnared by roommate scams. They simply believe the narrative that introduces the scammer who needs a roommate, and they accept the scammer's convoluted explanations of why he or she can't see the room before paying for it. Then they believe the further explanation of why the overpayment has occurred and why they need to send a refund immediately, before the scammer even arrives to see the room.

The same kind of pattern emerged in a series of exchanges from June 10 to March 28, 2015, on a website devoted to "Avoiding a Common Roommate Scam on craigslist" by Mike, who created the site after he was targeted by the scam but never became a victim (www.rentingoutrooms.

com/avoiding-a-common-roomates-scams-on-craigslist). He got a gut feeling after a series of fraudulent emails that they were not from legitimate roommates, and he found the same kind of patterns I observed, which mostly involved scammers claiming to be younger individuals, including students or young adults recently starting a new job. Perhaps the scammers adopted these characteristics because most of the victims seeking a roommate are young themselves, since they aren't yet established or earning enough to live on their own. And typically the scammers are ready to move in without meeting you and simply want to know the cost to hold the room, because this way they can arrange to pay you more than the required amount so you can send a refund for the difference. As Mike described it:

> The scammers or purported roommates make initial contact with you, stating that they are interested in renting your room, but cannot visit because they are overseas or have a tight time constraint and can't make the time.
>
> The scammer insists they are easy going and would like to move. They . . . have a very legitimate-sounding story. They might be a medical school or college student, or perhaps starting a new computer or modeling job, and they might even be arriving with their parents. Somewhere in the exchange of e-mails, they ask for you the total amount to secure the room for them to move in.[1]

If you do reply, the scammers send a check or international money order for more than the total amount needed to hold the room, and they provide an excuse, usually after the money has been sent, for why it is too much—such as because it includes an extra amount for their scholarship, employer's paycheck, or was a mistake. Whatever the excuse, you are supposed to send the difference back to them via Western Union or a MoneyGram, after deducting the amount from what seems to be a genuine check or money order. The bank may accept the check if you are depositing it or may even cash it if you have that amount already in your accounts, so you think the money is real. But you are really sending the scammer your own money, and once the bank discovers the fraud when your check doesn't clear, you are on the hook for the full amount. Either the bank will deduct it from your account or you end up owing a negative balance.

Thus, the key for avoiding the scam is the following:

- Always talk to any potential roommates on the phone and determine if they really are sincere in their interest. One way to show their sincerity is that they will normally want to see the place and meet you, though scammers may give a reasonable explanation of why they can't visit in advance and ask you to send photos or claim they feel comfortable with you from your email exchange, what they learned about you on the Internet, or phone conversation. Not seeing the place is a red flag, though not necessarily fatal, since some real roommates do make long-distance arrangements.
- Be cautious if the potential roommate is from another country, since scammers commonly live outside the United States so they can avoid being prosecuted. Not all foreigners are scammers, but it's a reason to proceed with caution.
- Look for any errors in the email, since scammers often make a lot of spelling and grammatical mistakes. Such mistakes could be because English is a second language or because of a limited education, and they are often a tip-off of a scam, especially if there is a disconnect between the educated person the scammer claims to be, such as a medical student pursuing graduate studies, and the mistakes in the email.
- Don't use Western Union or a MoneyGram for a transaction. Ideally, meet and personally exchange any initial checks, and if you get a check or money order in the mail, don't give any money back until the check or money order fully clears your bank, which could take two or three weeks. Advise your prospective roommate accordingly. Real prospective roommates will often make other arrangements to speed up the process, while scammers will commonly disappear.

Some Examples of Individuals Who Were Taken or Nearly Taken by the Roommate Scam

The enduring power of this scam is shown by the way victims keep falling for the compelling story line. However, some individuals were able to avoid the scam once they learned what to look for or were warned by a knowing bank official.

For example, Siddhardtha Das (September 29, 2011), reported how she escaped sending off a very large amount when her bank alerted her.

> OMG my bank just saved my butt from being scammed. A girl from canada claimed to be coming over and gave a check to me and when i went to the bank to deposit it, they just told about the room-mate scam and saved my butt of $3500.

Another woman began to feel suspicious about the overseas woman she hadn't met who wanted to rent her room, and she quickly realized the scam when she discovered an account of what to look for on the site for Renting Out a Room in Your House. All the signs of a scam were there, including the bad grammar and the prospective roommate wanting to ship her things and writing a check for more money than due. As addicted2u143 wrote (December 10, 2011):

> I just caught on to a scammer and of course I was not aware of this scam . . .
>
> It was a little fishy so I researched scams and it was a dead on match. . . . The girl was out of the country (Canada), wanted to send me a money order and reserve the room without seeing it. She said she was 28 yet gave me a 1985 dob . . . she was not willing to sign a lease till she got in town but she wanted to ship her things here, therefore she was making the check out for more than the rent due for the shippers, she had very strange grammer, she kept avoiding answering questions that she should have been able to answer, she did not have a scanner to send proof of identification or a camera to send a picture of herself. All signs point to scammer!

A giveaway for many prospective victims who escaped the scam is that they got multiple letters, often with the same story, even identical wording, in response to their ad for a roommate. As Teri wrote (January 28, 2012):

> I have received at least twenty scam responses in two days . . . poor grammar and form letter styles that duplicate each other . . . i am so frustrated that i started responding in a nasty way . . . I am on several roommate sites and they are all the same . . . Either same person with different

names or a form letter sold to scammers . . . it is very easy to identify . . . I just need a real roommate.

Here are some examples of scammers' stories, which some victims believe, so they send checks. If they didn't, the scammers would stop using those appeals. One story, reported by multiple people, is the story of a woman from Seattle who was born in Finland and now had to visit her sick uncle there. She has to move because she has gotten a job as a nurse in a local clinic and will have a car and some furniture to send, too. She wants to secure a place before she leaves for Finland, in order to have a place to come back to. To sweeten her appeal, she describes all the ways she will help, including doing the dishes, paying the rent on time, liking nice clean pets, and loving dogs and cats, though she has none now. While the letter is full of grammatical mistakes and typos, it is designed to make the scammer seem sincere, even caring and nurturing, since she is first caring for her uncle and then working in the health field to help others. Here are some excerpts from this "Finnish nurse from Seattle" letter (January 30, 2012):

I am Christina massengill by name and live in Seattle, WA. I would have been kind of happy if we can meet before making any plans, but am very busy and i have a lot of things to do right now . . . I will really appreciate it if you can tell me more about the place and tell me a little about you because my uncle is presently very sick, and i have to travel to Finland to see him but i want to secure the place down before going. He was involved in a crash with his new car some weeks back and now ill serious, I need to check on him and take good care of him . . .

I am moving cause of my job, am a medical Humanitarian nurse for united Nations. I work for CHRMC Children's Hospital in Seattle but will be working in a local clinic over there, More about me, am a neat type of person, honest, humble and responsible. I like honest, responsible and hardworking people while i hate the lazy, messy and uncaring people . . . well am a quiet and gentle going person to live with . . . I am 27 yrs old female, 5.4 in height, i like tourism and i don't keep late at nights neither i will have overnight guest around but am ok if you do . . .

I was born and brought up in Finland, i studied there i had my university education right there while staying with my uncle. I lived all my life in Finland before coming down to Seattle, WA have been living with my uncle from from age 12 . . . Then i was member of the Red Cross Association it really sounds interesting for me . . . Am sure You'll really like the person that i am, because i will also do the dishing if you like I work when i am to and relax when i am to, I also like sharing my thoughts also . . . paying rent on time will not be a problem as i will be making the rent fee before the month ends . . . I do not have any pet, i really like dog and cat but have none of it now, so there is no problem about that.

I must confess am comfortable with the price and I will want to secure the place down before my arrival . . . I also will want you to know that i have my car that i will be coming over with little of my furniture . . .

please let me know if there will be room for them . . . Let me also know how i can go about securing the place down before my arrival as i will also be busy from next week and let me know if you can take off the ad off the site as i am going to secure the place with a deposit.

One characteristic of these letters is that they readily morph in names and details, though the message is essentially the same. For instance, in the following letter, the Finnish nurse is now named Nicolle, not Christine; she is twenty-six, not twenty-seven; and she has been living in South Dakota, not Seattle. She also has a sick uncle, but here there is no car accident, and rather than working with the United Nations, she has served in the Paris Red Cross, in projects with orphans and sick children ages four to ten. Plus she is looking for a job, rather than already having one lined up, but she can still help with the "dishing." Here's a copy of her initial letter of August 14, 2012, along with a follow-up letter with the payment arrangements.

Thanks for your reply,I really do appreciateit,. I would have loved us to see u before making any plan but i really have a lot of things to do right now, But will be okay if you can tell me more about the place and you, as my uncle is presently sick and i have to go see him, but really want to hold a place down . . .

More about me again, i am a nurse,am 26 years old of age . . . I am the neat type,Ilike honest, responsible, trustworthy and hardworking while I dislike lazy,messy,uncaring people and I love pets so much, am quiet and easy going person to live with. I like tourising and,i don't keep late nights but i am okay if you do,I was born and bread in Finland as there was where i had my university education and stayed with my uncle there!!

I lived all my life way in Finland before coming down to South Dakota to stay together with a nurse friend, I grew up with my uncle since 15 years old . . . I've also wanted to be in the medical line since i was born, I served in the Paris Red Cross for 8 months, we have involved in projects that includes orphans,orphanages,heart related diseases in children between the ages of 4-10yrs . . .

I was looking to move over to your state because i need to live on my own . . . And i will be working with any hospital around as i am also making enquiries about that now . . .

Am sure You'll really like the person that i am, because i will also do the dishing if you like, I work when i am to and relax when i am to. I also like sharing my thoughts also . . . paying rent on time will not be a problem as i will also be making the rent fee before the month ends about the place,as i can't see it before my arrival . . . I also will want you to know that i have a car that i will be coming over with,and little of my furnitures, please let know if there will be room for them . . .

With all that i've said above,I have told you more about em and more picture of mine will be attach in the next email,Let me also know how i can go about securing the place down before my arrival as i will also be busy from next week preparing to come over.

When the person seeking a roommate emailed Nicolle asking her to fill out an application, "Nicolle" simply wrote back with much the same message, plus added information about how she would be sending the payment to secure the room, and attached a photo of a woman with dark hair. Here is what she wrote in part:

Thanks once again for the quickly reply, Really would have loved to call You but am leaving now to see my sick uncle, i can only communicate via email but I will make sure i call you whenever i get there but before that i will want to secure the place. . . . i smell the kind of person whom you are and i like you,I will want You to know that i am okay with the cost . . .

i believe that you'll be a nice person,I just have my dressers,computer table,kitchen utensils and a queen size bed,2 big luggages and my car to be shipped . . .

I got a message that my uncle is sick in Finland . . . and i have to go see him but i am making plans to secure place so that when i come back i'll just move in into the place, and with the way we've communicated,I am okay with you and i want you to know that i don't want to make any travel plans without securing a place down now,I will be signing a year lease for the start if you are okay with that . . . so i will be making payment to hold down the place and the mode of payment will be by United States Certified Money Order,so pls let me know if this mode of payment is ok by you.

And if YES pls provide me with the following information to get the payment to you . . .

So Kindly get back to me with this requested address contact information so that we can proceed asap bye for now.

When Hillary wrote back describing her requirements for considering a roommate (a completed application, a background check—which she would do because she worked for a government agency) and stated that the only payments she would accept were cash or PayPal payments, not money orders, she didn't hear back from Nicolle. Clearly, the scammer realized the scam wouldn't work and so quickly disappeared.

In other variations on the scheme, the prospective roommate was from England, Germany, Spain, China, Mexico, Canada, or another country. She was also seeking additional education or a career in the sciences or technology: getting an MA in Microbiology, beginning a career as a clinical Pharmacist, or doing further research. But much of the language was the same about loving pets, being easy going, and preferring cleanliness. The hook was similar too—the prospective roommate wanted to know the exact rent, make an advance payment, and ship furniture and/or a car, but there was no way to contact her or meet in advance, because she was in a remote area. And typically these emails came from free Yahoo or Gmail accounts, which can be set up by anyone in minutes under any name. To illustrate, here are a few more of these requests to be a roommate.

From "Diana Gibs" from London on August 27, 2012:

I'm Diana Gibs a 23yrs old female,fun loving, friendly,clean, caring,and respectful of others and a non-smoker don't do drugs i drink occasionally and drama free. I graduated last year in Greater London UK and I'm single and have no children.I do bible study and sometimes we do karaoko night with my roommates in park row! I go to church every Sunday so i need to secure the room before my coming and I'll be moving in with my luggage's. You seem to be a very interesting person and I must tell you that you will like staying with a girl like me in the house as i make people smile,So I need to be in the state before the ending of the Month and i will be staying for a year as i have programs to run during my stay. I am coming to continue my educational career Masters Degree Microbiology . . .

I was born in England (UK) my families are from London as well. I graduated from the University of Greenwich with a degree in Microbology Science specializing in Microbiology and Molecular Biology. I speak both English and French and I'm presently on a research work assistant . . .

I would have loved to call you but i can't make an international calls from my phone so it's kind of hard to call here and i don't want to waste much time as i really need to secure the room on time so I do love pets but i don't have any at the moment. I would like to see the room before renting but I'm okay with pictures so i wil be renting sight unseen . . .
Let me know the total amount of the room so that i can send your email to my dad for him to email you later because he is the one that will be paying the bills inform of a Cashier's Check . . .

Here's a similar one from Doris S. Jendy, reported on September 12, 2012. She says she's from "China" at the University of Technology, doing research in Guam, seeking a Master's Degree, but otherwise the basic structure of the scam is the same, since she can't call from a remote area, is fine with pictures, and wants to know the total payment, which will come as a US cashier's or certified check.

My full name is Doris S. Jendy i'm 25yrs old. (FEMALE). I was born in CHINA BEINJING i speak both language, my Dad is from US while my Mum is from China . . . I went to Beijing University of Technology china and i graduate last year in Beijing University of Technology. I'm fun loving, personal, friendly, clean,caring and respectful of others. A non-spoker, don't do drugs but i drink occasionally, am single and have no children. I go to church every Sunday.I amcoming for my masters degree, am presently on research work at Guam, but will be coming to the state for my master degree in October . . . I would have loved to call you but this is a remove area calls is hard to go through from here and i don't want to waste much time. I'm really interested in renting from you, i would have loved it see it but am very far, with pictures ill really appreciate it . . .

Please let me know the total payment of the place and, payment will be done by via US Cashier or Certified Check . . .

Not only are women seeking roommates in these scams, but men, too, and their language is much the same, such as this man, supposedly from Germany, though also doing research in Guam, ready to sign a lease, can't call because of the remote area, and wants to send a cashier's or certified check. As he writes in a letter reported on November 11, 2012:

I'm so glad to hear the room is still available for rent, here is little about me, my name is Eric Collins i speak both German & English, am single, fun, loving, clean, and respectful of others, don't do drugs. My father is from US and my mother is from Germany, am 21yrs old, sex male. I was born in Rheinland-Pfalz (German) i attend University of Hannover, and graduated a year ago.

I'm coming for a long term stay and am ready to sign a year lease as soon as I get to your house, but am presently on research work at Guam and will be coming for my master's degree from soon. I'll be arriving November 24, and pay for the deposit and one month rent up front, loved to call you but here is a remote area calls are very hard to go through, and also love to come and check at the room before renting but am very far, with pictures that will makes me happy and feel comfortable . . .

Let me know the total amount for the first month rent, because i will be paying upfront so that it will give you strong prove that am really interested in renting the room from you. Payment will be done via US Cashier's or Certified Check . . .

Then, on January 24, 2013, with virtually the same letter, Sona David, twenty-six years old, reported that she was born in Mexico, and while her dad was from the USA, her mum was from Mexico, and she went to the Universidad de Colima in Colima. Now after finishing her legal research in Guam, as a prerequisite for her master's, she was heading to the United States and her dad would be making the payment to hold the place for her arrival. In another variation, reported February 4, 2013, Jane Felix plove [sic], age twenty-one, claimed to speak both Spanish and English, and have a father from the USA and a mother from Germany, while she was born in Munich, Germany. Now she had just graduated from Hamburg University of Technology in Germany, but couldn't call because, where else—she was stuck in a remote area doing research in Guam.

And here's one from a French student born in Spain, who speaks both "España" and English, though she is doing research in Guam for her masters in Microbiology—essentially the same story nearly a year later, reported in August 15, 2013.

My name is Diana Arteta (F),I am 24yrs old, I am fun loving, personal, friendly,clean and respectful of others. A non-smoker, don't do drugs, I drink occasionally,and drama free. I graduated last year in France. I am single and have no children . . . I do bible study, and sometimes we do karaoke night with my roommate! i go to church every Sunday.

Am coming for my masters degree. I was born in Spain,Malaga(Los Asperones, my dad is from USA but my mum is from Malaga . . . I went to Malaga University (UMA) I speak both España and English, am presently on research work at Guam(USA), am doing it because its part of prerequisite for my masters in Microbiology. I would have loved to call you but this is a remove areas calls is hard to go through from here and i don't want to waste much time.

Am really interested in renting from you and i don't have pets but i don't care if there is any in the house. I would have loved to see it but am very far,but with pictures, I am glad . . . please let me know the total payment of the place and . . . I will send your email to my dad for him to email you later because he is the one that will be paying the bills but nevertheless,I will like you to send me your full Name and the mailing address, your phone number as well,so that my Dad will issue out the payment for the place as soon as possible.

Over the next year, this girl from Guam, with much the same message and even phrasing, morphed with different names, degrees, and locations. For example, in an email reported on September 6, 2013, the message came from Tessa Russell Morgan who was now thirty years old, open to both male and female roommates and similarly seeking a master's degree in Microbiology. But now she was born in Virginia Beach in Virginia, and while her dad was there her mum was from Canada, and the reason she couldn't call was because her mobile was disconnected because she had moved out of Guam. But her dad was still paying the rent and deposit fees.

Then, in an email of October 27, 2013, the prospective roommate was now named Aida Howard, and she spoke both English and German, while her father was from the UK (London) and her mother was from the US (New York), and she was now twenty-six years old, born in the United Kingdom, and graduated from the University of Oxford. Still she was ready to sign a year's lease once she arrived from her research in Guam to start her master's degree in November. Now she was ready to pay for the deposit and a month's rent, though she couldn't call from this remote area, but a picture of the room and surroundings would be fine.

Still another prospective roommate on this same date called herself Mellisa Johnson, age twenty-four, and said she spoke both French and English, while her father was from the United States and her mother was from France, where she was born in Paris, and now she had graduated from the American University of Paris. She, too, wanted to come for a long-term stay, sign a year's lease when she arrived, and she wanted to pay for the deposit and one month up front. But she too couldn't call from her research assignment in far-off Guam.

Even Diana Arteta surfaced again with exactly the same earlier message, though now she was seeking a place as of December 3, 2013.

Meanwhile, first reported September 12, 2013, a roommate request appeared from Debbie Rose who claimed to be half-Mexican and half-Spanish and a photographer on a photography assignment, although when one man receiving her email responded to her in Spanish, she didn't know what he was talking about and she didn't even have photograph of herself. Subsequently much the same message reappeared under other names. Here's what "Debbie Rose" had to say:

> I am happy to hear that the place is still available to rent out, I am not a student i am self employed. I am into cinematography and i do other businesses,I am sure paying my house rent won't be any problem for me.I am ok with the rent charges . . .
>
> I love reading, staying indoor, Love traveling right now i am on a tour to Egypt on a cinematography and photography work, i love going beach and meeting new peple, got no bf but hopefully i might one too because i just break up with my boyfriend which so i am just getting over it,i have never rented a room or a house before because i have lived with ma family all of my life, i mixed race, Spain and Mexico . . .
>
> Will the house cleaning arrangement will be made by me ? i have no problem cleaning the house and have no problem living with other potential roommate if available . . .
>
> Well i am okwith the amount charge, i am willing to make the deposit down to you so as to be able to hold the room for me . . .

However, when Marcus, the man seeking a roommate, wrote back to Debbie, who was supposedly half-Mexican and half-Spanish, in Spanish, she had trouble understanding him, as in this following exchange, which helped to convince Marcus this was a scam:

> Marcus: cuando va a llega en usa (when will you arrive in the usa)
> Debbie: I am U.S.A. citizen, ma, Springfield
> Marcus: si, pero cuanda va a llegal en usa (yes, but when will you arrive)
> Debbie: I don't understand your language

Then on November 13, Debbie sent the exact same message to someone else. Meanwhile, variations of the researcher in Guam continued to circulate, though on March 14, 2014, instead of Guam, the person seeking a master's degree was now doing research work in a small village in Alaska, such as in this letter from Beth Arteta from France and another from Melissa Douglas from Germany, though the rest of the letter is essentially the same. In still another variation, Julia Pritchard, a graduate from Scotland, was visiting a cousin in Kosovo. Here are some excerpts from their letters.

From Beth:

I'm interested in renting the room. My name is Beth Arteta i was born in France (Paris) i speak both French & English, am single, fun, loving, clean, loyal and respectful of others, don't have any pet. More about me, my father is from US and my mother is from France. I'm 24yrs old, sex female, i attend American University of Paris, graduated a year ago.

I'm coming to stay for a year, and am coming for my master's degree.I'm currently in Alaska in a village "Nunivak Island" on a research work and will be coming soon . . . i'll loved to call you but here is a remote area calls are very hard to go through, please send me some picture of the room because i will not be able to come over and check on it before renting . . .

i will be coming with my own car. Let me know the total amount for the first month rent, i will be paying upfront so that you can be rest assured that am really interested in renting the room from you . . .

My mode of payment is US Check . . .

I'll be waiting to read back from you with the information requested so that i can forward it to my father to issue out the check for the deposit and month rent upfront as soon as possible, with that you can hold on the place prior to my arrival.

From Melissa:

My name is Melissa Douglass from Germany, i speak both German & English, am single, easy going person, loving, clean, and respectful of others, don't do drugs. My father is from USA while my mother is from Germany, am 24yrs old, sex female. I was born in Stuttgart (Arkansas) and i attend University of Stuttgart, and graduated last year . . . I have my B.Sc and I'm coming for a long term stay and am ready to sign a year lease as soon as i get to your house. I'm currently in Alaska in a village

"Nunivak Island" on a research work and will be coming soon for my master's degree . . . I'll loved to call you but here is a remote area calls are very hard to go through . . .

Finally, here's the email from Julia, who shares the same basic message and language though with some new details:

My name is Julie, female and 24 years of age, fun-loving, outspoken, friendly, clean, caring and respectful of others, a non-smoker (but can hand-out in a smoky bar) don't do drugs, drink occasionally and drama free kind of person. I graduated last year from Edinburgh University, Scot and I'm single with no children. I would love to secure the room for myself before my arrival to the States. I like my roommate to be very caring and friendly. I will be in the States before the end of this month for the next two years as I'll be coming for my Master degree program. I was born in Scotland (UK) and my Dad is from Kahului, Hawaii, but he has been living in Scotland for over 27 years. I obtained my bachelor's degree (Economics) from the University of Edinburg and I speak fluent English with a Scottish accent. I'm currently visiting a cousin in Kosovo. . . .

Like the others, Julia then goes on to explain why she can't see the place in person, but some photos of the room are fine, and she will forward the information to her dad who is paying the bills from a US cashier's check.

In short, it is as if the scammers are copying the basic letters from a template and filling in their own information, though many are English-language challenged from their many mistakes in spelling and grammar. The major point is to describe themselves to be easy-going, fun-loving, but well-educated roommates who will be coming soon, can't call or meet beforehand to see the room, and want to make a payment up front to secure the room.

That's the essence of the scam. They overpay and ask the victim to pay for something in advance out of their check, though the amount may vary. For example, in a July 10, 2014, letter describing how she was twenty-four-year-old female who graduated from the American University of Paris and lived currently in the "Nunivak Island" village in Alaska, Katherine Roberts had this to say:

Once you receive the payment, go straight to your bank have the $2877.88 deposit into your account, after doing that please partially withdraw $1700 cash for my car. . . . Take the cash to the nearest Western Union store to make a money transfer to the car delivery agent information give below (in this case to a Roberta Fiore in Pine Bush, New York).

So that's the basic scam, and as of March 18, 2015, it was still going strong, with a letter from Marie Bowlers, twenty-seven, who graduated from Hamburg University of Technology. After being in the United States for a year, she was coming to the victim's state for a Master's degree, and couldn't call since she was in a remote area, but wanted to pay for the deposit and month's rent up front via a US cashier's or certified check.

Unfortunately, some victims keep falling for this phony roommate scam, or the scammers wouldn't continue to use this approach. And even more unfortunately, the victims are not only out whatever money they send the scammers in another country or in the United States, but they may end up paying bad check fees when any check they have deposited is proved fraudulent. Then they discover after a few weeks that they don't have a real roommate either—so they are doubly duped.

The Opposite Approach

A somewhat different variation on the phony roommate scam is the one where the "landlord" or "renter seeking a prospective roommate" is actually the scammer, though this really involves a different scam dynamic, where the victim pays money for a property, product, or service that doesn't exist. In this case, the victim responds to an ad for a place to share (or a place to rent as an individual). Then he or she receives information about the property if out of town or visits the property if in town, and sometimes even meets the purported landlord or roommate. The victim may even get a key that opens the door. Whatever the scenario, the place to rent seems very real. But in fact, the landlord or prospective roommate does not actually own the property. Rather, he or she is committing an elaborate fraud to make it seem that this is a rental arrangement.

After the victim pays the money, sometimes after signing an agreement, the scammer disappears and the victim discovers that someone else actually lives in the place or owns the property. Meanwhile, the scammer is long gone, so typically the victim is stuck for the lost money and law enforcement can't do anything. Though this scheme might seem like a variation of the roommate scam, it is more like the ersatz home repair, roofing, tree removal, or landscaping service scam, where the victim is persuaded to pay in advance for a service, usually by thinking he or she will be getting a bargain from a team that is in the area for a certain period of time. After the scammers get the victim—or a series of victims—to pay for the service, they skip town. Here, too, the victim is commonly out the money because the scammers are gone and can't be found.

Encountering the Phony Jobs Scam

These phony job scams take various forms, although one of the most common types is the cash-the-check version, where the victim gets an overpayment and has to send the balance via Western Union or a MoneyGram, which is untraceable, and after a couple of weeks, the fraudulent cashier's or certified check from the scammer bounces. As such, the phony job scam works much like the phony roommate scam, except that it is much simpler since it doesn't require a long personal story or exchange to build a relationship. The scammer simply presents the job offer, usually for a short part-time assignment or series of assignments— such as becoming a mystery shopper—immediately accepts the person to do the job, and sends instructions for carrying out the assignment and sending the scammer the money from the check he or she receives. Unless the victim's bank catches the fraudulent check before it is deposited or the victim becomes suspicious and decides to not participate further, within a day or two the victim sends off the money. Then, as in the roommate scam, the victim soon discovers that any money sent to the scammer is gone, while he or she is now responsible for any returned check charges and other penalties for depositing a fraudulent check.

The other phony job offers involve three different strategies. One is to get the job seeker to send an advance fee for the opportunity (the advance fee fraud). Another is to get the person to be a "money mule," where the victim is unknowingly recruited into receiving packages and shipping them or transferring money, which involves the victim in other crimes, such as sending stolen goods or ripping off customers from auction sites like eBay.[2] The third and most nefarious job scam is getting personal information from the victim, such as one's birth date, social security number, or mother's maiden name, to use for identity theft or identity fraud. In some cases, scammers may even ask the victim to fill out what appears to be a direct deposit form so they can make a payment in the victim's bank, but instead, they use the bank account and routing numbers to drain money out.[3]

However, despite the different strategies, characteristics of the email letters used are often similar. For example, scammers commonly use free Yahoo, Hotmail, and Gmail accounts rather than an email linked to a company domain. They often offer a high salary with no experience, and a job without an interview, whereas most employers only offer a job to those they have interviewed and assessed.[4] Also, scammers may ask you to pay a fee. Legitimate recruiters are paid by employers, not by job seekers.[5] Another possible scam tip-off is a work-from-home job, though some of these jobs are real.[6] Instant job offers are another warning sign, since normally job seekers have to wait a few days, or even a few weeks, until the application deadline closes or the employer looks through the applications to select a few candidates to interview by phone, if not in person.[7] Still another tip-off is if you get a job offer letter in the form of an image telling you that your profile has been selected.[8] Bad English is a sign of a scam, too.

But perhaps the most important tip-off is that "there will be money involved," in that you have to provide some bank account for your candidacy to be considered further,[9] or you have to send money in some form to the company, as in the overpayment scheme used in the phony roommate scam, except here the story is what you have to do to get the job or carry out the assignment. In either case, the basic structure of the scam is the same: in believing the scammer's story, you deposit an overpayment—usually a cashier's or certified check—and return money to the scammer via Western Union or another untraceable means of transferring money. You think you have a real offer, whether from an employer or a prospective roommate, so you accept the check, provide the necessary information to receive it, and send your own real money to the scammer, after which the scammer disappears and you are stuck with the loss of funds, which in some cases can be disastrous for the often low-income victims targeted by these scams. They are seeking jobs or roommates because they are struggling financially, and they need the job or roommate to make ends meet. Not only do they not get the job or roommate, since both are fake, but they also lose money, too, which can push some victims over the edge. And sometimes, making the fraud even worse, the scammer has obtained personal identity information, so the initial fraud can open the door to identity fraud, too—and even the loss of more money, since the scammer has obtained bank account information.

What makes this type of job offer based on an overpayment so compelling? How do the scammers commonly make their case? And what is the effect on the victims? Those questions will be covered in the next sections.

The Mystery Shopper Jobs Pitch

One of the classic phony jobs scams is the pitch to be a mystery shopper. What makes this ideal for a scam is that this is a part-time job that someone can do long distance by going to a selected destination, evaluating the shopping experience, and reporting the results—all online without meeting the employer. Also, what makes these pitches seem legitimate is that there is a real mystery shopper job and organization, so the scammer can reference the real organization and claim that legitimate, well-known firms, such as Walmart, Pizza Hut, and the Gap, pay for Secret Shoppers to go shopping and report on their experiences. However, the big difference is that legitimate shopping companies don't send out emails to people they don't know; instead people apply to them directly, and there is normally a face-to-face interview followed by a short period of training, so the shopper knows what to do. Additionally, job seekers pay no money to enroll in their training. Moreover, these legitimate companies hiring mystery shoppers never pay in advance, and they don't send out large checks asking people to send back the overpayment; rather shoppers advance their own money to make purchases and get reimbursed by the company. And the pay is typically $10 to $15 an assignment, never $200 to $300 for "a duty," so this job is definitely not a quick way to make some big bucks for an hour or two of work.

I first encountered the scam when I got a series of letters between November 21, 2014, and April 15, 2015, from different AOL accounts to four of my emails offering mystery shopping assignments, promising easy earnings of $200 to $350 per assignment. The amount was vastly more than a legitimate shopping assignment would offer, but it might be compelling to someone not familiar with the industry and eager to earn some seemingly quick and easy money.

I received three different messages to start the process, none addressed to me personally. One really short one that I got on November 21, 2014, and again on March 14, 2015, from two people with different emails and the same errors in grammar and space began with the subject line: "Job Offer . . . Are You Interested":

> We have a customer service survey assignment in your location for you. We will pay $200 per assignment which would come in the form of a cashiers check along with comprehensive details in regards to your assignment. The job Entails an Evaluation process such as visiting Wal-mart, Rite-aid,Walgreen e.t.c. Send information below to get started if you are Interested"
>
> Full_Name
> Full Address (No PO Box):
> City:
> State :
> Zip Code :
> Phone_Cell
> Gender_Age :
> Email_Address:
>
> Thank you for participation:

It was signed by the HR Manager for the Customer Service Evaluation Team, and one of them included "The Premier Mystery Shopping Company" followed by a Copyright 2014® sign, a sign of a scam, since one doesn't copyright the name of a company nor use a $^®$ registration mark for a copyright. Another tip-off of a phony letter is that the name in the email didn't match the name of the person signing the letter or the supposed company. For example, the email from Tom Mathre came from arade5831@aol.com, while the email from Alex Pratt with the Premier Mystery Shopping Company came from Elmahouseclean@aol.com.

A somewhat longer letter from "Todd Bennett" with the subject line #Offer said the following, which includes the errors as well as the first word "Opening," as if this is a script sent to the scammers to advise them what to send in their email. Intriguingly, in the letter the scammer uses a gmx account, though the email came from an AOL account at ovabus@aol.com.

> Opening People todd.bennett@gmx.com We are accepting applications for qualified individuals to become MysteryShoppers. JOB DESCRIPTION: 1. You will receive funding for the assignment. 2. You will receive the Instruction for your assignment via email on the location and details of the assignment. 3. You are to complete the assignment as fast and discreetly as possible. 4. You will be asked to visit abusiness location to conduct business be it a restaurant, shopping store etc. PAYMENT TERMS: You will receive a flat sum of $250 per assignment. The company will furnish you with all expense needed for the assignment and any other expense incurred during the course of executing your assignment. Note : Send information below for Sign UP Your Full Name:_____ Your Address:_____ City, State:_____ Occupation:_____ Phone:_____ Number:_____ Age:_____ It's fun and rewarding. There is no charge to become shopper and you do not need previous experience and you would be paid $250 for everyduty you carryout, Thank you. **Todd Bennett** Secret Shopper LLC.

In addition to these two letters, I received nearly twenty almost identical pitches from different "Recruitment Specialists" with two different companies. One was "Sights on Service Inc" from January 6 to April 7, 2015, which began with the subject line: "Job Offer," "Job Offer!," (the most common), "Secret Shoper®," "MYSTERY SHOPPER 2015!!!" "Secret

Shopper 2015!!" and "2015 Offer." The other was from the "Platinum Corporation" from March 28 to April 3, 2015, with the subject line "MYSTERY SHOPPER 2015!!!" The only difference in the content of these letters was that the paragraph breaks were slightly different in the "About Us" section, but otherwise the copy was exactly the same, except for payment of $300 per duty for Sights on Service and $250 per duty for Platinum Corporation.

Unlike the other brief letters, this letter went into extensive detail to suggest the legitimacy of the service by citing a real organization, the Mystery Shopping Providers Association (MSPA), the professional trade association for the mystery shopping industry. The letter also refers to the real Secret Shopper organization at www.secretshopper.com, which has a registered name. However, this website also indicates that being a mystery shopper is strictly a part-time job, with payments of $12 to $25 per assignment, and secret shoppers need to pass a Basic Certification Test to show they are familiar with the requirements of being a secret shopper and the policies and procedures of the Secret Shopper organization.

Thus, the scammers build on the reputation of these legitimate organizations to lure people into the scam, which involves immediately hiring the person, paying $250 or $300 per duty, and asking for extensive personal information up front. Then, if the person responds, the scammers ask the victim to deduct the fee for their duty from the total they send after depositing it in their bank. A company hiring real Secret Shoppers pays about $10 to $25 per duty, along with the shopper's expenses in buying the products. If anyone does check to verify the information in the letter, they can think they are dealing with a representative of the real organization, when they are only corresponding with the scammers, who are providing documentation to lure the person into the scam.

For many victims, that appeal can be quite convincing, given the number of letters I collected in just six months. However, the signs of a scam are readily apparent in the detailed personal information collected up front in the initial "recruitment" letter, before the person actually shows any interest in the job. Another indicator is the discrepancy between the name of the "Recruitment Specialist" in the letter and in the email, and even when emails come from two different accounts for the same person. One recruitment specialist even sent letters from different emails for different companies.

Here's an example of the basic letter, followed by examples of these emails from different accounts, with different names from the purported "Recruitment Specialist." Though the description of the secret shopper and the Mystery Shopping Providers Association are correct, the scammers have no real connection to them.

I am **Robert Lawson**, Recruitment Specialist with Platinum Corporation. We have a mystery shopping assignment in your area and we would like you to participate". Secret Shopper® has been in business since 1990. We are a charter member of the Mystery Shopping Provider's Association (MSPA), the professional trade association for the Mystery Shopping industry. There is no charge to apply to be a Secret Shopper® and information is protected. Secret Shopper® is accepting applications for qualified individuals to become mystery shoppers. Its fun and rewarding, and you choose when and where you want to shop. You are never obligated to accept an assignment. There is no charge to become a shopper and you do not need previous experience. After you sign up, you will have access to training materials via e-mail, fax or postal mail.

ABOUT US

Secret Shopper® is the premier mystery shopping company serving clients across America and Canada with over 500,000 shoppers available and ready to help businesses better serve their customers. Continual investment in the latest internet and communication technologies coupled with over 16 years of know-how means working with Secret Shopper® is a satisfying and rewarding experience. Secret shopping as seen on ABC NEWS, NBC NEWS, L.A.TIMES. Since 1990, Secret Shopper® has delivered actionable intelligence to our clients, helping to drive exceptional bottom-line performance. Nearly 1,000 shoppers have registered this week, performing millions of mystery shops throughout North America and the Caribbean. When coupled with our continual investment in the latest internet and communication technologies, you can rest assured that working with Secret Shopper® is a satisfying and rewarding experience.

Secret Shopper® is also a charter member of the industry trade association, the Mystery Shopping Providers Association (MSPA). Benefit from partnering with Americas premier mystery shopping company. We have been building our tradition of excellence for two decades. Stores and organizations such as The Gap, Walmart, Pizza Hut and Banks. One amongst many others pay for Secret Shoppers to shop in their establishments and report their experiences. On top of being paid for shopping you are also allowed to keep purchases for free. Secret Shopper® NEVER charge fees to the shopper. Training, tips for improvement, and shopping opportunities are provided free to registered shoppers. Mystery shoppers are either paid a pre-arranged fee for a particular shop, a reimbursement for a purchase or a combination of both. Secret Shopper® has available for immediate assignment an inspection of the customer service of any walmart in your area. You are to shop secretly. This fee will be paid upfront to you by Check. During this shopping, you will visit a location and make several observations as regards the customer service. You will be required to interact with the shopper clerk. You may conduct the shop alone or as a couple. The assignment will pay $200.00 per duty and you can be able to get up to 2- 3 duties in a week depending on how fast you are able to execute the first assignment. Kindly Fill Out the application form below and we will get back to you shortly with the assignment:

PERSONAL INFORMATION:
First Name:
Middle Name:
Last Name:
Street Address:
City, State, Zip Code:
Cell Phone Number:
Home Phone Number:
Age:
Current Occupation:
Email Address:
We await your urgent response. Thank you your willingness to work with us. We look forward to working with you.

Best Regards
Robert Lawson

However, Robert Lawson sent this letter from a chtonys at AOL account on March 17, and on April 3 from a kbonsu12274596 AOL account. Similarly, Kelvin Joans sent out a February 2 letter from a kimsports1 AOL account and again on February 5 from smartrabit at AOL. And other name and AOL mismatches were even more blatant, such as Eric Zimmerman with mmkkale, Greg Eather with saragolias, Jenny Richardo as wallison09, Mark Wood as peterfveltman, Douglas Neil as croony, John Panes as RSCHUMAN, Jimmy Grabby as Steviejae7, and Robert McCarthy as leahch4. A few also combined their email names with several numbers, such as Eagan Phillips (jambk736) or Jacob Livington (revjgt106). Besides the warning flags in the copy of the letter (such as the high amount to be paid up front and the request for detailed personal information in an initial letter), these email mismatches are another giveaway, even if someone didn't get multiple copies of almost exactly the same letter from different people.

Whether the same scammer is using different aliases and emails or multiple scammers are using a template for these letters, the scam has continued by targeting a great many prospective victims with the same basic message—carry out the steps to doing a mystery shopping assignment, deposit the check we are sending you, and send us the money by Western Union or MoneyGram, the same untraceable sources for sending money used in the phony roommate scam. The steps and time required for becoming a victim are much simpler in the phony jobs scam. It takes just a day or two to lure in the victim and get him or her to act as a shopper. Then, another hour or two is needed for the victim to send off the money, and that's it. But depending on the size of the check sent in advance, the victim can lose about as much—from several hundred to a few thousand dollars. The story and setup are different, but the outcome is much the same. The victim cashes the phony check and is out whatever money he or she sends to the scammer—and it is gone, with virtually no way to get it back, since sending a Western Union or MoneyGram is untraceable, and even if it was, the scammer could be out of the country. Moreover, individual losses of a relatively small amount in different states means that law enforcement is not likely to get involved. The victim's loss is just one more small claim in a backlog of many thousands of cases.

The Effects of the Scam

Despite all these warning signals, if the victim goes along with the scam, law enforcement can generally do little to pursue these phony job scammers, and the effects of the scam can be devastating for the victim, especially since the target is someone seeking a job. In many cases, these victims are literally living on the edge, so the substantial loss of a few hundred to a few thousand dollars can be enough to push someone into deep poverty or homelessness.

Suspecting the Scam

At least a few people become suspicious about the offer or were warned by their banks that the checks were fraudulent so they didn't fall for the scam, though they reported their experiences on the Ripoff Report. Here are some examples of their letters.

From Mrs. Battle in Bellwood, Illinois (July 7, 2014):

> My husband responded to a Work at Home ad for Mystery Shoppers / Secret Shoppers. The person or persons behind this scheme trick people into depositing a fake cashiers check in the amount of $1400 into their bank account first. Then you are supposed to go a Walmart, CVS, Kroger or 7 Eleven to purchase 2 money pak pins for $500 that are $4.95 each, your payment is $300, and after the purchase and your payment there is $80 left over, and in the bogus letter they send you there is a statement at the end that says they will contact you with information on what to do with the remaining $80. . . .
>
> I googled the address and checked the street view, and this address is a raggedy looking house. . . .

Though the company letterhead has an address in Greensboro, NC, the phone number that they tell you to text once you receive the cashiers check & instructions via UPS Next Day delivery is . . . a California number, and when I called it, I learned it was a number they set up through Google. . . . There is no phone number or website on the phony company letterhead. After searching the company, I found it didn't even exist.

I called the bank that the cashiers check was supposedly purchased at. . . . The person I spoke with confirmed the check was fake. . . . She stated that someone has copied and falsified their cashiers checks; and she asked me to fax her a copy of the check and the letter. . . .

I know how hard people work for their money and do not deserve to be sucked into a scam like this. Those who have the audacity to prey on innocent people because they are too sorry to get a job need to be put under the jail.

Another woman, Alyce, in Farmington, Utah (December 15, 2008), quickly suspected a scam when she got an email saying she had been selected to be a mystery shopper, when she hadn't even applied for the job. She also got a check for nearly $5,000 to cash and was asked to send back the difference. Then she noticed even more discrepancies: the company was in a state in the United States but the letter came from Canada. As she wrote:

I received a letter stating I had been selected for a mystery shopper, though I had not applied for or inquired about this job. Along with the letter was a check for $4,995. All I had to do was cash this check and send most of it back by moneygram as my first job.

This is A Scam!! The company is supposedly in Texas, but the letter is postmarked from Canada. If you receive anything from this company, Do Not cash the check. You will be held responsible for returning all of the money.

Still another way that some email recipients recognized the scam is by noticing a discrepancy between the supposed location of the company, the person sending the check, and the bank on which the check was drawn. Why should three different states be involved? This led them to suspect a scam. One man from Pine Knot, Kentucky (April 14, 2015), decided not to further participate in the job offer. As he described it:

I received an acceptance letter with an evaluation form on the back and a check for $1972.18 to be a secret shopper. Instructions were to call Peter Williams before I deposited the check so that it could be activated. The amt breakdown was salary $322.00 and survey funds needed for the job $1650.18. This was for 2 stores. My income potential stated could be up to $1000 per week.

The company listed is in NY, the check was from an art gallery in MD, and the bank in DC. . . . I did not call or deposit the check because it sounded like a scam to me. I started surfing the web regarding this company, and it sounds like it is what I thought, only this time the address is slightly different. (Instead of 20th floor, it is listed as 10th floor). I just do not want anyone ripped off by this company.

In some cases, those suspecting the scam altruistically sought to warn others, as well as protect those companies that were unknowingly linked to the scam to help protect their reputations. Peter from New York (July 21, 2014) wrote this:

Please be aware of e-mail or priority mail regarding an opportunity to become a mystery shopper. There is an offer of $200, but you are also requested to send more money than that - $1350 or $1400.

This scam may reference Buckingham Rseearch Group, however. The group . . . has no relationship to this scam.

Others became suspicious because they couldn't find anything about the company on the Internet—another good way to assess if job offers are from real companies or are scams. Some companies put up a phony website to seem credible, though they may lack contact information with a real person. For example, TiredofCreeps from Harvest, Alabama (July 14, 2014), provided this warning against one company involved in the scam:

I just received a letter today from Joe Corning at National Survey Studies they request that I become a mystery shopper in my area. They include a check for $1658.00. So I googled the company name and could not find anything there. Then I googled Joe Corning and found a lot of information on the Mystery Shopper scam with Global Test Market as the company name. Therefore, decided to write this report hoping that the National Survey Studies will get associated with the same scam.

Still others who had been ripped off before were more wary when they got the mystery shopper offer. So they were determined to wait this time until they got real cash and were pleased to discover a warning report about the scam on one of the scam report sites. Krazeehors from San Antonio, Texas (August 15, 2014), wrote this:

> I received an email from Mr. James Giles, claiming to manage a program that pays people to be a 'Mystery Shopper.' . . .
>
> I signed up for this program and then received yet another e-mail saying, 'Your Check Is On the Way!' along with 'instructions for my assignment.'
>
> I was also told to 'cash this check at MY BANK,' then send HIM a check for $150, telling me that I could keep the item I purchased, and additionally saying that I would be 'Paid' a sum of $200 once he received my 'report,' via email.
>
> As I have been ripped off before, I determined NOT to do ANY shopping until I received the check, cashed it at a public check cashing store (not my checking account), deposited the CASH into my savings account (I set up a new one for this specific purpose), and then would complete the assignment.
>
> Thank you for posting your reports on James Giles. I was almost taken in again.

Of course, after acting upon suspicions, James Giles never got back in contact with Krazeehors.

Some individuals not only suspected a scam, but after checking, they took further steps to stop it by reporting it to the authorities, in this case the Federal Trade Commission. However, as with most scams, law enforcement can do little, since the scammers are often overseas or move around in the United States, and have multiple victims in multiple locations in many states with relatively small losses each—generally under $500 to $2,000. So these are difficult, costly cases to bring with uncertain results due to elusive suspects. At least Sharon from Tennessee (September 25, 2014) tried.

> Received email relating potential mystery shopper position in my local area, as I have performed this task before . . . I answered the ad. A priority USPS envelope arrived with my FIRST assignment along with a check for $1690. The fact that there was not a date, company logo or signature was my initial concern, but as I read through the letter I was sure this was too good to be true. Contacting the credit union USAlliance Credit Union after verifying the routing number, the live chat person 'Mario' was not very helpful.
>
> With further research I found this is a regular scam. I will be reporting this to the federal trade commission as well as turning over the cashier's check to my local bank.
>
> The letter instructions said to "text" 832 318 0209 once the letter/check was received and again when the check was deposited with available funding date. I did text this number to inform them I was reporting them!

In some cases, information from the scam report sites is what led individuals to realize they might be a potential victim of a scam after they did some online research about the company that contacted them, so the scam failed, as reported by Peter in Miami, Florida (November 13, 2014). He became initially suspicious after discovering the website didn't exist and that the domain name had been registered only three weeks earlier. As he described it:

> I witnessed a real case of a scam case about "Green Dot MoneyPak Cards." My roommate signed up with a mystery shopping company that goes by the name of "Retails Active Marketing Inc." . . . email address: hr@retailsactivemarketing.com.
>
> 1. The website does not exist.
>
> 2. Domain name was registered on 24-Oct-2014.
>
> Anyways, he received a Navy Federal Credit Union cashier's check for $2,350. He was instructed to deposit the check and use $2,000 to buy Green DotMoneyPak cards and keep the difference as paymeant.

The assignment was to:

- go to the nearest stores like: CVS, Walmart, 7Eleven, Walgreen
- buy the cards in values of $500 to $1000
- scratch the back of the card to get the pin numbers
- send these numbers by email with a report of his shopping experience

Thank God, the scam failed. After doing a search online, we found the right info to quit the ongoing steps and discovering the whole plan.

Getting a Tip-Off of a Fraud by a Bank, PO, or Check-Cashing Service

In some cases, potential victims who were about to go ahead with the scammer's offer were prevented from doing so because they encountered a bank teller, postal clerk, or check-cashing service rep who shared their own suspicions, leading the potential victims to escape being scammed. In turn, this revelation led some to expose the scam to others by reporting it to law enforcement and the scam reporting sites.

That's what happened when pwwrew from New York (August 23, 2014) received an offer and tried to cash the money order she received but was turned down four times—by two banks, a check-cashing store, and the US Post Office, where he was finally shown why the money order was fraudulent, since it was missing a watermark. After that, she was so angry she notified the Postal Police and FBI. As she described what happened:

> We received a letter from Dr. Pat Rice who indicated that she was the President of a company called TPROOF SURVEY. She asked us to be a mystery shopper to do an evaluation. She sent by priority mail what appeared to be a US Postal Service money order. We thought since she was willing to send us a $985 money order this was legit.
>
> The instructions we were given was to cash the money order or deposit the money order in our bank account and to evaluate the service we received and report on that. We were also asked to take $30 of that money and buy something at Walmart and report on their service as well, and the remaining amount of money which was

$805 was to be sent to someone known as Smooth J Robert (obviously an alias).

Yet even suspecting an alias, pwwrew went ahead with the instructions. As she described it:

> We tried to cash the money order at two of our banks, cash checking place, and the US Post Office. We were turned down by all these. The post office also was reluctant because the money order we were given was on paper that didn't feel right to them and it was missing the watermark of Benjamin Franklin that you can see when you hold it up to the light. We would then have been confronted with depositing the "false money order" into our bank account and withdrawing our own money for the money that was asked of us.
>
> This is exactly what they wanted us to do. I have traced back the IP address of the email that was sent to us and have alerted both the Postal Police and the FBI. If there are others of you who have information that would help track down these perpetrators of this fraud so that they can be brought to justice please send that to the authorities. It's unfortunate that a small few criminals in our society make it bad for legitimate work at home opportunities for the rest of us.

In a few other cases, an astute banker provided the tip-off by noticing the check was fake, and sometimes the bank that allegedly issued the check reconfirmed this, as occurred for Rose from Cleveland, Ohio (December 19, 2014). As she reported:

> [Two] tasks. One was to send $2850 by Western Union to a receiving agent and the second task was to use $150 to shop at one of 10 stores. The rest was to cover expenses and pay me for my services. None of this was to be done until the check cleared in 24-48 hours, I was told. I went to my bank and asked if it was a legitimate check and was told that it wasn't.
>
> Then I called the bank in N.C. that was shown as having issued the check to see if it was legitimate and was told that it was fake. This company tried to scam me out of almost $3000.

Likewise, Paula in Princess Anne, Maryland (February 19, 2015), escaped being scammed because the banker at her bank refused to let her deposit the check, advising her that it was fake. She was angry that the fraudsters tried to scam her and hoped something would be done to stop them. As she commented:

> I am reporting this company as a scam because they sent me a check for being a mystery shopper for $1876.45 and the check was a fraud check, and I was very upset about this, because as I went to my bank to deposit the check like the directions told me to do, my bank told me it was a fake check. I really think this company needs to be sued for this because they have all of my information and my address and everything about me and anybody could be behind this scam and i want to make sure they never do this again to anyone because it's very embrassing and it is very upsetting when you think u have something good coming to you and really it's nothing but a scam or someone just playing around with you and this could really get us the innocent people into trouble when we go to our bank and try to deposit these checks. something needs to be done asap with this company.

Experiencing a Financial Crisis

Unfortunately, some of the people who could least afford it got sucked into the scam, and it caused a crisis in the lives of a number of them. In fact, some of these people were sucked into bigger and bigger pay-offs by the first couple of smaller checks going through, so they were ready to pay out an even larger amount, leading to their financial crisis.

That's what happened to Sheila Nguyen from Phoenix, Arizona (August 1, 2014), who described her situation on the Ripoff Report thus:

> Ive been contacted by Dennis childers. Thru email he was telling me about his company. It seemed legit so I went thru and did two checks for him and I got a bigger amount of $3880. I did what I was suppose to like the last two. But the bank told me it was fraud and he keeps calling me to and telling me I have to do it by tonight. This all happen

this morning. He told me to send it to a person name Timothy Ayew. So now my bank shut down and lock the account on me. I have to pay rent and more thing but no I cant do anything. And I hae[sic] to pay the bank back with interest. I hope they catch him before he do this to many more people.

Likewise, Marilyn E. Thompson of Carmichael, California (September 10, 2014), found the loss of money from to the scam especially difficult, because she was a retired senior citizen living on a small fixed income. As she reported:

The assignment was to cash a postal money order and complete a bank evaluation. Go to Wal Mart and make a purchase. Remaining money order balance less $150.00 for payment as mystery shopper assignment was to then be wired to Smooth J. Robert in Chicago through Western Union Victorville California.

I received a Priority mailing envelope at my residence address. Inside was a typewritten one sheet paper with instructions as a Mystery Shopper assignment and a postal money order in the amount of $985. The sheet indicated my assignment was to cash the money order at the bank and prepare a bank evaluation to include information of what the particulars of the transaction were. I was to claim $150 of that money as my pay for completing the remainder of the assignment.

Next, I was to make a purchase from Wal Mart and not to exceed $40 for my purchase. The remaining funds were to be wired through Western Union to Smooth J. Robert . . . in Chicago, Illinois. The money order was signed by Shawn Conne . . . Victorville, California. Upon sending the wire transfer I was to pay out of the remaining funds the fee for sending.

The typed written sheet which was a part of the directions included a breakdown on what to do with the money and how and where to effect the assignment.

I took the money order to a local bank and opened an account for checking and deposited the total check. The next day I removed all of the funds except $50. When I went online to transfer more funds into the account I discovered my account was debited the money I deposited and was charged a transaction fee.

I am livid. This was a new account I opened and now I owe a fee in addition to the monies I withdrew. I am a Senior Citizen, retired, living on a fixed income and have been scammed. I am extremely upset . . . now what?

Unfortunately, Marilyn's "now what" question cannot be answered successfully for her or anyone scammed by this scheme. The money is gone, and the banks hold the victim responsible and potentially liable for check fraud, though any such claim is unlikely. Rather, the victim is out the money and owes any overdrafts to the bank, unlike the credit card scam, where victims can often get their payments back by claiming an unauthorized purchase was charged to their credit card or debit card. The scenario and particular instructions may differ, but in the end, the essence of the job scam is the same: getting the victim to deposit a phony check and send the money order to a selected recipient before the fraudulent check is discovered by the bank and the victim realizes he or she is being lured into a scam and doesn't deposit the check.

The detailed instructions are like a cover to get the victim to think he or she is performing an assignment exactly as requested; it helps to make the victim think this is a real job with real pay, and many victims fail to question the underlying premise of the scam—deposit the phony check and send us your money before you discover you have lost it all. Another reason that some fall for the scam is because they have worked as mystery shoppers for a legitimate company or worked at a company that was reviewed at times by real mystery shoppers, so they didn't recognize the key difference that made this a scam rather than a real opportunity— the big check payment up front and the requirement to send their own money via Western Union or another money transfer service.

For example, JHanna of Newberg, Oregon (September 10, 2014), described being enticed into perform a series of steps only to find the next day that she had been scammed.

Mystery Shopper Training—I was to deposit $1689.15 in to my account then spend 100 dollars for shopping at your choice of 1 out of 6 stores. Then I was to send western union to the named 'mystery shopper' then my job was filling out 2 surveys about each of the stores customer service that you experienced. When done faxing in your paperwork and your receipts . . . you would earn 400 dollars for training—then the 21.15 was for the service charge on the western union.

My bank just called me today and now my account is overdrawn and i got a charge of 6 dollars for a refunded check. I called the number on my paperwork and it is now no longer assigned to anyone. I hope no one else falls for this trick. I really thought it was legit because . . . when I worked at subway back in my high school days we had mystery shoppers that came in quite frequently.

In another case, a woman and her boyfriend ended up feeling desperate after losing around $1,800 to the scam. She was even pressured by the scammers to quickly go through with the transaction that led to this loss. But soon after she put the check in her bank and sent the money as requested, she could no longer contact the scammers. She couldn't pay her bills and was afraid she might lose her car—all because she wanted to earn a little extra money. SamB from Madison, Virginia (January 29, 2015), described what happened:

Sent a letter in the mail, detailing a job offer for a myster shoper[sic], enclosed with a Check from Hancock Bank. Was told to deposit the check, and take enough out to complete the tasks. Tasks were completing a transaction with Moneygram, spending $100 at Walmart, and spending $100 at Sears.

Company adamantly called over and over when Moneygram task was not completed in the first hour. They called me from a cell phone number and texted my phone as well. . . . Whenever I call this number now, there has been a busy signal, and then a message saying that this number is no longer available.

After the tasks were completed, I did not hear from the company regarding the CSET (Customer Service Evaluation Tool) that we were supposed to fill out. The following day, the check that they activated and instructed us to take money out of to use, had been stopped. Bouncing the account around $1,800. I cannot pay my bills. I fear losing my car, all because I was interested in making a little extra money.

We have direct deposit, and the bank has informed us that my boyfriend's entire check will be taken, plus we will still owe around $900. I am almost in tears writing this report. I don't know how we are going to pay for anything now.

Revictimizing the Victim

In some cases, victims who try to stop the scam get retargeted for being scammed again or are threatened by the scammers to go through with the scam, even after they are aware the offer is a scam.

For example, Skywavebe from Bensenville, Illinois (December 4, 2014), got contacted multiple times with the same job offer, though he already knew the offer was fraudulent. As he reported:

I was contacted for another time by an individual named Bob Thomas this time to become a Mystery Shopper agent. They want all kinds of information but the last time this same scam took place the certified check was sent from Florida and drawn on a bank called the Texas Gulf Bank that is Florida.

Their hope is that you will wire the money via Western Union to a place like China within 48 hours where these characers really are and then when you find out in 10 days that the check is returned to the bank no good, you are the one responsible for the money that you sent. In other words it is a rip off and fraud.

What is more, once you get on the list you keep on getting hit with several Job Offers with different names but the same form letter. If you go looking to see if the legitimate Secret Shopper company works like this it does not and you have to pass a test to become one of their shoppers. These thieves are just using the name of good companies or those that are like it to fool you. The best thing to do with these E mails is to delete them or send them a reply that they are being recorded as a scam and reported on the Internet like I am doing. (Otherwise they will contact you again and again).

Whether or not individuals respond, the scammers may repeatedly go after the same individual once they have their email, since I got nearly two dozen emails, most exactly the same. In some cases, they won't let go of the person who has discovered the scam and is trying to disengage by using coercive tactics to get the person to participate in their own victimization. That's what happened to Theron from Spring Creek, Nevada (August 9, 2014). As he reported:

> JAMES GILES HAS CONTACTED ME NUMEROUS TIMES INCLUDING LEAVING A MESSAGE ON MY PHONE AFTER I DEMANDED HE CALL ME BEFORE I COULD COMPLETE MY MYSTERY SHOPPING ASSIGNMENT. HE SENT ME A POSTAL MONEY ORDER FOR $970.00 AND WANTED ME TO DEPOSIT IT AND IMMEDIATELY WITHDRAW THE FUNDS AND SPEND $50.00 AT WALMART, TAKE ANOTHER $150 AND KEEP THE SHOPPING ITEMS AND THE REMAINING AMOUNT WAS TO BE SENT VIA WESTERN UNION TO TEST THEIR SYSTEM TOO! I TOLD HIM THEY HAD A HOLD ON THE FUNDS AND HE STILL DEMANDED I COMPLETE MY SHOPPING ASSIGNMENT. I HAVE THREATENED HIM WITH REPORTING THIS AS A FRAUD AND HE IN TURN THREATENED ME WITH THE FBI FOR KEEPING HIS MONEY . . . LOL. PLEASE CATCH THESE PEOPLE THAT ARE TAKING BILLIONS FROM AMERICA.

Other Job Scams

Besides the mystery shopper scam, there are other kinds of job scams, although the mystery shopper scam is potentially the most costly—causing people to lose thousands of dollars.[10] Some other phony job offers are used for other purposes, such as to get personal information, including a social security number, credit card, bank account information to access the person's bank account, credit cards, or to steal his or her identity,[11] which will be discussed further under personal information scams. The basic ploy that there is a "job opportunity," though the steps to the scam differ. Usually, the goal is to get personal information, although some scams involve the victim buying something, either by making a direct payment or withdrawing funds from a fraudulent cashier's check, such as to purchase training materials. The scams typically start with an ad on the Internet, Craigslist posting, or other jobs forums, and often they use the name of a legitimate company, and an email address similar to the real company is named.[12] Following is a brief description of other types of job scams.

The Credit Card Scam

This scam begins with a job posting, to which the individual responds. Then the victim gets a letter discussing the job opportunity, but in order to proceed to the next step in the hiring process, he or she needs to have a credit score check. To do so, the victim is directed to a website where he or she is asked to put in personal information, including a name, address, and social security number.[13] A real job interviewer wouldn't ask for such information at this stage. There would be no credit check, at least until the person was seriously considered for the job after a hiring interview, and no social security information would be requested until the person was hired. The purpose of this request for information is to steal the person's identity, since there is no job.

The Pay-for-a-Background-Check Scam

In this case, the job seeker is told that he or she has to pay for the cost of a background check using a prepaid Visa debit card and send it to the interviewer to pay. Sometimes the job seeker may be told that a position has just opened up in a phone interview,[14] but the scam can also be conducted online after the victim has responded to an ad with a résumé. Then, the recruiter simply emails the victim to ask for payment with the prepaid Visa card.

The Pay-for-Software/Program Scam

In this scam, the job seeker is told he or she needs to buy some software or a special program for the job briefing or interview,[15] though the scammer might give another reason the victim has to pay for this software or program. In any case, the victim has to buy this material in advance, and then the company will reimburse him or her. Depending on what the person has to do, the scam could simply be getting a payment for unnecessary material for a nonexistent job, or it could involve getting additional information for an identity theft.

The Pay-for-Online-Training Scam

In this scam, the victims are told they need some online training to be able to do the job, in some cases because the job they applied for has been filled, but now there is an opening for another job that requires this extra training. So the victim has to pay for this in some way, such as sending money or providing credit card information.

The Pay-for-Training-Materials Scam

This is similar to the pay-for-online-training scam, except that victims are told that the company will send them some software so they can work at home. In some cases, the scammer may tell the victim that he or she needs this training after he or she has participated in interview tasks, such as taking a test on accounting or other questions.[16] But instead of sending the package of training materials directly, the company sends the individual a check to deposit into his or her bank and then withdraw the funds to send via Western Union to get the "training materials." So this is a variation on the other phony check scams.

The Direct Deposit Scam

In this scam, the individual is told that the company needs the applicant's direct deposit information, since all employees are paid via a deposit, and often the individual has to do this before even having an interview or being offered the job. Then the scammer directs the victim to a website to enter this information, as well as indicate a preferred date and time for the interview if there is to be one.[17] Obviously, this scheme is to get bank account information that can be used to take money out of the victim's account.

The Trial Employment Scam

In this scam, the victim is told that he or she has been selected to go through a short trial period, such as three weeks. The company name and website seem legitimate, so the individual thinks he or she has the job. But then the company asks the victim to fill out a contract that requires personal information, including a social security number.[18]

While many of these phony job offers use job search websites such as Craigslist, or social media postings such as Facebook and Twitter, others send emails directly to the individual's email address, often from a free email account such as Yahoo, AOL, Gmail, or Hotmail,[19] which was frequently used in the roommate and mystery shopper offers I received. One tip-off that the job offer is a scam, whatever the job, is that no company will offer anyone a job without knowing who they are.[20] Then, too, some email scams use "spoofing" techniques in which they include a link to a posting that seems to come from a legitimate job search site, but in reality, this is a fake site dressed up to look like a real one.

Thus, these job offers can take multiple forms, although the mystery shopper approach is especially costly for victims. Whatever the exact details of the scam, the scammers are basically victimizing job seekers in three different ways:

- Getting victims to cash phony checks and send them money, as in the roommate and other phony check scams.
- Collecting private and confidential information to use for identity theft or for accessing the individual's credit card or bank account to charge or withdraw money.
- Getting the victim to pay for unneeded, overpriced, or substandard services or supplies by either using his or her own money, a credit card, or cashing a phony check and sending the balance.

Recognizing the Scam

Unfortunately, it can be difficult to distinguish between many legitimate and fake jobs because some scammers have become so effective at appearing to be legitimate, such as by creating websites that make them seem real or using names that are the same or similar to the names of real companies. Thus, the first line of defense is to be aware of these different types of job offer scams and look for signs that the company may not be what it seems. Also, recognize the techniques that scammers use with various scenarios, such as getting people to give up personal information or cash checks and send them money.

Besides the job scams listed here, there are dozens of other potential approaches you can read about, such as those listed in "Job Scams List: A-Z" prepared by Alison Doyle, a job-searching expert on About.com's About Careers section.[21] Here are some of them:

- Craigslist Job Scams
- Craigslist Writer/Research Assistant Scams
- Credit Report Scams
- Data Entry Scams
- Direct Deposit Scams
- Email Job Scams
- Employment Scams
- Entry Level Job Scams
- Fake Job Scams
- Internet Job Scams
- LinkedIn Scams
- Money Job Scams
- Nanny Scams
- Personal Assistant Scams
- Phone Call from a Recruiter Scams
- Shipping Scams
- Unemployment Scams
- Visa Scams
- Work at Home Scams[22]

In short, for many types of jobs, there are scams that appeal to job seekers who are sucked into giving out personal information, cashing fake checks, sending information, or a combination of these activities. They become victims because they are eager for a job, are too trusting, don't recognize the warning signs, and do not sufficiently check out the individual or company making the offer. And once someone is scammed, law enforcement can do little more than collect information on a particular individual or company scamming others. Unfortunately, by the time law enforcement collects enough complaints and is ready to take action, the scammers are long gone or perhaps creating another scam or using different names to perpetrate the same scam—and many are out of the country, out of reach of any enforcement action. It may be possible to get your money back if you are duped in a credit card scam, since the credit card company or your bank will cover your losses. But if you send any real money, that is gone.

Thus, the best strategy is to be cautious and recognize the potential for being scammed in the first place. In the case of the phony check scams, whether they involve fake roommates or fake jobs, these are some warning signs there's a scam ahead—and many of these cautions apply to fake job scams generally:

- Recognize that no legitimate company will send you a cashier's check "out of the blue" or require you to "send money to someone you have never met."[23] So don't cash the check or send money to anyone you haven't met.
- Realize that scammers use realistic-looking documents, emphasize the "secret" nature of the mystery shopper or special investigative job, and put pressure on the job seeker with a forty-eight-hour deadline to cash the check and wire the money. This push to act quickly is so the scammer gets the money before you or the bank can determine that you have received a fake check.[24]
- Be wary of secret shopper, mystery shopper, or investigative shopper companies that advertise their jobs on the radio, in a newspaper's classified or help wanted section, or in an unsolicited email asking you to perform this task, since legitimate secret shopper companies generally do not advertise in this way.[25] Normally, prospective job seekers initiate the contact with them.
- Consider it a warning sign if a company guarantees you the job if you apply or charges a fee for you to apply or to get job information.[26]

- Be very cautious if the company or person contacting you appears to be located outside of the country and does not have an established office nearby that you can visit in person.[27]
- Check with the Better Business Bureau to see if the company has a listing, and if so determine if it is a good one. While having no listing is not necessarily a problem—since many small legitimate companies aren't listed—if the company has a low score, reflecting a number of complaints, stay away.
- Avoid fake cashier check scams, which have a variety of scenarios providing reasons for cashing the check and sending money. As Judy Hedding describes in an article on avoiding the "Mystery Shopper Scam," these are things not to do, so you don't get scammed:[28]

  - Do not depend on the funds from a cashier's check from a source you do not know.
  - There is usually no legitimate reason for someone who is giving you money to ask for money to be wired back or wired to a third party. Don't do it.
  - Do not rely on the fact that the check was accepted for deposit by a financial institution as evidence of the check's authenticity. It can take up to a week or much longer for a financial institution to determine whether a check is good, especially if the check is from an institution outside the United States.
  - Consumers are responsible for the deposited fake check, even if it was a cashier's check. When the check bounces, the bank deducts from the consumer's account the amount that was credited with the fake check—often with charges added. The bank will not take the loss.

So there you have it—how to be aware of and avoid being caught by the cash-the-check scams, which take various forms—from roommate to phony job scams. And if you are a victim of these scams? Figure that you can't get back any money you paid out. But you can always report your experience to any of the scam sites or to your state attorney general, FBI, or other authorities who deal with Internet crimes.

Notes

1 Mike, "Avoiding a Common Roommate Scam on craigslist," June 14, 2010. http://www.rentingoutrooms.com/avoiding-a-common-roommates-scams-on-craigslist

2 "Fake Job Offers," That's Nonesense.Com, February 2, 2009. http://www.thatsnonsense.com/viewdef.php?article=fake_job_offer_scams

3 DarkSyke, "Job Seekers Beware of the Fake Job Postings," *Daily Kos,* Feb. 9, 2014. http://www.dailykos.com/story/2014/02/09/1274938/-Job-seekers-beware-of-the-fake-job-postings

4 "How to Recognize a Fake Job Offer Letter," *Career Addict*, http://www.careeraddict.com/3116/how-to-recognize-a-fake-job-offer-letter

5 Angela Rose, "5 Tips to Avoid Fake Job Postings," *Hcareers,* http://www.hcareers.com/us/resourcecenter/tabid/306/articleid/904/default.aspx

6 Susan Kihn, "How to Determine if a Job Offer Is a Scam," *Career Miner,* http://careerminer.infomine.com/scammers-are-constantly-on-the-prowl-how-to-spot-a-scam-job-from-a-real-job/

7 "How to Spot Scam Emails," *Total Jobs.com,* http://www.totaljobs.com/careers-advice/unemployment-advice/how-to-spot-scam-emails

8 "How to Recognize a Fake Job Offer," *Computer Essentials for the Commons,* https://sites.google.com/site/raysaibal/how-to-recognize-a-fake-job-offer

9 Ibid.

10 Laureen Miles Brunelli, "Mystery Shopper Scams," About.com: About Parenting, http://workathomemoms.about.com/od/workathomescams/a/Mystery-Shopper-Scams.htm

11 Alison Doyle, "List of Fake Job Scam Examples," About.Com: About Careers, http://jobsearch.about.com/od/jobsearchscams/a/fake-job-scams.htm

12 Ibid.

13 Ibid.

14 Ibid.

15 Ibid.

16 Ibid.

17 Ibid.

18 Alison Doyle, "Email Job Scams," About.Com/About Careers, http://jobsearch.about.com/od/jobsearchscams/a/email-job-scams.htm

19 Ibid.

20 Alison Doyle, "Job Scams List: A-Z," About.com/About Careers, http://jobsearch.about.com/od/jobsearchscams/a/email-job-scams.htm

21 Ibid.

22 Judy Hedding, "Mystery Shopper Scam," About.com/AboutTravel, http://phoenix.about.com/od/scam1/a/mysteryshop.htm

23 Ibid.
24 Ibid.
25 Ibid.
26 Ibid.
27 Judy Hedding, "Mystery Shopper Scam," About.com/Mystery Shopper, http://phoenix.about.com/od/scam1/a/mysteryshop.htm

CHAPTER 4

AUTO REPAIR SCAMS

Another major scam, sometimes called the "Number 1" scam in the United States, is the auto repair rip-off. This can take many forms, from being overcharged to being advised to have unnecessary repairs to having a mechanic repair a car improperly. A key reason for these scams is that car owners typically know little about cars, so they are vulnerable to what a mechanic or shop owner tells them. Often, they have to get a repair done quickly because of a car breakdown or accident. As an article on "Auto Repair Fraud" offered by MyAutoRepairAdvice.com notes: "The easiest people to rip off are the ones who know nothing about their car or what is being done to it. When you lack knowledge on a subject matter, you're more likely to believe whatever you're told and therefore stand a higher risk of being ripped off."[1]

Another factor contributing to rip-offs is there are so many auto body and auto repair shops, many of them unlicensed or without any local business affiliations. Even licensing or local business memberships may provide no consumer protections, so it is difficult to keep track of consumer complaints. Thus a perfect storm of factors make it easy for auto repair scams to flourish, especially since there is a lack of enforcement by any auto industry organization or law enforcement. As a result, it is largely up to the consumer to take steps to avoid being scammed—such as getting local references, obtaining second opinions, and checking scam report sites—so as to stay away from shops with a dubious record. In the case of auto repair problems, reports of fraud to banks and credit card companies often won't work, since the customer has commonly signed a contract authorizing the repairs or has given a verbal go-ahead; it becomes a matter of dispute about what was done and how well, so any outcome is uncertain if the customer goes to court. The car owner could well lose, in addition to spending the time and expense of taking a complaint to court. Thus, most victims can do little besides avoiding the scammer in the first place.

Ironically, getting trapped by an auto repair scam is what inspired me to look into scams generally and write this book. In my case, not knowing much about cars, I took in my old Toyota with 140,000 miles on it for an inspection to see if it would be safe to drive about 500 miles to Las Vegas from my house in Lafayette in the San Francisco Bay Area. When the mechanic told me the car should be fine, I got the air conditioning fixed, knowing it would be hot. I was going there for three days to meet the director, cast, and crew for a film I had written and executive produced—SUICIDE PARTY: SAVE DAVE—and if my car hadn't gotten a clean bill of health, I would have flown there.

So I drove there, and after three days and forty more miles in Las Vegas, the radiator, thermostat, and hose gave out and the car broke down the day before I planned to drive home. I spent eight hours at a Toyota dealership deciding what to do, because even if I fixed the cooling system, a Pep Boys mechanic told me there was a fifty–fifty chance the engine could blow, too. If that happened, not only could I not afford any additional repairs, but I feared risking a drive across the very hot 250-mile Mojave Desert, since any breakdown could be deadly. So I ended up buying a new car I couldn't really afford after I barely qualified for a six-year car loan, which I am still paying off.

But when I called the auto repair shop to at least get a refund for the repairs I wouldn't have gotten if they hadn't said the car would be fine after their inspection, the auto repair shop would take no responsibility. Later I discovered that experts hired for their advice do have a duty to warn—such as about the risk of taking an old car into a very hot location. They refused to reimburse me for the air conditioning, which I only got because of the trip, since the air conditioning still worked. They also claimed that once the car left the shop there was no way to predict what might happen to it, so they were only responsible for what they actually fixed—the air conditioning system, which worked. The owner even insulted me for not realizing that it was not a good idea to take a car with 140,000 miles on it on a long trip to a very hot place, and since it was up to 116 degrees in Las Vegas, what did I expect? But that's why I took the car in for an inspection, and the mechanic who inspected my car gave me no warning. The owner even dared me to take him to court and sarcastically added: "Why not claim we're responsible for paying for your new car, too?" after which he added, "And when you lose in court, we'll get our expenses for our lawyer, too," though lawyers are not allowed in small claims court.

But rather than put the time, effort, and expense into suing, I incorporated what happened into a suspenseful murder mystery thriller called *The New Car* and began researching and writing about auto repair scams, first for a Huffington Post blog and then about scams generally for this book. Plus I filed a really negative Yelp report about both the company's Lafayette branch, which did the inspection and repairs, and its home office in a nearby town.

As I wrote in my first article:

Typically, an auto repair scam involves advising you that you need unnecessary repairs, not doing the stated repairs, or increasing the bill by adding repairs after you get a quote. Commonly auto repair shops can get away with these extra repairs and charges, because consumers generally don't know very much about what's going on inside their car. But what about doing extra unneeded repairs, when an auto repair shop leads you to think that your car will be okay to drive after they complete the repairs, but they don't warn you of the risks if you drive it? That's what happened to me, which led me to think about the problems pervasive in the auto repair industry, though most repair services are quite reputable.

In brief, what happened to me is this. I took my car in for an inspection at a service center, because it was an authorized service for my type of car, which I had for over 30 years. When I brought in my car, I told the manager I wanted to be sure my car, with about 140,000 miles, would be safe for a 500 miles trip I was planning from the Bay Area to Las Vegas, which gets very hot during the summer. After the inspection, the manager said the car would be fine, so I got the air conditioning system fixed, a repair I wouldn't have made if not assured the car would be okay. But then the car broke down my third day there due to the failure of the radiator and coolant system, and even if I got these repairs, a big chain repair services advised me of a 50-50 chance of another break down due to gasket and engine problems. So rather than risk a potentially deadly breakdown in the desert, besides the cost of more repairs, I bought a new car I couldn't really afford. Then when I told the service owner what happened, he claimed no responsibility for anything, even the unnecessary repairs I ordered because of his manager's assurances my car would be safe. If he had mentioned any risk, I would have left my car at home, flown to Vegas, and rented a car.

This situation led me to look at auto repair scams generally and consider what consumers can do to avoid them.

One discovery is that auto repair complaints are the largest type of consumer grievances, and many involve car repair scams. According to the National Highway Traffic Safety Administration, consumers lose "tens of billions of dollars each year due to faulty or unnecessary car repairs" (www.fraudguides.com/auto-repair-scam.asp).

A key reason for this high complaint rate is that many people like me know little or nothing about their cars and don't understand what is being done to them, so they can easily be persuaded to get repairs they don't need or be subjected to other scams, such as getting a "bad" part that isn't really bad replaced or not having the agreed-upon work done (www.myautorepairadvice.com/car_repair_fraud.html).

Even some of the biggest auto repair chains have been found cheating customers, as revealed by a four-month undercover investigation of Jiffy Lube by NBC4 NEWS in 2013. Though an NBC4 exposé seven years earlier had led Jiffy Lube to apologize for cheating customers and promise changes through its system, in its 2013 [investigation], the NBC4 team uncovered new tricks and tactics, some violations of the law. For example, the I-Team's hidden cameras discovered Jiffy Lube employees charging for repairs that were never done, rigging diagnostic tests to say the car needed repairs, or urging customers to get unnecessary repairs (www.nbclosangeles.com/news/local/You-Were-Robbed-NBC4-I-Team-Exposes-New-Tricks-and-Tactics-at-Jiffy-Lube-Stores-207304771.html). In fact, the investigators found that seven out of eleven Jiffy Lubes they went to engaged in deceptive practices, suggesting a continuing system-wide abuse at the biggest U.S. car repair chain with about 22 million customers at over 2000 franchises nationwide (www.scpr.org/news/2013/05/13/37244/investigation-7-out-of-11-jiffy-lubes-scam-custome/).

While I wasn't directly advised to get unneeded repairs, the manager's failure to advise me of the risks on a long trip after an inspection of my old car led me to get unnecessary repairs to take the trip, which led to my car's breakdown.

So what are the biggest unnecessary auto repair scams and what can you do about them? According to Angie's List, an online service that reviews local companies, one scam is claiming you have a dirty air filter, and to prove it, a mechanic will show you a black and dusty filter, but it may not be yours. Another trick is the oil change scam urging you to upgrade to a premium synthetic oil. An even more expensive scam is a company giving an initial quote to investigate what's wrong and then claiming you owe money for all the repairs done and you can't get back your car until you pay (www.angieslist.com/articles/beware-these-3-common-car-repair-scams.htm). Still other scams include luring you in with low-cost specials and padding the work order with other repairs you don't need or want (www.huffingtonpost.com/jason-alderman/steer-clear-of-auto-repai_b_3720395.html). Or a service might advertise a reasonably priced check-up or preventative maintenance service and then suggest expensive and unneeded repairs (www.fraudguides.com/auto-repair-scam.asp).

What can you do? One strategy is to check out listings on Yelp or Angie's List to see if other customers think this is a reputable service or not, and these websites can also suggest other services in your area with higher ratings. The Better Business Bureau's website can be another good place to check. Or a victim can report scams to sites like My Auto Repair Advice.com (www.myautorepairadvice.com/car_repair_fraud.html), which has a Facebook page for auto repair scam stories: www.facebook.com/myautorepairadvice.

Another precaution is asking for a written estimate before you authorize repairs, required in most states if a repair is over $100 or exceeds an estimate by 10%. Also, get guarantees in writing and don't authorize any repairs unless you are sure a repair is needed (www. fraudguides.com/auto-repair-scam.asp). Plus check that the work order clearly specifies the repairs to be done, along with all fees including parts and labor based on a flat rate or hourly fee. Consider getting a second opinion and ask for diagnostic or assessment charges if you do this. If the shop says a part is bad, ask to see it or where it fits, so you avoid one of the easiest rip-offs—claiming you need a replacement part when you don't and even showing you a part from another car to prove it. Just seeming knowledgeable and asking questions can help you avoid many of these frauds.

And here's my scathing Yelp review, although I have taken out the name of the company to conceal their identity.
First my original review:

I went to the company's Lafayette branch to get an inspection before driving my old car to Las Vegas to be sure it was safe, and indicated that this is why I was getting this inspection. They recommended a minor inspection and since they assured me the car would be safe, I got the air conditioning fixed. Had I not relied on their assurance, I would not have gotten this fixed and would have flown to Las Vegas and rented a car.

But two days after I got to Las Vegas, the car broke down because of leaks in the radiator and thermostat problems, leaving me with the option of paying about $750 for repairs. But even then I was advised the car might not make it because a gasket could blow, requiring another $1600 for repairs. Rather than driving home as planned, I spent about 10 hours dealing with the breakdown and getting an assessment of the problem from a gas station mechanic, Pep Boys, and the Toyota service center in Las Vegas. Due to the cost and safety concerns of getting stuck in the 250 mile Mojave Desert, I bought a new car I couldn't really afford.

I felt that ********* had some responsibility for what happened given their assurances my car would be safe to drive to Las Vegas. Then, when I contacted the company based in ****** about at least getting a refund for the air conditioning repair which I wouldn't have gotten had I not driven to Las Vegas, the owner not only refused to take any responsibility or provide any refund, but was insulting to me, disparaged my detailed letter of problems which had been reviewed by an attorney before I sent it, and claimed that if I tried to take this to small claims court, he would bring his lawyer and I would have to pay his legal expenses (when in fact, lawyers aren't allowed in small claims court).

Here's my response to the owner's comments:

First, my name is Gini. Secondly, my car had 144,000 miles on it, not 180,000 miles. Third, the heat in Las Vegas during that period was 105 degrees not 116. Fourth, and most significantly, I originally brought the car in for what Toyota calls a mini or minor inspection to make sure my car was safe to drive to Las Vegas. I advised the service manager of my plans for this trip and my concern that the car be safe to drive there. I was aware that the car hadn't been serviced for some time, since I only drove about 2000 miles in 2 years and I didn't need an A/C repair for local driving. It was only after I was assured the car would be safe to drive to Las Vegas that I authorized the A/C repair due to the high heat there. Had I had any warning of the risks of taking my car to Las Vegas due to the heat, I would not have authorized the A/C repair which I didn't need for local driving and I would not have driven to Las Vegas. I would have flown and rented a car. I have since done extensive research, and there is a duty to warn under certain circumstances, such as when one looks to someone who claims to be an expert in something, as would be the case in taking a car to a mechanic for an inspection or repairs. I have very little knowledge about cars, and so I looked to your service manager or mechanic for this advice in asking if my car would be safe to drive to Las Vegas, and only drove it there and arranged for these repairs based on those assurances. Knowing about the risks of taking an older car there, as you have suggested in your response to me, the manager should have given me a warning, but didn't, perhaps because I would then not authorize the repairs.

I initially only asked for a refund of the cost of repairs, which I would not have made but for the assurances my car would be safe to drive to

Las Vegas with these repairs, and that would settle the matter. I did not originally ask for anything for the cost of the car which I had to purchase, given the cost of additional repairs to the radiator system, and the dangers of other systems in the car failing on the drive through a 250 mile desert, which could be deadly. The possible problems in these other systems were not identified in the inspection. But in your phone call to me you responded to my offer with insults and threats of legal costs should I pursue this, though there are no lawyers involved should I take this to small claims court or seek a refund through a claim to my MC account. You also did not respond to the letter from my lawyer affirming my claim for a refund.

Also, I originally used your service, since your sign to service Toyotas suggests you are acting as an authorized, certified, or otherwise sponsored representative of Toyota, and I have long had an excellent relationship with Toyota for over 30 years. So this may have been an inappropriate use of the Toyota name to imply this representation, and had I been aware of this lack of authorization from Toyota as well as the negative Yelp reviews, I wouldn›t have used your service.

So my own experience set the stage for my more extensive review of the different ways auto repair scams occur, including examples from victims who have been scammed, and a discussion about what to do if you become a victim of one of these scams.

The Many Different Auto Scams

There are a vast number of auto scams, and according to several sources, including Fraud Guides, these repairs make up the largest group of consumer complaints. As Fraud Guides reports, according to the National Highway Traffic Safety Administration, "consumers lose tens of billions of dollars each year due to faulty or unnecessary car repairs." Although most auto repair shops are honest, the results of undercover car repair stings reveal dishonest mechanics and auto repair shops victimizing consumers in most areas of the country.[2] In fact, a *Consumer Reports* survey in 2013 found that 27 percent of the respondents were dissatisfied with their experiences, according to their Annual Auto Survey of reports of more than 67,000 service visits to independent mechanics and 101,000 visits to dealerships for the past twelve months. The main reasons for the dissatisfaction were high prices, cited by 38 percent, not getting their problems fixed properly, for 20 percent, and getting repairs that didn't "hold up," cited by 18 percent.[3]

Key reasons for this high level of consumer dissatisfaction with repairs are that it is relatively easy for an auto mechanic to convince a car owner that he or she needs unnecessary repairs, to perform various bait-and-switch tactics such as substituting used parts for new ones, or to not even make the repair. If unauthorized repairs are made, the shop can refuse to return the car until the excessive payment has been paid. Vacation and business travelers are especially vulnerable to these scams because they are out of their local area, where they can take their time and get references before taking their car in for repairs. But in a faraway location, they can't do so. Plus they may feel stranded and that they have little choice but to rely on what the mechanic tells them to do. Commonly, they aren't in a position to get additional opinions and estimates since they are in an emergency situation calling for quick action. In fact, they may be stuck with the only repair shop for miles. So they are like sitting ducks, easily hit by whatever an unethical mechanic or repair shop owner might shoot at them.

Following are descriptions of these major scams, followed by examples from victims who have experienced different scams, and lastly some recommendations on what to do to avoid being scammed.

The Highway Vandal or Bandit

The scam here is that the highway vandal or bandit, who either owns or works for a service station, actually damages your car, and then you have fix it yourself. They victimize the motorist who stops for air or water. While the motorist may think that this is a routine stop, suddenly he or she discovers all kinds of damage, so the car now needs some repairs. For example, larcenous mechanics may spray or drip oil under a car and then claim it leaked from the victim's car, requiring some fixes to whatever is causing the "leak." The bandits may also puncture tires or cut water hoses and fan belts, so the victim has to buy new ones. In turn, motorists commonly fall for these schemes because they fear what may happen if they don't make the repair, and when the scammer makes the unnecessary repairs, often the prices are inflated, so the motorist is doubly victimized.[4]

Repair Overcharges

One of the biggest scams is inflating the cost of the repair beyond the original estimate. This can occur in several ways.

One type of overcharge occurs when the mechanic provides a verbal estimate that sounds reasonable for the cost of the repair when the consumer brings in the car. But when the consumer arrives to pick up the car, the repair bill is much higher, which could seem legal, since the mechanic could have found additional work. However, in that case, the shop is supposed to call the customer for an authorization that is higher, generally more than $50 or 10 percent more. But if the original estimate was verbal, it is hard to prove what it was.

Another approach to overcharging is for the mechanic or shop owner to leave the estimated cost of repairs section blank when asking the customer to sign an authorization for the repair. Unfortunately, the blank estimate on the form leaves the door open for filling in an inflated amount, or even further descriptions of the problems by the mechanic or shop owner, after the customer leaves.

Still another way that car scammers can jack up the prices is by advertising a low-priced repair job, such as an engine tune-up or oil change, at a very low price that brings in the consumer, anticipating a great deal. But once you bring in your car, the mechanics find other problems in your car that need to be fixed, so the sales manager or shop owner gets you to agree to additional repairs and increases your bill accordingly. This is an example of the classic "bait and switch" scam, where you are drawn into a store by a low offer on one product and are then convinced to buy another product at a higher price.[5]

Unnecessary Upgrades

A scam related to overcharges is getting you to agree to an upgrade rather than the usual product you plan to get, so you end up getting a premium product, such as a better grade of oil that your car doesn't need. One way this works is that you bring in your car for an oil change, which you do need. But soon after the mechanic looks at the car, you get a call that your car needs a premium or synthetic oil, and you have to approve getting this better-quality product. The mechanic might even tell you about the potential problems you might experience if you use a low-grade oil, thereby convincing you that you need this upgrade. In some cases, you might even be asked to come back to the shop to speak to the manager to sign an agreement to show you approve, and then the manager might tell you about further problems that were encountered once the mechanic lifted your car on the hoist. So now you are persuaded to approve fixing these issues that weren't detected before, since they are "hard to see, highly technical to describe," and they are very expensive to fix.[6] But now, since the mechanic has presumably discovered these problems in time and seems to be especially adept in discovering them, you are convinced you need to pay to repair these unneeded upgrades—and any additional repairs.

Unnecessary Repairs

Often a way to get customers to agree to unnecessary repairs is by using verbal agreements, blank repair sections, and bait-and-switch tactics, as previously described. But scammers use other strategies to get customers to make these agreements, which may seem perfectly legal—however the catch is that the mechanic or shop owner misrepresents the facts. They can readily do this, because the average customer knows very little about how to repair or maintain a car—and given the recent technological improvements of the last few years, cars have become more complex than ever, making the average person even less knowledgeable about what is going on under the hood. So an unethical mechanic or repair shop owner can easily deceive most customers about what they really need.

For example, when I took my car in for an inspection, I was the perfect candidate for any kind of deception, since I knew little about my twenty-two-year-old car. Aside from knowing I had to keep water in the radiator and oil in the oil tank and knowing that something was wrong if I heard an unusual knocking or clunking or saw steam rising up from the radiator, I knew little more. Then, after I got a new car after my old car expired in Las Vegas, I knew even less. The car salesman gave me a fifteen-minute overview of how to turn on the ignition, raise and lower the automatic windows, adjust the mirrors using buttons to change the angles, and stop and go. That was it, except for giving me a 700-page car manual, which I still haven't read.

After about nine months of owning the car, I have learned how to respond to unexpected things, such as when the horn suddenly honks for some reason, though I still don't know why. I have learned to stop that by putting a key into the front door lock and turning it. But mostly, I have learned the bare minimum needed to drive the car safely. So, an auto repair shop owner or mechanic could tell me just about anything, and I wouldn't know whether a repair was truly needed or not.

A great many other drivers are in a similar situation. They really don't know what is going on in their cars, making them easy targets for an unethical shop owner or mechanic.

Problems with Parts

Another type of scam involves the parts that the mechanic is supposedly putting in your car, when the parts aren't what they are claimed to be. Then you might be charged not only for these parts but also for the labor to install them.

One version of this scam involves charging for parts that weren't used, along with the labor for the nonexistent replacement. Another version is to install substandard or used car parts, while claiming these are new and even premium parts and charging accordingly. Then, too, counterfeit parts might be used instead of the standard high-quality parts from reputable manufacturers. Again the customer pays the full price. Aside from paying more, there can be a danger to the customer when substandard, used, or counterfeit parts are put in your car, since they can be unsafe due to wearing out sooner than genuine parts due to their inferior quality. But when you don't know about cars, it can be very hard to detect these fraudulent parts, and recognizing counterfeits can be especially difficult because the counterfeiters commonly stamp on duplicate or only slightly altered trademarks, so only experts can tell the difference.[7]

Even asking to see the parts taken out of your car may not help, since sometimes unethical mechanics and shop owners will show you a part that they claim is damaged, but it is not actually a part from your car. Rather, it is one of a series of parts kept on hand to defraud customers into thinking something is wrong with a part in their car. Unsurprisingly, the shop has exactly what the customer needs to replace it.

One variation on this scam is the dirty air filter scam, according to an Angie's List article, "Beware of These 3 Common Car Repair Scams." The scam occurs when you bring your car in for regular maintenance or repair and the mechanic reports that your air filter is dirty. This filter could be the engine air filter, which protects your car's most essential moving parts from dust and debris, or it could be your cabin air filter, which is attached to your HVAC or heating, ventilation, and air conditioning system and cleans the air as it comes in through your vents. In either case, the scam occurs when the mechanic tells you how dirty your filter is and shows you a black and dusty filter. But the trick is that it's not the filter from your own car, so you will be duped into buying a filter you do not need.[8]

Another parts scam is using used parts instead of new ones. While used parts can often be an effective replacement for worn out or broken parts, what isn't legitimate is charging you the full price for a new part, while using a used or lower quality part purchased at a lower price, so the shop profits from the difference. Then, too, mechanics and shop owners sometimes significantly mark up the cost of the parts, along with the labor, since customers commonly don't know what a part really costs.[9]

Other Common Upsells

Still other common unnecessary repairs and upsells are these, according to another Autoblog.com article, "Don't Fall for These Auto Repair Tricks."[10]

The Flat Tire Replacement

In this scam, a mechanic or salesperson tries to sell you a brand new tire or pair of tires after you bring in a car with a flat, though most flats are due to screws, nails, or other sharp metal objects that penetrate the tire, and generally the tire can be repaired by simply removing the object or covering the break with a patch that costs around $20.

Replacing Your Radiator Coolant

This scam typically occurs when you take your car in for a routine oil change or when you are doing a periodic maintenance inspection. In this case, the mechanic will recommend that you replace not only your oil but also your radiator coolant. However, this additional purchase is unnecessary, since radiator coolant is made from water mixed with antifreeze and it doesn't degrade as does oil, which requires periodic changes. The only time you need to replace your coolant is if it has been contaminated or if it hasn't been replaced in 100,000 miles.

Replacing Your Oil More Frequently as a Preventative Measure

In this scam, a mechanic or shop owner advises you to change your oil more frequently than necessary, say in 3,000 miles. But this oil changing is unnecessary and costly, since modern cars don't require such frequent oil changes, and modern oil products last much longer than they used to. So if your newer car requires synthetic oil, you can typically go for up to about 15,000 miles before you need to change your oil—not every 3,000 miles.

Unnecessarily Replacing Your Air Filter

Aside from using the trick of showing you someone else's dirty air filter so you will replace yours, mechanics and shop owners may recommend a filter replacement without even seeing your old one or they may charge extra for doing an inspection. The only time an air filter needs to be replaced is if it is clogged with dust and grime, and to determine this the mechanic should visually inspect the old filter to see if it really is clogged, and if it is, he should show you the old filter so you can inspect it to see if there is any dust or debris trapped there. Moreover, the mechanic should do this inspection without a special inspection charge, since a visual inspection on most cars only takes a minute or two.

Recommending a Fuel Injection Service Every 15,000 Miles

Replacing a fuel injection system this often is normally unnecessary, since a fuel injection system should last the lifetime of the car or at least 100,000 or more miles[11] if you use good quality fuel, as most customers do. So if a fuel injection system is performing poorly, the usual cause is a dirty fuel filter, which is much cheaper to replace.[12]

Replacing an Air Filter at Every Oil Change

In this case, it's a waste of money to replace the air filter so frequently. Rather it should be replaced once a year or every 12,000 to 15,000 miles, but a mechanic or shop owner might recommend a more frequent change to make more money.[13]

Getting an Unnecessary Engine Flush

In this scam, a mechanic might tell you an engine flush is necessary because your oil is dirty, but if he does, according to *Reader's Digest*, he's lying. The only time to get an engine flush is if you have been "driving the car for several years and notice a buildup of greasy material under the oil cap." But otherwise you don't need it.[14] In "Common Auto Repair Scams to Avoid," Aaron Crow notes: "Spending $20 on an engine flush is wasted money on a service that's not part of normal maintenance unless you've neglected your engine and don't change the oil when needed. An engine flush gets rid of sludge in an engine, which is something your engine won't likely need if you've taken care of your car."[15]

Getting an Unnecessary Auto-Transmission Flush

This kind of flush is also unnecessary according to the same *Reader's Digest* feature, because most cars have filters that keep the transmission fluid flowing freely. So there's no need to even consider such a transmission flush until you have driven at least 60,000 miles.[16]

Recommending Gas-Saving Devices

The scam here is that these devices don't work. The way to save gas is to accelerate gradually, avoid unnecessary braking, reduce the weight in your car, and learn to coast effectively, according to the *Reader's Digest* feature "Car Repair Scams to Watch Out For."[17]

Overcharging for Replacement Parts

In this case, the shop charges an extra high markup on the cost of the parts, in addition to its charges for labor. Shops can get away with these overcharges because most consumers don't know about the cost of parts, although they could avoid being scammed by comparing the prices in a repair estimate with the prices at a local auto parts store, and buying the needed parts in advance if the cost is substantially less. Or just being a knowing consumer might lead the auto repair shop to lower its price for parts, since they know you know the fair price for these parts and can go somewhere else to get them—or you might even go elsewhere for the whole repair.

Poor Workmanship

Still another scam is offering to fix something—perhaps in the course of replacing parts—but not fixing it very well. Then the customer has to bring the car back in to repair the previous repair or any other damages to the car due to the poor workmanship. Adding insult to injury, you have to pay for further repairs each time you bring the car back to the shop. The problem is due to the mechanic's or shop's negligence, but you still have to pay to fix the damages, sometimes because the shop blames you for doing something wrong that led to further repairs.[18]

Making Expensive Fixes without Your Approval

Another trap is when you discover the shop has made additional repairs you didn't formally authorize after you drop off the car to be fixed for something else. A common modus operandi for this scam is to carry out these repairs after you leave and you weren't given a written list of what you authorized the shop to do. According to Doug Bonderud in "Beware of These Common Car Repair Scams," one way this scam occurs is when you bring in your car because it is "acting up" and you want the shop to look at what's going on and call you back with their findings. That's what an ethical shop will do before fixing anything, whether this is a free or paid diagnosis. But in the scam, the shop will call back to tell you the inspection found a great many problems that have now been fixed, so you owe the company hundreds or thousands of dollars. They may put you off with a technical explanation of what they had to fix. As Bonderund notes: "They may talk about tubes and gaskets, spark plugs or transmissions, but the bottom line is they want you to pay for all the repairs."[19] All you should really owe is for the initial inspection and the labor to conduct this investigation. You shouldn't have to pay for work done without your written permission, but commonly customers will feel stuck with the bill, or the repair shop will threaten to hold the car until the bill is paid.

Damaging Your Car to Create More Repairs

While this scam is less common, some dishonest mechanics will damage your car so you have to pay more for repairs. A type of damage is creating a broken axle boot by cutting these boots, which you can spot by seeing a clean cut, whereas a real tear is jagged and dirty.[20]

Upping the Hours for the Job

Still another scam is to charge more for labor, since mechanics commonly charge by the hour rather than the job. So it can be easy to inflate the number of hours, such as claiming that a job that should only have taken an hour has taken three. In fact, some mechanics jack up the prices by working on multiple jobs at the same time and charging the full time for all of them. Some mechanics may take a break for lunch on your dime. And sometimes a shop will tell you a repair took longer than estimated because of complications, so you have to pay for the extra labor time.[21]

Taking Your Tires

Although rare, one scam is to take your good tires and swap them for older tires that are around the shop, since it's easy to take off your tires and switch them, and the shop owner knows he can sell your like-new or slightly used tires to another customer to make a profit. Meanwhile, the tires on your car will wear out and need to be replaced more quickly—perhaps even at the shop that switched your tires.

Verbal or Bogus Estimates

Apart from overcharges, unneeded repairs, faulty parts, and bad workmanship, another scam that can contribute to these other scams is giving you verbal or bogus estimates. Sometimes you may get a verbal estimate when you first take your car into the shop, or you may later get a verbal estimate when the mechanic calls to tell you about another problem discovered during an inspection or repair job. Then, when you go to pick up your car, you find the price is higher than you were originally given or heard on the phone. In the case of the bogus estimate, you may get a repair estimate in writing, but the shop leaves the estimated amount blank and still requires that you sign the document. Later on, the mechanic or shop owner might write in a changed estimate for additional repairs.[22]

False Advertising—Or the Art of the Great Deal

In this scam, an unwitting customer is drawn in by what seems like a great deal from an ad or sign at the shop, such as an oil change for $10 or a tune-up for $40. Or sometimes the promotion is for a free alignment check.[23] This ad is really a promotional offer to get you to come to the shop. Then the mechanic finds all kinds of problems that need to be fixed, and if you agree, the great deal can turn into paying hundreds or thousands of dollars due to inflated prices, unnecessary repairs, and the many other ways that some auto repair shops scam customers.[24] For example, the Coalition Against Insurance Fraud reports that "dishonest repair shops advertise super-low prices on specific repairs or check-ups, then use these specials to bilk their customers. A simple oil change and lube job can turn into expensive and unneeded repairs."[25]

Not Honoring a Warranty or Other Promises

Then there are the many scams when auto repair shops don't honor a warranty and don't provide the services or charge you for the repair work that should be covered. Plus, shops may make other promises but not keep them, such as telling you the shop will provide free towing or a free rental car during repairs but then charging you for the towing or the rental. Still another unkept promise may be claiming that the repair services will be completed by a certain day in order to get you to leave your car to be fixed, but then the services aren't completed by that day.[26]

Getting Your Authorization When Your Car Is Up on a Lift

This scam is a little bit like kidnapping your car and then seeking your authorization to proceed with the repairs. Once your partially disassembled car is up on the lift, you may feel forced to authorize the shop to go ahead with the overpriced repairs because otherwise you take the risk of "getting your car back in a disassembled and unusable condition," or you have to "pay a large and unexpected fee to have your vehicle reassembled, only to discover it no longer runs at all."[27]

Holding Your Car until You Pay Up

In this scam, which often accompanies these other scams for overcharged, unneeded, or shoddy work or for damages to your car, your car is held hostage until you pay the repair shop's bill. Some victims have ended up without their car for weeks or months as they struggle to raise the money. The irony is that you generally don't owe all or any of this money, because you have not authorized the repairs or because the damage to your car far outweighs the cost of any repairs the company has done. But usually owners do pay because they are afraid they company will hold their car. Normally companies can't hold a car for a questionable repair that could be fraud, but owners don't know this, so they pay. However, if they call the police or threaten to do so, the shop will generally release the car, because the last thing they want is an investigation of their operation by the cops.

Summing Up the Many Varieties of Auto Scams: Let Me Count the Ways

In sum, there are a vast number of auto repair scams. Besides the ones commonly listed, there could be many more.

While the vast number of auto repair shops and mechanics may be honest and ethical, it is easy for those that are dishonest and out to profit as much as they can to scam unwary customers, because most people know little about cars, especially the modern ones with the new technologies. It can feel like piloting a rocket ship, with so many electronic and mechanical devices that could potentially stop working correctly. I used to know little about my car that died in Las Vegas, after being assured it would be safe to drive by a shop that assumed no responsibility when it wasn't. And now that I have a 2014 car with all kinds of electronic devices and a 700-page manual, I know even less.

So, unethical mechanics can easily take advantage of the lack of general knowledge with all kinds of scams, including holding your car for payment if you resist paying for overcharges or unauthorized or unnecessary repairs.

In turn, consumers can feel truly helpless as well as angry when they have been victimized by a scam. The following section illustrates a wide sampling of these consumer accounts on just one of the report-a-scam sites—the Ripoff Report (www.ripoffreport.com)—over just a few weeks in April 2015. And the forty or so complaints I reviewed are just the tip of the iceberg. There would be vastly more complaints if these reports were obtained over many months or years and at multiple scam sites. Still this sampling shows the many different types of scams victims experienced and their inability to do much except pay and share their anger by reporting the scam.

Commonly, the complaints combined multiple problems—notably bad repairs, overcharges, failures to honor warranties and promotional offers, and refusals to return a car if the person didn't pay even though they disputed the charges.

A Bad Repair and Overcharges

One major complaint was that the repair shop not only did a bad job but then overcharged the victim. For example, Lance from Largo, Florida, had this to say about his repeated visits to install a new air conditioning unit. After the unit installed didn't work, the company was unwilling to redo the work, even when Lance provided a new unit he bought himself. As he described his updated April 1, 2015, complaint:

> After having a new air conditioning unit installed in my car, I took my car to Platinum Wrench to have the system finished up and recharged. I paid $160 for this to be done. The new unit burnt out after only a couple of weeks. I returned the parts to the auto store where purchased, as it was under warranty and [I] had another new until installed, thinking the 1st was faulty.
>
> I went back to Platinum Wrench to have them finish up and recharge the 2nd until as I have been going to them for years. Once again I paid $160 for the service. Once again the 2nd new system only worked for a couple of weeks and burnt up!!
>
> At this point I decided to get a second opinion so I took it to another auto repair shop. This mechanic asked me if Platinum Wrench flushed the system, and stated that they should have advised me that all new systems need to be flushed when replacing. Platinum Wrench never advised me that it [the system flush] needed to be done or offered to do it.
>
> I asked Platinum Wrench to install another new unit that I [would] provide, flush it and recharge the system free of charge this time, as they have caused me considerable time and expense to replace 2 units already. They refuse to stand behind their work and told me no. They stated that I did not ask for a system flush.
>
> I am NOT a mechanic, so there is no way for me to know that the system needed [to be] flushed. Isn't this why mechanics get paid the big bucks?? Never in my life have I had to tell a mechanic how to do their job or what needs to be done.

So after $320 in charges I have to pay another company to install another unit and then flush and recharge the system. . . .

I advise everyone to take your business to a company that stands behind their work and avoid this business completely!

An ex-employee, Joel, even chimed in on March 27 to echo Lance's original March 26 complaint, and he pointed out that not only did the company do bad repairs, but it also overcharged customers and provided poor service. As he wrote:

As a former employee at Platinum Wrench, I will sum it like this. The owner of the company is a non-legit multimillionaire that worked his way up by overcharging customers, shortcutting services, reverse engineering other companies products, several frivolous lawsuits, and a dozen very lucrative insurance claims. . . .

I have personally seen used transmissions painted and sold as new units to unsuspecting customers. I have seen . . . block seal used and the customer was charged [parts and labor] for a head gasket job . . .

I hope that I have opened your eyes to Platinum Wrench's antics. Stay away and DO NOT bring your car there.

Damages to Car

Some victims reported that the shop even damaged their car, but they still had to pay.

For example, okrepair from Enid, Oakland, described on April 4 how the shop not only damaged the car's fuel tank so their car was no longer working, but now he and his wife had to pay to get a new fuel tank. The company took no responsibility for the damage, and told him that their price was lower than getting it fixed at a dealer, because he took on the risk of being responsible if something went wrong. As he described the situation:

We [my wife and I] thought we could save money by using this company. My wife called and they seemed real nice over the phone and we told them we need a new fuel pump. We gave them all the information and they came back with $150 for the labor. We already bought the new fuel pump. . . .

[A few days after we dropped off the fuel pump] I got a call from them and they said sorry but we damaged your fuel tank and things like this sometimes happens and this is why dealerships are so much higher in quotes to make up for these kind of things, but you are going to now need a fuel tank. GM is the only place to get them and it will cost $610 more dollars on top of what we have already done.

I asked if our car is currently working. They said "No" . . . [I] called them back and asked them, "Why it is not running? The car was running when we brought it to your company." Their response was, "We are not going to argue with you about it. You can either come get it or have it towed."

We spoke to a dealership in town on how often this kind of thing happens, and they said the only time this could happen is if you had a crack in the neck of the fuel tank. You would know this because your car would have leaked gas in the driveway and had a gas smell when the car engine is on. We had none of these problems. They tried to make us pay $610 for a mistake they made. NEVER AGAIN will we recommend or go back to this company.

In another damage case, Cynthia from Bradenton, Florida, described on April 6, 2015, how a car company broke her windshield wipers after she brought the car in to replace several parts, and wanted her to pay $604 to fix that. Subsequently she discovered that the mechanics had taken out the fuse box and a fuse that could be replaced in seconds was loose. So she suspected that a mechanic had tampered with the fuse box so she would pay for new windshield wipers. She describes what happened:

I went to Cox Chevrolet in Bradenton, Florida. I had gone there because I received a recall notice for my 2005 Chevy Malibu; three parts needed to be replaced. . . .

While waiting for the service I used my windshield wiper to wash something on my windshield and turned them off when the customer service representative approached me. I gave them my keys. It took 3 hours for them to replace the parts. . . .

Prior to getting home I decided to wash the car and when I went to use my windshield wipers they were not working. . . .

Cox Chevrolet ask me to bring the vehicle back . . . and without reviewing the possible cause of the wipers not operating they decided that a diagnostic test was necessary. . . . After waiting 20 minutes the service advisor returns and tells me that the motor to the windshield wipers had ceased working and needed to be replaced at a tune of $604. I was shocked and could not believe that . . . when I brought the car into Cox Chevrolet the wipers were working fine, in fact, they are brand new wipers and were operable. I decided to pay the fee of $122 for the diagnostic test and decline on any further repairs.

I took my car three days later to another mechanic to find out what was wrong with the wipers and to see if they would agree with Cox Chevrolet's diagnostic results. Well, the first thing the mechanic did was open the hood, open the fuse box and noticed that there was a fuse loosely placed inside the fuse box. He . . . replaced [the fuse] where it belonged. He asked me to turn on the car and try to turn on the wipers. Well, to my amazement, they were working. Cox Chevrolet mechanics had taken out the fuse to the wipers . . . and left it loose inside the fuse box. . . . It took my mechanic a second to replace the fuse and my wipers to begin working.

I believe Cox Chevrolet uses recalls to deceive and manipulate customers to get work done that they themselves have caused. My wipers were working and after I left Cox Chevrolet they were not. A mechanic who is ASE Certified [should be] honest and will not attempt to deceive a customer by taking out the wiper fuse, leaving it loosely inside the fuse box and attempt to tell the customer that they need to replace the motor . . . at a cost of $600 because it is no longer working. If they were in fact honest and competent mechanics they would [have] remembered that they themselves disconnected the fuse that operated the wipers and replaced it, and I would never [have] had to pay for a diagnostic test that was in fact unnecessary and deceitfully diagnosed. . . .

[The] recall did not cost me a thing, but Cox Chevrolet wanted to find a way for me to pay for the time it took to replace the recalled parts. They purposely removed the wiper fuse, manipulated me to have a diagnostic test knowing beforehand that they were the cause of my wipers not working. Cox Chevrolet are deceitful, dishonest, fraudulent, and incompetent, and I would tell all customers to be aware of the ripoff scam. Cox Chevrolet uses recalls to deceive customers into repairs that they do not need or purposely removes parts in order to have the customer pay for unnecessary repairs.

Other damage complaints began with radiator and transmission flushes that led to serious problems; the service center would take no responsibility for what happened. Instead they blamed the customer for lying or doing something to the car that caused the damage.

Here's what Jon of Escondido, California, had to say on April 6, 2015, about how his car overheated after a radiator flush because the mechanic forgot to put the cap back on, causing blown gaskets. As he described it:

> Firestone Complete Autocare forgot to put cap back on reservoir after radiator flush. Car overheated, blown head gaskets.
>
> Took in my car for radiator flush. Took car back, and that night . . . [it] overheated. Two days later car overheated again. Checked under hood. There was no cap on coolant reservoir! There was coolant almost up to the brim and bubbles were surfacing. If the cap had been blown off by pressure—as Firestone kept saying—there would have been coolant everywhere. There wasn't.
>
> Called Firestone and took it in per instructions. Comes back blown head gaskets. Went through their shady claims process, and basically they are calling me a liar in the end.
>
> Their only defense is that they don't have proof that the cap was not put back on after service. It's been almost two months now. Now my car is complete garbage, and I ride a skateboard to work—takes three hours. I'm on the verge of seeking a polygraph test, and if they don't honor it through their claims dept., I will be seeing them in court. I really hate Firestone—they've made an enemy for life with their lack of honesty and integrity.

Here's what Joe of Phoenix, Arizona, had to say, also on April 6, 2015, about how a routine transmission maintenance that included a flush at the Sears Auto Service Center destroyed his transmission. Later, he learned

from other mechanics that Sears never should have done the flush, while
the auto center blamed him for causing the problem due to metal shav-
ings in the transmission, so they would not reimburse him for the costs
of repairs, which he couldn't afford to pay himself. As Joe reported:

> I took my 2002 Honda Accord to Sears Auto Service Center . . . for
> routine transmission maintenance. The first thing I did when I talked
> to the guy at the front counter was ask him if he thought I could get
> my transmission flushed and/or drained and filled. He stated for the
> flush he would have to speak to his 'expert' service advisor because
> of the high mileage on my car. He came back and stated his 'expert'
> upon evaluation of my car said I could indeed have the transmission
> flushed. . . .
>
> Needless to say that flush destroyed my transmission. I then went to
> three different transmission specialists and they all said SEARS NEVER
> should have done the flush. . . .
>
> Sears played the run around game for over a month not taking
> responsibility for their actions resulting in the destruction of my trans-
> mission. Yes, they did state if I wanted to pay out of pocket and it was
> determined they caused the problem they would reimburse me. I'm on
> a fixed income which I explained to Sears Management and could not
> afford to do this and it fell on deaf ears. I was told without a doubt
> SEARS caused the problem, but here's the game these sort of shops play.
> Even if you get an actual receipt showing fault, they say that there were
> metal shavings in the transmission to begin with and that's what caused
> the problem. Mind you, those shavings would have stayed on the housing
> of the transmission had they not flushed it. STAY AWAY FROM SEARS
> SERVICE CENTERS. THEY DO NOT TAKE RESPONSIBILITY
> FOR THEIR ACTIONS.

Max from Hazelwood, Missouri, similarly found, as he reported April
14, 2015, that a service company wouldn't take responsibility for the
damage it caused after it replaced a new power pump. After the company did so, his car lost all the power steering fluid, which leaked onto
his rack and pinion, so he would have to replace that. But even after
the company replaced these items, his engine began smoking because

the mechanics didn't replace that properly, and he ended up not being able to drive his car. But the company took no responsibility for that. Though Max found other complaints against the company, he couldn't cite them in small claims court and lost his case. As Max described what happened:

> I took my 1996 Lexus in . . . for a small power steering leak. I was told upon inspection that I needed a new power steering pump at a cost of $885. After one week I lost all of the power steering fluid and my car began to make noises from the pump. I returned to the shop and I was then told that the fluid had leaked into my rack and pinion and I needed to replace it as soon as possible.
>
> I then asked why they were not responsible for the problem and [the mechanic] told me that he could replace the rack and pinion for an additional $885, and he would not charge me for labor.
>
> I replaced the rack and pinion but the problems became worse. My car began to smoke from the engine and the tailpipe. I took it back to 2 other locations and one location informed me that the rack and pinion had not been properly secured and my engine could go out any minute.
>
> Let me point out . . . that my car had been inspected one week prior to the work [being] done. . . . They actually ruined my car. I can no longer drive it.
>
> I took the owner to small claims court and the judge immediately stopped me from talking about the complaints from the Better Business Bureau and others. . . . [So I] lost my case in small claims court.
>
> I would like to start a class action lawsuit against this company and put them out of business because people are losing a lot of money dealing with this company. . . .
>
> People, please stop doing business with this company.

A Bad Repair and Other Problems

Many other victims claimed a bad repair job, and commonly they reported overcharges and a refusal to give a refund. In some cases, the bad repair job was due to a bad diagnosis and accompanied by delays in fixing the car. A few reported being insulted or blamed for the problem, and one man faced not getting back his car if he didn't pay. Here are their stories.

J Demore of Houston, Texas (April 8, 2015), described how he bought a transmission on eBay that didn't last for thirty days. Then he didn't receive the promised replacement, and he was subsequently scammed by a local transmission shop that used paint to conceal a transmission that wasn't rebuilt. Since the shop never paid the freight company, the freight company turned the bill over to collections, which is billing him. Here's his story:

> I am warning the general public . . . under any circumstances [do not] do business with the above mentioned company. They are scam artists and you will be defrauded. Research and you will see for yourself they have quite an abundance of complaints. . . .
>
> To summarize my experience. Earl Lucket . . . sold me a transmission for my F250 Diesel track through ebay. . . . My 1300 EOD transmission did not last 30 days nor did I receive my replacement as promised. . . . I called and called no response until the phones were disconnected.
>
> I had a local transmission shop rebuild his . . . transmission [but it] was never rebuilt. It was a worn out piece of crap with a coat of paint.
>
> 3200.00 dollars later my F250 is back on the road. Well, some say you get what you pay for. 1300 for a coat of paint!!! And to boot they never paid the freight company. Now I'm being billed and turned over for collection. . . .
>
> Earl has quite the reputation of defrauding the public. Watch your back Earl. . . . Google his name run through a few pages. Save yourself the headache.

In his case, Louis of Santa Cruz, California (April 8, 2015), found that after an automotive service company replaced his high-end transmission with a low-end one, he could only drive up to sixty-two miles per hour. The shop overcharged him by $862. When Louis questioned the quality of his work, the owner became insulted that he would question his work and screamed at him, so Louis ended up retreating, stuck with the bad repairs and overcharges for the poor work. As Louis reported:

Henderson Automotive Greg Henderson . . . replaced my hi-end transmission with a low-end transmission. Now my top speed is 62 MPH at 4500 RPM. He also charged me $862 more than what we agreed on and when disputed he became very irate and started screaming and yelling at me using racial slander and about every one of the worst swear words known to man. . . .

He became very irate and angry that I was questioning him about the work. I tried speaking rational with him but he became more angry and started using racial slurs towards me, then progressively got louder and used about every worst swear word known to man. He jumped up from his chair with [his] fist clinched and started walking towards me, then threatened to call the Sheriff on me if I didn't leave his property right away.

He continued screaming at me as I was driving away calling me a ****** and ********, which I am neither.

I strongly recommend anyone to find a different "more stable and honest" auto repair shop. Greg Henderson is hostile.

Lonnie in Columbus, Ohio (April 13, 2015), also experienced a bad repair job after he had a number of parts replaced, including an air charge sensor and spark plugs, but his truck didn't run more smoothly as promised and after a few days it stopped running entirely. The manager not only wouldn't give him a refund but charged him for further repairs. As Lonnie described what happened:

Took my truck to Meineke Car Care Center . . . for service engine check light. They replaced air charge temp sensor and spark plugs. Eight days later same problem . . . The manager told me the truck would run a little rough until about 40 mile then would run smoother. On the way home the truck began to run rougher. I called the manager to inform him of the problem. The next day while I was taking the truck back to the shop it stopped running. . . . I had to call a tow truck to carry it back to Meineke.

I told the manager that I felt I was overcharged for parts, and he charged me for repairs that was not the problem. He refused to return some of my money. I called Meineke customer service to file a complaint. . . . They . . . stated that it was up to the manager and he refused to return some of my money. [Two days later] the service light came on again. Therefore the problem is still there.

Frosty of Gainesville, Florida (April 16, 2015), after spending almost $4,000 in repairs, discovered that the shop used all kinds of faulty parts and shortcuts and repeatedly lied to him when he bought a car from them that had all kinds of mechanical problems. As he explained:

Smitty's Auto Service and Parts owner sold me a lemon VW. Smitty swore to me the car had no mechanical issues. I just spent 4000 dollars in repairs to fix the car.

I bought a car from this business owner a couple of months ago and I've had a laundry list of problems ever since . . . . I just got my car back from the shop and spent almost 4000 dollars getting it properly serviced and fixed. Smitty swore to my face that it was mechanically sound. Smitty claims to be a VW certified tech. He installed a gas transmission in a diesel car, used wire to hold up shifting cables, used electrical tape to try and seal [a] bad brake line [which could have caused an accident], used gas bolts that don't fit a diesel engine, used gas axles on a diesel engine so I had to replace these as well, and the list goes on. Smitty does not practice ethical business practices, and lied to my face multiple times.

For Ron in Hollywood, Florida (April 18, 2015), there were all kinds of problems in fixing his transmission, including not fixing it properly, not deducting a promised amount, delays in getting the repair done, and then getting blamed by the shop owner for the problems because Ron tried to rush the mechanics. Here's how he described the multiple problems:

Transmission King in Plantation Florida misleading dishonest deceptive ripoff. [They provided] delayed unreliable poor workmanship [and] poor service.

I decided to go to Transmission King in Plantation Florida after speaking with three other transmission shops. . . . My vehicle's gear shift was slipping out of fifth gear into neutral while [I was] driving on 95 to work doing about 70 miles per hour. Certainly not safe . . .

I . . . spoke with a woman by the name of Cheryl [who] . . . was so pleasant, nice and charming, I thought she was honest just based on her demeanor but did she sock it to me.

Cheryl told me that she would charge 400.00 just to take out and replace [the] transmission if I decided not to get work done and this charge would be deducted from [my] total bill if transmission was done at Transmission King. I left my car there and picked up a rental car. . . .

Anyway three days went by and no word on my vehicle so I called on the fourth day and pressed the issue that I really needed my vehicle and this was taking longer than expected. Cheryl explained that her transmission builder got sick and she had to send my transmission to another builder to get the repairs done and needed my okay. I asked Cheryl what was the cost to fix. She told me 2200 for new factory parts and 167 for refurbished synchro kits plus a brand new clutch assembly. I told Cheryl since my car was a 2001 to repair transmission with refurbished parts and install brand new clutch assembly and let me know when it was ready.

So I called quite a few times to check on the vehicle's progress and Cheryl told me she would call me when the car was repaired and road tested by her mechanic. I got the call late in the evening on the fifth day that my vehicle . . . was ready to go.

I was ecstatic. . . . When I arrived at Transmission King . . . I spoke with Cheryl and paid a total of 1767.00 without getting the 400.00 deducted from the total bill. So in my mind my vehicle was going to run exceptionally well. Surprise!!! While driving off the car lot . . . I could barely get the gear shift to go into first gear and this went on until the following day. Not Happy!!! . . .

When I called the following morning and explained to Cathy the problem she responded by scolding me, saying "this is what happened when you rush my mechanics to finish your car." So she is blaming me for the car not being repaired properly the first time? Really???

Wow! I would not recommend anyone not even my worst enemy to take their car to Transmission King. . . .

For Tony from Roebling, New Jersey (April 19, 2015), the problem was that the mechanics made a series of mistakes in incorrectly diagnosing the problem, and the repairs they made did not fix the problem—a burning smell, smoke from the turbo area, and the smell of raw fuel when the weather was cold. But despite all of the repairs costing almost $3,000, the car still didn't work. As Tony described it:

> Haldeman Ford and Subaru Vehicle was not repaired. Car is worse than before I dropped it off. Ripped off for almost $3000.
>
> I brought my car back 4 times for the same problem and they still didn't fix it. I had a burning smell that blew into the cabin, smoking coming from or around the turbo, and the smell of raw fuel in cold weather. They forgot to bolt parts back in that caused damage to the coolant reservoir that wasn't damaged in the first place. They also forgot to put on the splash guard that goes underneath the entire engine and had to order another one.
>
> They first said it was the head gaskets. Then they said it was the oil pan. Then they said it was the power steering pump. . . . I have detailed records of everything.
>
> I also had a new fuel filter installed that did not fix the raw fuel smell. I also opted for new brakes, rotors, and timing belt thinking my car would be drivable after the first time. On the phone, they pretended to know what was going on, but the results proved otherwise.
>
> They have been playing guessing games and making mistakes at my own expense. I was ripped off for almost $3000 and have a car sitting in the driveway for over two months without being driven. I don't know anybody that would drive a car with a visual of smoke, smell of raw fuel, and missing bolts. . . .
>
> I will never ever recommend their services to anybody.

JTroll of Anaheim, California (April 20, 2015), similarly experienced repair problems when several new parts weren't installed or were installed incorrectly causing more problems, and he never got the refund he was promised. As he complained:

> Quick Response Automotive & Diesel Repair . . . charged me for several new parts that were never installed and not only recreated the conditions

that initially caused the wheel to fall off but worsened them by installing a stripped broken ball joint bolt. A full refund was promised but never given. The owner . . . knew we would continue traveling at high speeds and put a life in danger . . .

. . . The front driver's side wheel fell off my car due to a ball joint bolt that was never torqued after the car was serviced in New York. . . .

Graham the owner of the company told us what was needed to fix the wheel knowing we would be back on the Interstate driving at speed limits around 70 to 80 mph. He gave us an estimate and told us he could get the parts he needed within a day and have us up and running in two which was about the only promise he kept.

We picked the car up from Graham but noticed a knocking in the gears as we drove. Uncomfortable to get back on the Interstate with this noise, we took the car to [another service center]. . . .

Once the car was put up on a lift the mechanics immediately notified us that no new parts were installed and that the ball joint was not only not torqued again [but] the bolt they installed was stripped and unable to be torqued or even tightened at all. When the wheel fell off the axel[sic] shaft, [it] ripped out the transmission. Quick Response . . . charged us for an axel[sic] shaft, lower ball joint, wheel hub, trans seal, speed sensor, wire plug, and 7 quarts of transmission fluid . . . [The inspection of the other service center] revealed [our car] to have old broken parts and none of the parts said to be replaced on the Quick Response . . . receipt were new.

I immediately called Graham at Quick Response . . . and told him what was happening and sent him picture of his work. He blamed [his] mechanics and said one of them had returned the parts he purchased himself for one reason or another. He asked for a day to find out what was going on. He personally came to our hotel and promised a full refund. He signed our receipt, returning all charges in full. . . . Weeks passed and every time I called him he had another excuse until the day I called and his number was no longer his.

The man lied about the parts, lied about the refund, and put broken parts on a car he knew would be traveling at high speeds the minute it was fixed. He put my life in danger and if it wasn't for the sound in the transmission I believe a much worse incident would have happened.

In some cases, these complaints about repair scams can be very complicated, as the charges mount up due to mistakes in diagnosis, faulty parts
installed, delays, extra charges for towing, getting a car back to its original condition, and promises made but not kept. That was the experience
of Dianamhm in Lawrence, Georgia (April 6, 2015), who reported these
series of events and only learned afterwards that there had been all kinds
of complaints against this company. As she described what happened:

> Mr. Transmission RIP OFF—SCAM . . .
> Charged me over $900 to diagnose the problem on car and left with the
> transmission in a box, car towed, because I will not pay a cent more to
> have this company do anything for a vehicle of mine.
>
> After paying $450 to "fix" the transmission issue, [which took] over
> almost a whole week more than it was supposed to, they then told me it
> would be no additional charge to diagnose the issue by going into the
> transmission. Once they quoted another $1500 to "fix" the new found
> issue of four parts needing to be replaced, I indicated I wanted to take it
> somewhere else for a 2nd opinion and the car was working fine previously
> except for the jerk from 1st to 2nd gear so I would continue driving it
> until I decided what to do. At this point, I was told it would be another
> $500 to get my car back to driveable condition. . . .
>
> Anyway, called back to speak with the owner . . . and was then told
> it would be $457 to tow the car and take the transmission in a box and
> $718 to drive it out in the condition it came in. This is on top of the $450
> cash already paid. . . . The police had to enforce that we would be leaving
> with a proper receipt which then took them over an hour to produce.
> They tried to bring down/close all the garage doors while our vehicle was
> still inside—my husband physically stood in the door. The police went
> and stood in the office asking them what on earth was taking so long and
> what they were up to. . . .
>
> How this business remains in business with all of these complaints
> is beyond me but please if you're reading this in advance, run. This is
> NOT a reputable business by any standards. Do your homework with
> BBB, Yelp, here and Gwinnett County.

Often the initial pitch to get business is so convincing that the victim thinks he or she will be getting a good deal, sometimes because the higher price suggests higher quality, while more commonly victims are lured in by offers of lower prices. But after the shop owner gets the victim's money, the victim experiences many excuses, labor problems, failures to repair the problem, and a bad repair, resulting in continuing problems for the car, as reported by Jonathand of Silver Springs, Maryland (April 7, 2015).

Mid America Diesel did not meet deadlines as promised, would not answer phone calls, furnished an engine with the wrong configuration and no power . . .

I was shopping for an engines remanufacturer and I went with Steve Spencer over his competitors, at a much higher price . . . as he was very convincing and knowledgeable. He stated that he had a core block on the shelf and would return a rebuilt industrial engine back to me in two weeks.

After he received my money, he had excuse after excuse, labor problems, facility problems, and 'the block on his shelf had a hair line crack and he had to acquire another block.'

After three months, he had stopped answering my telephone calls and I would call him on different numbers, of which he . . . did answer. I finally sought legal counsel and threatened to sue him. With an ultimatum to perform or I would file suit, he finally produced an engine. Ten weeks late, the engine that he supplied was from a wheel loader instead of a crawler loader and had less horsepower. Additionally, the installer had to change the turbo location on the block. The engine runs well but has no power, which is resulting in me giving up on this loader and sending it to the auction. . . .

I would never do business with this company again and I would recommend that you run, not walk away from any consideration of doing business with Mid American Diesel. I had many sleepless nights, frustrating phone calls with the office manager and general manager when he was playing hide and go seek with me. This is not the way you do business and not the way you treat pre paid customers.

Sometimes the new parts that are recommended at a high cost don't fix the initial problem, and then the shop owner claims that something else is wrong with the car, which isn't the real cause of the problem. Then, should the customer complain, the company doesn't treat the customer with proper respect, as Jody in Porter, Texas (April 16, 2015), complained:

> NTB lied about what their parts and services would do to repair my car . . .
>
> I recently took my 2009 Toyota Corolla in for a front end alignment because the front end started shimming when I got up to 60 mph. NTB tech called back an hour after I dropped off the car and said I would need struts, brackets for the struts, front end alignment, and a complete brake job. . . .
>
> I asked if this would stop the front end from shimming and he said yes. Several hours later I picked up the car and paid the bill which was just over $1400. I took the car up on the freeway and got it up to 60 mph. The front end was still shimming.
>
> I took it back and the store manager acted is if [he] really didn't want to hear my complaint and so another tech came and talked to me. He said he would have a mechanic look at it. They came back and said it was the new tires I had just bought at Discount Tire. They said the tires were no good.
>
> I took the car to Discount Tire several days late and they took all four wheels off, spin balanced them, and put them back on the car at no charge. Took the car on the freeway and it no longer is shimming at 60 mph. NTB not only sold me parts and services I didn't need, but treated me with disrespect when I came back.
>
> It is obvious that NTB's . . . store managers are only interested in making commissions and not customer satisfaction.

Sometimes the many complications that result from bad repairs and misinformation can lead to extensive delays and increased costs that far outstrip any discount promised in the beginning as an incentive. In some cases, the customer can end up with an undriveable car that the shop blames on the customer. That's what happened to Alfreda in Norfolk, Virginia (April 6, 2015), who was originally lured to one company that was offering a 20 percent student discount. But ultimately, she didn't get this discount either. As Alfreda described her saga:

Indian River Auto & Transmission Repair promised a great working car, but I no longer have a drivable car. . . .

On 12-10-2014 I was looking up different companies for [a] Diagnostic Check on the Internet. The second one that popped up was Indian River Auto & Transmission Repair. What caught my attention was that it [said] that they give free Diagnostic Checks and I also qualified for a 20% discount because I was a student in school. To me that was the best deal compared to all the ads. . . .

I brought [my car] in 12-11-2014. Tom [the customer service rep] gave me a paper to fill out called the Customer Intake Form. . . . It asked me what problems I noticed wrong with my car. I wrote oil leaking and knocking noise under the hood. I told Tom that I wanted a full Diagnostic Check for any problems. . . .

Two days later Tom said . . . they found a lot of things wrong and the bill would be near $1700 not including the 20% off. So I told him I would come over there so he can give me a break down of everything the car needed. Tom said o.k. . . .

When I got there, he started writing everything down that needed to be done plus the amount of time it would take down on the Customer Intake Form. The total ended up coming to $1623.93 plus tax not including the 20% off. I asked him how much it would be if I got the parts myself. Tom said 'near $1000.' I said o.k. I will be getting my own parts. He seemed disturbed about that.

I requested that he give me a list of all the parts I would need. He wrote it on a little business card. I was supposed to get a Timing Chain Kit. I asked him what that consisted of. He wrote Guides, tensioner/gasket. I told Tom I wanted to make sure I got everything I needed. Also on the list was Gasket/valve cover, oil sending unit, shocks [rear] 2 and Belt [drive].

I bought all the parts from Advance Auto Parts and Auto Zone. On 12-13-2014 I took all the parts to Indian River Auto. I asked, did I get everything that was needed? Tom said 'yes' and he claimed [my car] would be ready in two days. I came up there 12-15-2014 and he said everything was not done. I needed another part. It was something with the guides. He called over to Auto Zone, a few doors down . . . I immediately went and purchased it from them and brought it back to Indian River Auto. . . .

Tom said [my car] would be ready by the end of the day. . . . But it wasn't until 12-18-2014 and when I was dropped off there [to pick it up], it was still not ready and I still had to wait for another two more hours for the car. Tom claimed "he threw in a free oil change for inconvenience." Plus he did not tell me that I would need any of those things when I purchased all the parts. . . . The total he came up with was $817 which did not include the 20% off. I asked him to call the owner since that is the only one that could change the prices. Tom said he would and I waited for almost an hour and a half, [but] he never called at all. This on top of the two hours I had already been waiting for the car to be finished. So I went and paid them.

Tom told me to come back for the two week checkup. I said o.k. When I left about 10 minutes later I called the shop and said I was still hearing the knocking noise under the hood. The very same noise I wrote on the Customer Intake Form. He said to give it a couple of days. It would blow over. It should stop soon, because the car has not really been running. I responded alright, but the noise still sounded the same.

Next the oil light came on. I called Tom and . . . he said it was because they never reset the electrical unit for the dash board. I bought some oil and put it in. The light clicked off and I told him his people never put oil in it. Tom swore they did change the oil.

The two week checkup was due on 1-05-2015; they said they were busy so I came on the 7th with a friend. They did not check [the car] . . . [they just] reset the electrical component. Tom said 'it should be good now.' They did not fix or or check the knocking noise or the oil. . . . Two weeks later around 1-19-2015. . . . I called and told him that the engine light was coming on and off along with the oil light. . . .

I kept calling to see when I could bring [my car] in and to [ask Tom to] fax the total breakdown of everything they did to my car, which was written on the back of the Customer Intake Form. I never received it. He told me the problem was that I did not buy all the right parts for the

Timing Chain Kit. He said he wrote [this down], which he did not. I found the cards he wrote on. I asked him why he did not call and tell me about it. He said he thought I could not afford it. . . .

The oil and engine light came on again. I bought 2 quarts of oil and the engine light went off but the oil light stayed on. I kept calling, telling Tom that they did not put oil in it and about the engine light. He reminded me that they did that free of charge. . . .

I stopped driving my car for a while and went out of town. . . . On 2-11-2015 while I was on my way to work both the engine and oil light came on. I checked the oil stick and it was bone dry, so I went and bought 5 quarts of oil to put in the car. I proceed to go to work, five minutes later the car starts jerking back and forward. This had never happened before. I continued to go to work and parked the car. When I got off work at 1:30 a.m the car would not start. . . .

[When I threatened] to call The Better Business Bureau and report them to Service Pal, [Tom] said to "let us look at the car again. I will get it towed back here today."

I waited a week. They did not notify me, so I called them around the 19th of Feb. Tom said the car would try to start but would not turn over. He told me that the car needed a starter. . . . He . . . called Auto Zone to see if they had one. I went to pick it up. . . . Tom said everything would be done by Friday of that week.

I received no call. [When I called him] Tom said the car still would not start and that the starter was not the problem. . . . It was the engine. The engine was sucking the oil in it but was not returning back to the correct place and that messed up the engine. . . .

Tom called me 3-2-15 and said I needed a whole new engine and it would be almost $2000 for just the engine. Then he said that he would call the owner and see what kind of deal he would work out for me. No one contacted me back. I went up there to get a couple of things out of the car and everyone was busy. I noticed the engine was still [in] the trunk. . . .

On 3-13-15 the owner Travis called me back. I tried to explain to him how I felt that it was not my fault that the engine stopped working. Travis interrupted me and said that it was not their fault but he was willing to work something out with me. . . .

I told him that I felt like it was their fault that they found nothing wrong with the car. I complained about the oil problem and knocking noise under the hood. Tom tried to blame it on two other things before he said it was the engine. Travis said he did not believe me . . . and he had not heard anything about my situation until yesterday.

I said "well can you get my car towed back to my house?" Travis told me that he was not in the business of doing work for free and I would have to get it towed myself. I called a company and got my car towed home.

I feel like Indian River Auto & Transmission caused the engine problem in my car or at the very least made it worse than it was. . . . They have showed poor customer service toward me. Not calling me about the missing part should not have happened. Or not keeping me informed of the progress of my car . . . I don't believe I owe them for any repairs. They didn't put the engine back in my car; it is still in the trunk of the car. It was not in the trunk when it was towed there.

I am not used to this type of service/customer service. Usually, when a shop or business tell me they are going to do a job, it is done right. If there is a problem I can talk to management and get it resolved.

All I wanted to do was get my car repaired. Their ad sounded like the answer, no it seems that was not the case.

No Refund

For some victims, the problem of bad work or not doing the job is compounded by the failure of the shop manager or owner to provide a refund. The circumstances vary, but the basic complaint is the refusal to give a refund, and if the customer persists, the manager or owner denies any responsibility or the customer gets a runaround. In some cases, the victim is steered into buying products or services he or she doesn't need, even ones that could damage the car, but still the manager or owner won't give a refund.

In one case, Gloria from Romulus, Michigan (April 1, 2015), reported that after she paid a deposit to fix a cracked radiator, someone took her car for a joyride over the weekend, which was obvious from the ashes and pine needles all over the car. Even so, the shop denied that anyone had driven her car and claimed the mechanics were already working on it. But on seeing her car, she realized the work hadn't started. Still, the shop denied that anything she claimed had happened and wouldn't return her deposit, telling her she could always take the matter to court. Of course, she never did, not for that small amount of money. As Gloria reported:

Sam's Auto Master took my truck for a joy ride over the weekend and refused to refund deposit after not completing repairs.

3/28/15—took vehicle to Auto Master's and was told that the radiator was cracked and they could not in good conscience let my fiancé drive it as it was and [I] was promised a delivery date of 3/29/15 . . . Left $250 cash deposit.

3/29/15—Never received a phone call. Went to Auto Master's around 5 pm and shop was closed and nobody would answer telephone.

3/30/15—Auto Master's phoned my fiancé at approximately 8 am informing him they had ordered the wrong part and that they were currently working on it. Approximately 8:30 am my fiancé stopped into the shop to see progress. Upon viewing my vehicle the work had not even started. My vehicle had been washed and detailed, ashes and pine needles [were] all over [the] hood and windshield (no pine tree near shop or our home). My fiancé asked why it was driven if it was not fixed. Shop had no reply. He then took my vehicle off premises and requested a refund of the money paid. Owner would not give it to him and called the police.

At 5 pm I went to the shop to get my money back and they were closed. I inspected my vehicle over the weekend. [It was] smoked in with ashes all over . . . pine needles all over, scratches on the driver's side, gas missing and mileage changed from [when I] dropped [it] off. I had filled my gas tank when it was dropped off and reset the trip meter. The trip meter now reads 319 miles driven . . . my vehicle does not even get that amount on a full tank. It gets 297 maximum.

3/31/15—Went to the shop to get my money back and was told they had no idea what I was talking about. After I refreshed [the manager's] memory I was informed that I would need to speak to the owner. When I asked his name I was told he would not give me that information. I asked for a number to call him and also was told no. I then asked for him to call the owner and was once again told no. He went on to laugh and tell me it was a civil matter and he would love to see me in court.

For dcc178 from Staten Island, New York (April 11,2015), the problem was a terrible paint job after he bought a used, pre-owned car that was supposed to be fine from a dealer. But then the paint started peeling off, and after another dealer repainted it, that also began peeling off. The shop owner refused to repair it and told the victim he had to take care of the problem himself, and, of course, he offered no refund. Here's what dcc178 had to say:

> Very disappointed and disgusted with Paragon Acura. I bought a 2010 certified pre-owned Acura TL in 2011. When asked if there were any issues with the car, I was told everything was fine. . . . About 2 years later, my clear coat was just crumbling off of my roof. Apparently the car had a terrible paint job done on it and I was not informed of it at all.
>
> I had to go to another Acura dealership where they had a device that can tell if it was repainted, which it was. They repaired that, but now it is crumbling on the side, which was also repainted.
>
> They now tell me they don't have to repair it and basically tell me I'm on my own, washing their hands of the situation. For what I paid, this issue and how I'm being treated is completely unacceptable. They sell me a shoddy product and don't even take responsibility. I'm absolutely disgusted with this place and regret going there and giving them my hard earned money.

ScottG of Los Angeles (April 20, 2015) similarly got a bad paint job and wasn't able to get it fixed or get a refund, since the manager who had originally taken his order had moved to a new shop—and now he felt he had been overcharged as well. As ScottG complained:

> I was involved in an accident back in 2014. . . . So along with the repair of the back bumper, a 1350 fix, I paid an additional 2600 dollars to have the whole car painted. The manager at the time took longer than usual and I was not happy at the poor job. There were spots all over the car and the car was not painted as how they told me it would be, with dents and dings removed, and the whole car would be painted. I had to bring it back twice to get it good enough, so that I would accept it. About 4 months later, the

car paint started to peel. I notified the manager and he told me to bring it in to have it fixed.

When I brought it back, the original manager was not there and the owner Fred had taken over. [Fred] stated [that I should] try getting my car fixed by him and if not I will take care of you. So I contacted the old manager. Of course he said I had to take it to the place he was employed at the time. [But then Fred, the new owner, wouldn't fix the car.]

THIS [Fred] GUY IS A COMPLETE SNAKE AND LIAR. HIS COMPANY OVERCHARGED ME IN THE FIRST PLACE AND THE PAINT STARTED TO PEEL 4 MONTHS AFTER I PAID A TOTAL OF $3,800 AND HAVE A CAR THAT LOOKS TERRIBLE AND HAS PEELED PAINT EVERYWHERE. PLEASE DO NOT, I REPEAT, DO NOT GET ANY WORK DONE THERE. HE IS A CROOK. I AM FORMER NAVY. I URGE ANY OF MY SERVICE MEMBERS TO STAY AWAY.

In another case, Drew from Philadelphia (April 10, 2015) was advised to get an engine flush when he took his car in for an oil change, only to find that car manufacturers recommend against doing an engine flush because it can damage the motor, including destroying the rings and gaskets. After the flush, Drew heard knocks in his engine and got his oil changed two more times to get rid of the chemicals from the engine flush. But when he complained to the manager, the manager would not give him a refund for the cost of the oil change and flush, despite the problems it caused him. As Drew described what happened:

Speedy lube engine flush scam . . .

I went to Speedy Lube for an oil change. I was told that I need an engine flush. So I asked why. They told me because of sludge build up. So I said OK go ahead and clean my motor, thinking I'm doing what the tech recommends is good for my truck.

The service is complete and I am paying and the tech now tells me I need new brakes, but I just had new brakes put on a month before, so this tips me off that I am being scammed.

So I investigate this oil flush process and come to find out that this can destroy your motor and they never mention this to me. I start researching engine flush and find out that the only way to find oil sludge is to look at the pistons and they never did anything like that. They just told me the oil is dirty because of sludge. I look up in my owners' manual and there is no maintenance schedule for engine flush.

I come to find out that every car manufacturing company recommends against doing this [flush] because it can damage the motor and void your warranty. I asked a few mechanics about this and they said [doing this flush] is bad. It will break up sludge and cause seals to leak, and if you think about this using common sense, if you put a chemical in your motor to break up sludge in five minutes, imagine what it does to your rings and gaskets. It will eat them up.

I have also found a report done by the news on this scam. It is on YouTube under Jiffy Lube is still scaming customers, and it goes over the whole engine flush scam.

I went for an oil change and they sold me a service I did not need and may have caused motor damage. I can hear a small knock in my motor now, and I believe it is from this engine flush.

I went back and talked to the manager and asked for my money back, because I had to go and get my oil changed two more times to make sure all of the chemicals they put in my motor are out. He would not pay me back a single cent. My oil change wound up costing me $150 dollars. The manager would not explain why the car manufacturer recommends against this service. I will never use Speedy Lube again.

Not Honoring Warranty

As many scam victims report, besides other problems, such as a poor repair job, the repair shop won't honor their warranty. In some cases, the shop blames the customer to avoid facing its responsibility.

For example, L. Wilkins of Austin, Texas (April 9, 2015), had this experience when he saw flashing lights on his dashboard followed by smoke coming from under his hood after he pulled over. However, while the shop identified the problem as a temperature sensor that fell off, causing his coolant to leak out, and resulting in severe engine damage requiring a new engine, the shop wouldn't cover the approximately $12,000 in damages under his three-year extended warranty. The shop claimed it was his fault because of continued driving, even though he pulled over as soon he could on the freeway. Here's what L. Wilkins had to say about this situation:

Roger Beasley Volvo attempt to place blame on customer so as to not use 3yr extended warranty.

I was driving on the flyover of 290 West, about to exit, when all of the lights began to flash on my dashboard. . . . I began to frantically try to merge to the right to pull over. By the time I had pulled over, I began to see smoke billowing out from under my hood. Meanwhile, I had compromised my own safety to stop as quickly as possible, which happened to be on the shoulder of the flyover exit. . . . As cars zoomed past me, I waited for the tow truck to arrive for over an hour.

The next day I get a call from Jim Benton at Roger Beasley, who tells me that nothing is for sure as to the status of the engine yet. However, they were able to find the original culprit to be a 'fatigued temperature sensor' which had actually fallen off and in turn all of my coolant had leaked out immediately.

This would be covered by my $3000 3yr warrant. But I had to wait for the inspector to come by to make his final verdict. A couple of days pass and I hear from Jim again, who informs me that the damage to the engine was so severe that it will need to be replaced. . . .

I finally hear from them and what do you know—NOT covered by warranty because of "continued driving." [But] the faulty temperature sensor did not notify me that anything was wrong. Thus, I did not pull over until my car began to start flashing other lights on the dash at me.

I reached out to a local mechanic who had this to say: "The engine coolant temp sensor inserts into a plastic thermostat housing and is held by a clip. When it pops out the coolant is lost quickly. . . . There is no low coolant level sensor for [a] warning and when coolant is lost rapidly the damage is done before you can know there is a problem. Getting [the] vehicle to [the] roadside without risk of personal injury takes time. You could not have caused this to fail. The clip that holds in the temp sensor is not a maintenance item nor is it accessible for you to have touched it causing it to be loose. He [the shop owner] is acting in bad faith per the terms of the insurance coverage contract."

Now I'm stuck with a bill of $12,000 from Roger Beasley Volvo (not even sure where they came up with this outrageous number) and a warranty that apparently doesn't mean Sh*t!!

Mark from Grand Terrace, California (April 20, 2015), similarly found his warranty wasn't accepted after he bought a replacement turbo that failed after he drove only 1500 miles. They blamed him for the problem due to contaminated oil, so they claimed that wasn't covered under the warranty. As Mark reported:

Virgil's Auto RV Diesel & Repair would not stand by their work or warranty claim. . . .

I recently had an issue with my truck. . . . The turbo went out so I had it towed to Virgil's for replacement. $2200 dollars later I was back on the road. Everything seemed fine until a few months down the road I am dealing with the exact same issue as when I brought it in. . . . I had only put 1500 miles on the truck.

I called Virgil's and wanted to claim a warranty for the turbo going out and I sent them the turbo in the mail. They received it and . . . they basically told me they have never had a turbo fail and blamed it on the oil being contaminated.

I will never recommend this diesel shop to anyone ever! And I hope people see my complaint as well as others on this shop. These guys are rude and do NOT stand by their work at all.

In another case, Wrage from Phoenix, Oregon (April 9, 2015), was talked into buying an extended 100 percent bumper-to-bumper warranty. But after his air conditioner went out, he was told his warranty didn't cover the $100 repair charge, which was difficult for him to pay, since he was permanently disabled and his only income was a small SSI monthly check. As he reported:

Crown Motors sold me an overpriced extended 100% bumper to bumper warranty, and now they won't honor my repair.

In 2011 I found the truck I was looking for at Crown Motors. I paid $20,000 cash, but that wasn't all. They wanted to sell me an extended

100% bumper to bumper warranty. I told the two girls no I didn't want to spend that much more money. Then (since my son and his wife who were with me had a Costco Card), the sales lady said she could offer me the exact same warranty for about half the original price. I then agreed and that was that.

Now my air conditioner is going out and the sales rep said I purchased a cheaper policy and even though it's between the bumpers it's not covered. . . .

I took it to a Ford dealership as instructed by Crown Motors [when this happened]. They looked up my warranty and kept my truck for the day. I returned to pick it up, and they charged me $100, then told me my warranty did not cover the repairs.

Being lied to by sales people has got to stop. I'm permanently disabled and live on a small SSI monthly check. Now I need the coverage I paid for. I'm being ripped off again.

In some cases, the warranty problem is due to a change of ownership in a chain of stores, so that the new owners or the owners of the chain won't honor it, even though the original store still has the same employees who did the original work on the car. As ExposingWrongDoers from Houston, Texas (April 7, 2015), reported:

AAMCO College Station . . . would not honor warranty from previous owner and retains the mechanics who ruined my transmission. . . .

Scott Smith is a liar when he says he warrantied the prior owner's work. What he does or you have to do is contact AAMCO Headquarters . . . and tell them the previous AAMCO store went out of business and you need work done on your car as per your warranty. That is the only way he will honor the previous owner's warranty, so he can get paid.

He did not do this for me. In fact, he told me when he took over the business, he has in his contract he does not assume any liability from the previous owner. Fine, but don't keep the previous owner's staff who screwed up my car. . . . They screwed up my car's transmission, the PCM, the electric system pinching and crossing wires to the fuse box that cost me $2300. For six months, I kept having the same transmission error codes that were electrical, putting my car in limp or safety mode, costing me more money, because I tried to get other AAMCO stores to work on my car and they refused.

Do a search on AAMCO and you will see they are the worst car repair company in the country. I went to five AAMCO stores in three states and they won't honor warranty repairs if it is a transmission electric problem or . . . inside the transmission. Two, AAMCO won't work on your car if you had a problem with the original store and if you try to get warranty work done at another location, they have to call the store who did the work, and [that store] will try to get out of paying for repairs, so the warranty is useless.

This is what I went through. To get my car worked on, I had to sign a release with AAMCO corporate that I don't make a claim against them or College Station AAMCO. There is nothing I could do since the previous owner went bankrupt and I had to take what I could get at the time. Scott Smith operates in the same building paying a franchise fee using the AAMCO name and he kept the previous owner's mechanics who ruined my car. Therefore he is responsible.

Overcharges

Another complaint from many victims is overcharges or extra charges beyond an initial estimate. Sometimes these charges are added because the company claims the problem was more involved or the job took longer than expected. Or the company may claim they never gave the lower quote if it was given verbally. Another big problem is that the company may go ahead and do work that hasn't been authorized or is only authorized if the car is under warranty. Sometimes it doesn't do the work it has charged for. And some victims later do research and discover a number of similar complaints about overcharges and work not being done. Thus, there can be many different reasons for unexpected overcharges, as reflected in the following examples.

For Nadine from Hiddenite, North Carolina (August 15, 2015), the problem was that the cost of the repair mushroomed to almost double the original estimate—from about $500 to $950—because the shop owner claimed the repair was more involved, although the owner had promised her that the mechanic would not do any work on the car unless she approved it. But now he expected to be paid anyway, and she did pay, but left feeling furious about being ripped off. As Nadine reported:

Meineke doubled the price of repair.

I brought my pickup in for brakes. . . . I took it to Meineke to have it looked at. . . . I was given the cost of $539 to repair it. The owner Bobby said that they would not do any work until approved by me. I said go ahead with the repair.

They called later that day saying the supplier shipped the wrong part and it would be ready the following day. It is a second vehicle, so I said no problem.

The next day they called to say it was ready. When I went to pick it up and pay, the bill skyrocked to $954. They claimed it was more involved blah blah blah. I was not prepared for that bill. I would have waited to have it done but they just went ahead and did it. I will NEVER go there again. And the owner Bobby was just not professional at all.

In the case reported by Steve from Belding, Michigan (April 6, 2015), the salesman originally said there would be no charge for installing a part that Steve bought to replace one that fell off his van lift when the company's mechanics previously worked on this car. But when Steve came over with the part, the company wanted about $70, although the bill backed up his claim that there should be no installation charge, so eventually he returned the part and after three months still didn't have one, because he is handicapped and on a limited income. As he reported:

Clock conversions. They have you over a barrel, so they squeeze you for every penny.

I'm a handicap individual who just drove over 70 miles to have a piece put on my van lift. It was quoted at $37.50 and I asked if they could put this on at no charge because I'd spent over $850 there in the last few months getting work done on my lift. I also said that this piece has been on my van since 2002 and it only fell off after they worked on it.

I was willing to purchase the part but am not capable of installing it as I can't reach down that far. They said that a sales man or someone would be able to put that on, as it's only a 5 minute job and it just slides into place.

When I got there, they wanted $69 for the part because it also needed a gasket of some type, but they were unwilling to install it without a charge. (I think that the gasket is $7 on Amazon). I told them that they had said on the phone that they would install it at no charge. In fact the bill had a note that said installation is $0.00. Then the person I had talked to said that he had talked to me and said that they would have to charge to put this on (not at all true).

I live in the handicap community and Clock is not highly thought of for just such actions. I returned the part and still don't have one after a three month's wait, [because] I refuse to knuckle under to their deceit and abuse.

Similarly, Tony of Roebling, New Jersey (April 19, 2015), found that he got a verbal quote that was later denied when he got to the store, resulting in the company charging him nearly twice the $160 several customer reps quoted him on the phone. As he described the situation:

I spoke with several different representatives from both PA and NJ on several different occasions. I informed them that my insurance won't cover any of the replacement cost and that I will be paying in full.

Each conversation (at least 3) I was quoted $160 out of pocket. I was very clear that my insurance wouldn't cover it. They still said $160. So you can imagine my shock when they charged me over $300 after the window was installed.

It is illegal for them to do this, but it was their word against mine. I filed a complaint with their customer service and they said they didn't have any record stating the quote of $160. I now record all my business conversations in NJ.

In the end, I was charged $269.

In Mauricio's case, the company took his money but didn't do the work. As he reported:

Santa Fe Auto Service [was guilty of a] truck repair that he never performed and I paid for.

Hugo Silva . . . the mechanic that owns this business . . . had my van for 7 weeks. [He] never worked on it, kept lying that he was working on it, and was almost done. I finally had to have it [the van] towed to a shop that fixed it in a day. This is my business van, he knew that. I needed it every day to work, without it I couldn't work, and he knew that too.

At the same time that I took my van there, I took a friend's truck to have the alternator replaced. I gave him $130 so that he can pick up a new alternator, and he said that he would replace it the next day. He took the old alternator out, never replaced [it], would not answer my calls or texts and never gave me my money back. I had to purchase another alternator and had the truck towed to another shop where they installed the alternator for me in 15 minutes.

He abandoned my van and the truck in the parking lot of his old shop. . . . I then found out that he was evicted from that shop by the location manager due to not paying the rent. . . . At the beginning, [Hugo] kept telling me that he was out getting parts. That's why he was not at the shop, when in fact he was locked out of the shop by the building manager.

He owes money to 3 tow truck drivers that I know of and hasen't[sic] paid them. ($450 to one and the other amounts unknown.) . . .

In the process of my investigating, I met 3 other people that he ripped off: Gary who gave him some money towards the end of last year to fix one of his vehicles; he never did the work and he never gave Gary his money back; Carlos who did some work for him at the shop, but never got paid; Pancho, who gave him an SUV to sell for him; Pancho never saw any of that money. Hugo Silva is a con man and is in the habit of ripping people off.

In the case of gunrunner from Hazel Green, Alabama (April 15, 2015), his car was supposed to be under warranty for some repairs and the shop was not supposed to do anything not covered by the warranty. But the owner did some additional testing that was not covered and tried to charge him the full non-warranty price for the test, though gunrunner thought this payment excessive. Though gunrunner was able to get his price down, he later found a loose door panel. Though the shop owner claimed he didn't touch the door, gunrunner found his handprint on the bottom of the door, which indicated that he did touch it. As gunrunner reported:

> Dennis's One Stop Auto Shop . . . My vehicle was damaged while in for repair; not the same price as agreed on.
>
> I have a 2000 Dodge Neon. I had a rebuilt jasper brand engine installed a little over 1 year ago that is still under warranty. I was having an issue with the oil light coming on at idle. The people at Jasper Engines told me to find a shop to take the car that would work under the warranty guidelines of $60 per hour shop rate and did not mind waiting for their money until the warranty check could be sent to the shop after repairs were finished.
>
> I found an automotive repairs shop close to me that installs jasper engines. . . . I took the car in to them with a hand written note from me that gave the $60 per hour amount, the claim number from Jasper Engines, and a note at the bottom that said in caps: DO NOT DO ANY REPAIRS NOT COVERED 100% UNDER WARRANTY.
>
> The next afternoon I got a call from Dennis's and he (the shop owner) said the problem was not covered under the warranty because the oil pressure was fine. The problem was coming from a bad oil pressure sending unit and not the oil pump, and I owed him $107 for checking the oil pressure, since it was not a warranty covered issue. I asked if he had seen the note to not do anything not covered under warranty. He said he did see it, but this had to be done to find the trouble. . . .
>
> I told him $107 was high for an oil pressure test. Then he said it was for [ordering] a new oil pressure sending unit and tightening a loose belt, and it broke down to $70 per hour for shop labor and $25 for the new oil pressure sending unit, [though] being a mechanic I already knew if the problem was not the oil pressure it had to be the sending unit, so I had already checked prices on the part, and the oil pressure sending until would only cost . . . $12 and change at the local auto parts store . . . so at this point he was trying to charge me $70 per hour instead of the agreed $60 per hour; he was trying to charge me $25 for a $12 part; and he was trying to charge me for tightening a belt that on my car is SELF-ADJUSTING.

He said the agreement of $60 per hour was with Jasper and not me, [so] . . . it would be $70 per hour. I told him I did not want the new sending unit installed and not to adjust any belts. He said in that case it would only cost me $70 for 1 hour labor for checking the oil pressure (which BTW is only ½ hour to do according to [the] labor hour guide book).

I told him I would pay the $70 just to get my car back. . . . I got there, gave him his $70 and got in my car to leave, when I noticed my driver's door panel had been partly pulled loose and was shaking when I closed the driver's door. I went back in and told him about it, and he said: "I did not do anything to your door. I can't help you."

When I got home and looked over the car, I noticed he had a handprint on the bottom of the door where he was under the car and had grabbed the door to get up off the ground. His other hand was braced . . . on the door panel when he was getting up off the ground and had pulled the door panel loose!!!

I would have done this work myself but I have a bad back, so don't work on cars much anymore. But from now on, I will grab a pain pill . . . and do it myself before I will go through this kind of crap again, warranty work or not!!!

Holding a Car for Payment

Unfortunately, when victims dispute a charge or overcharge, the auto repair shop or towing company can hold their car for payment, which many do. In some cases, a shop may refuse to turn over personal property in the car, even if it may not be legal to do so, in order to extract payment from the victim. So generally, since they need their car back, the victims pay up, as much as they feel they have been cheated.

That's what Jim from Hillsboro, Oregon (April 6, 2015), thought after he paid $4,000, since the shop owner not only didn't finish the work but wanted $4,300 more to do so, which was more than the going rate for the work. Thus, while Jim planned to take the owner to small claims court, he felt it unfair that his car would be sitting in the shop for four months until the court date, and the owner would only take cash for the full amount to return the car. As Jim described his plight:

Hot Rod Garage overcharged, did not finish work, will not release vehicle . . .

Had work done on my 1932 Chevy Roadster. Was overcharged and work was not finished. I paid $4000 and he wanted $4300 more. Checked other certified mechanics and was told about $2800 to $2900 is what I should pay when the job is finished. . . .

I'm taking him to small claims court. Car is sitting in his garage till July when there is a court opening. The car is valuable. I do not know what he will do to it. He will not take credit card or check, cash only. He is not listed in the Oregon state business registry.

Renata from Colony, Texas (April 14, 2015), encountered a similar situation after she paid $3,500 up front to a body shop to repair her car, but then the shop owner wanted even more money, though she had difficulty paying any more as a single mother of three who was trying to survive without any child support. As she described the problem:

All Star Auto Clinic . . . has collected the money requested up front but will not release my vehicle in an attempt to scam me for more money.

Here's my story. . . . I am a single mother of three and I am the sole provider; no child support or assistance at all. I am being scammed by a person I considered a friend. His body shop repaired my vehicle and they have received 3500 up to date.

They are continually trying to scam me out of more money. I have emails and text showing the total of repairs being $4000 in full and then saying they were only charging me $3000.

These people will not return my car. I have had to dip into the savings for my children to pay for rentals and my bills. I cannot go to work, and am hitchhiking with three little kids. The stress has also taken a toll on my health.

I am able to provide text messages and Facebook post from myself and this company to show proof they have lied and said I have not paid, but my bank account says differently.

Mazde quoted me the price upfront as all repair facilities do and Joe has continuously tried to scam me out of more money. It's not right how this company is operating, because now from the stress from all this I don't sleep. I'm under doctor's care and this is affecting me being able to provide for my babies. [Joe] has also stated he attempted to assist me by offering a payment plan but on the text you will see that is not true. [Besides] why would I need a payment plan when the amount he quoted was collected plus 500 more? I still don't have my car. I can provide over 160 text and emails to prove what I am saying is facts. [The company has] also continued to harass me to the point [where] I had to request a cease and desist.

Finally, in one more refusal-to-return example, slogan63 from Saco, Maine (April 15), complained that a towing and auto repair company wouldn't return the personal property of his son who was injured in an auto accident until they were paid the towing fee, despite a state law requiring the release of all personal property. As slogan63 explained the situation:

Southern Maine Towing & Auto Repair unlawfully seized personal property in towed vehicle pending payment of towing fees.

This company towed my son's vehicle after he was severely injured in a single car accident. When we asked to be allowed access to the vehicle to obtain his personal property, including clothing and medications, the company responded that it would only release his 'keys and papers' until and unless he paid the towing fee. Maine law requires the release of all personal property, including clothing, except business equipment, tools, or machinery. Despite having no legal authority to do so, the towing company has seized his property.

Taking No Responsibility for Stolen Property

Another problem for some victims was having their personal property stolen out of their car while it was in the shop. But the shop owner denied that anyone from the shop had taken the property or claimed no responsibility for the loss.

For example, Susan W in Kennesaw, Georgia (April 13, 2015), dropped off her truck for a simple oil change, walked across the street to get a manicure, and when she returned, her gun was missing from the car's console. But the owner did not check the station's video camera, which might have

shown someone stealing the gun, interview the station's mechanic or customer service person, or check around the shop for the gun. But then the
owner seemed unconcerned and took no responsibility for the theft. As
Susan W complained:

> American Service Station. I dropped my vehicle off and walked across
> the street. My valuables were stolen during my absence.
>
> On the afternoon of April 7, 2015, I dropped off my truck to have
> an oil change and walked across the street to get a manicure. When I
> returned and got into my car, I noticed that the Glock gun model 36 was
> missing from the center console of my vehicle.
>
> I immediately requested to speak to the GM, David, who came out
> to assist. I showed him where the gun had been previously located. I was
> a bit concerned when David didn't seem alarmed or show much empathy
> for my missing gun. He said he would check the video the next day and
> call me. He indicated that video cameras would identify any theft. I was
> surprised that David didn't interview or question the mechanic and the
> customer service person. Further, David made no attempt to search or
> check around the shop either. He was leaving to go home and didn't seem
> very concerned. He did commit to call me the next morning, which he
> failed to do. . . .
>
> My husband, Cliff, since we never heard from David . . . called the
> Marietta Police Department and had them come down to the station to
> take a report. The Policeman interviewed the GM but it was my word
> against his. David stated no theft was identified in the service bay when
> reviewing the video footage. However, I am certain that the gun was taken
> while parked on [the] premises, outside of the service bay, where there were
> no cameras. When I got out of the truck, I locked my car and handed the
> keys to David, but unfortunately never saw my property again.
>
> In closing, I am amazed in the total lack of professionalism or com-
> munication from the GM. I have registered several complaints on social
> media and contacted the Better Business Bureau. I want to warn other
> consumers, do not use this service. If you do, I believe you will be sorry.

In another stolen property case, Robert of Soperton, Georgia (April 17,
2015), reported that all of the personal property in his car, including a

laptop and radio, were taken when he dropped off his wife's car for minor service, and the owner claimed no responsibility. The owner even pointed to a sign on the wall saying, "Not responsible for theft," although Robert believed that one of the people working there—a kid, a senior citizen, or the owner himself—took the property. As Robert described what happened:

> Beckum Automative . . . is a total ripoff and the owner is a thief. . . .
>
> I took my wife's car in for minor service, and when she picked it up, it had been cleaned out of all personal property, like a laptop and other personal items along with the radio. When I went back and asked [the owner] about it, he just pointed to a sign on the wall saying "Not responsible for theft."
>
> [The car] was inside his shop the whole time and only him and a kid and a senior citizen were working in the shop. How can you not be responsible for something you did? And the next day I was looking the car over and noticed they even took my spare tire.
>
> When I went back again . . . [the owner] wanted to act like a bully and push me around. I would not recommend this place to anyone at all. BAD PEOPLE AND A BAD BUSINESS.

Excessive Delays

Finally, some victims report excessive delays in which their cars are literally held hostage. Meanwhile, the shop owners keep the victim waiting by making promises that the car will be done soon, don't respond to phone calls, and otherwise put the customer off after they have their money up front.

That's what happened to Reginald Kizzee from Dallas, Texas (April 17, 2015), who described how he was strung along thus:

> I went to Brenspeed in December 2014 to get me some work done to my 2008 mustang. I talked to the owner Don Jones and Cliff . . . about getting some more horsepower . . .
>
> Cliff told me they had a special going . . . and it was a Paxton Supercharger for $5300 and you will get about 450hp. I said I want that then. At first my car was quiet. You couldn't hear the supercharger.

After a month the supercharger started making noises. I took it back to Brenspeed April 16, 2015 . . . Everything is under warranty, so they said they will take off the supercharger and send it back to Paxton.

I told them I don't want to be without my car for no 2 or 3 weeks. My car has been down there for over a month now. All I was getting was lies from George [the mechanic]. I was going to Brenspeed at least 2 times a week asking how long will it be. All they would say is we have to ask George what's going on with my charger.

I called George. He wouldn't call me back, and when he did call me, all he was doing was just lieing to me after 3 weeks. I called Paxton myself to see what's going on with my charger. Paxton employee told me we just got your supercharger March 30, 2015. I called George to see why they waited 3 weeks to send my charger back to Paxton.

He didn't answer my calls, so I went to Brenspeed and asked Cliff what's going on, why it takes 3 weeks to send my charger back. He said George never got back with him to tell him what to do with it.

Now it's over a month my car is still at Brenspeed and they are still lieing about my charger. I got a call today saying they got my super-charger back from Paxton . . . but it's in Indiana and I'm in Texas, so I got 5 more days to wait.

This is bad business. I'll never use them again. I'm telling everybody I know, don't use Brenspeed because once they get your money, you're going to get nothing but lies after.

The Dynamics of the Auto Repair Scam

While the auto repair industry is sometimes accused of being the "Number 1" source of scams, these scams are very different from the credit card and phony check scams, which are designed by con artists seeking to trick victims into giving them credit card information or cashing a phony check and sending them money. Then these con artists are on to their next victims, using alluring ads, offers, or emails to suck them into being scammed. And often these scammers move frequently, use different ads, names, and emails to scam victims and evade any legal or law enforcement efforts, and commonly are located in other countries, where it is almost impossible to track them down, much less prosecute or institute legal action against them.

By contrast, the auto repair scams are generally perpetrated by owners or managers of established enterprises that have a physical presence in the community, and they may have an inventory of products that they offer customers through their auto repair or body shop facility. They also may have many legitimate customers who feel satisfied with their services, although these customers may not be aware that they have been convinced to pay higher prices or obtain additional services they may not need.

Thus, while some customers may feel ripped off, often these auto repair and body shops are not actually doing anything illegal. And it can be hard to prove any of these scams because they are often based on verbal disputes, such as when a victim claims an owner made certain promises about what repairs are needed and provides a cost estimate but charges more than that amount, while the owner denies making those promises. Or in many cases, the owner or manager may refuse to honor a warranty or to accept any responsibility for damages to the car on the grounds that the customer was at fault for continuing to drive after the problem developed. Or the owner or manager may claim that the problem developed a few hours or days after the customer got the car back, so there is no causal connection between the repairs and the problem that developed. As further leverage, the owner may refuse to return the victim's car until the amount in question is paid or a lower amount is negotiated.

Another problem with these auto repair cases, in contrast to outright scam cases, is that the auto is a complex technological system of parts, especially the newer models with all kinds of electronic controls. As a result, it can take extensive training to become a skilled mechanic who can identify what is wrong and fix it. Further complicating these cases is that mechanics sometimes differ as to what the problem is and how to fix it. And when the customer has some background in repairing cars and may even have been a mechanic, things can be even more complicated when the customer has a different opinion or perceives flaws in what the shop's mechanic has done. Further complications can occur when customers buy their own parts to save money, because they don't always get the right parts—or the owner or manager may not give them the complete or correct information about what they need and then blames the customer for any mistakes. At the same time, customers are very vulnerable to actually being a victim or feeling victimized, whether they are or not, since many customers know very little about cars. So they can be easily exploited, and this vulnerability can lead owners, managers, and employees to upsell customers, so they buy more products or services and sometimes agree to buy things they don't really need.

Adding to the potential for becoming a victim is the way many shops blame the victim or deny responsibility when things go wrong. Even though the victim may perceive a direct connection between taking their car for servicing and a problem that develops soon after that—such as a car that stalls, a knocking noise in the engine, windshield wipers that suddenly don't work, a radiator that boils over, a leaking gas tank, or a loose door—the shop owner or manager can readily claim the shop wasn't at fault. For example, they might claim that this occurrence was due to the customer's faulty driving, a different problem with the car than originally fixed, or another incident that occurred after the customer drove the car from the shop. As a result, according to the shop owner or manager, the customer has to pay in full for any future repairs, and the shop has no responsibility to fix them without additional payment—and if there was any warranty coverage, it no longer applies.

Thus, in these auto repair scam cases, victims often feel they can do little other than suck up the costs despite the serious hardships these costs may have for them—such as when victims have limited earnings, are subsisting on SSI checks, have kids to raise, or suffer a high level of mental and emotional turmoil due to their precarious situation, exacerbated by the extra auto repair costs. And even if victims take these cases to small claims court, which few do, they may lose because of the difficulty proving fault.

For many victims, filing a report on one of the scam sites, like the Ripoff Report, can be a way of venting their anger as well as alerting others so they don't get scammed by the same company they feel scammed them. Plus, they may feel some satisfaction in causing the company to lose business. Yet, in general, before their scam experience, most victims did not check out the companies they did business with on these sites.

Rather, they generally picked companies in their local area or responded to their ads or websites; in some cases, they were attracted by a company's promotional offer such as a free check-up, discounted services for a certain time period, or a 20 percent discount for students. However, once they responded, they were offered other products or services that they might not have needed or wanted, that later did not work well, or that were not sold at the promised prices. Thus, the scam commonly occurs over a period of time as the customer seeks to get his or her car fixed, rather than being a more limited or single event, as is the case in many other types of scams. These include scams in which the victim's response to a pitch sets the scam in motion by providing a credit card or cashing a phony check and sending money to the scammer.

The Major Types of Auto Repair Scams

As the previous examples have shown, there are a number of major types of scams experienced by customers who feel they have been victimized. Often many of these scams go together, such as when a victim feels he or she has experienced both shoddy work and has been overcharged. Should the victim resist paying for any poor work or overcharges, the auto repair shop may hold his or her car. In many cases, a shop owner, manager, or salesperson will not only sell the customer on getting products and services he or she may not need or want, but there will be overcharges for installing them. If a part turns out not to work very well or a car is damaged, the company may refuse to take responsibility or to work with the customer to fix the problem. And often there may be delays or lies when there are problems, because the owner, manager, or salesperson gets busy with other things or wants to hold off admitting the problem to the customer.

The major types of auto repair scams reported by the victims sharing their experiences included these common scams identified in articles and blogs:

- damage by a highway vandal
- bait-and-switch promotions
- unnecessary upgrades, repairs, and upsells

- installation of used parts instead of new ones
- nonreplacement of parts at all
- damage done to a car to create more repairs
- bills for repairs without authorization

In addition, victims reported more complex scams with many variations in the services and parts involved. To sum up, here are the major types of scams they reported:

- A repair was done with poor workmanship, and the bill included overcharges for the work.
- The car was damaged as a result of the repair. Though some scams involved intentionally damaging a car so the victim had to pay for additional repairs, these were primarily inadvertent damages due to errors by the mechanics working on the car. Commonly the shop denied responsibility and sometimes blamed the customer.
- The car was badly repaired, and this was combined with multiple other problems, including not deducting a promised amount, delays in getting the repair done, using faulty parts, an incorrect diagnosis, repairs that didn't fix the original problem, a failure to get a promised refund, and the shop's failure to honor a promotional deal.
- The shop refused to give a refund, honor a warranty, or fix a poor repair job at no charge, resulting in future problems, commonly because the shop blamed the customer for causing the problem after leaving the shop or denied the shop did anything wrong, despite evidence that some of its employees took the car for a joyride or painted a car with paint that soon began to peel off.
- There were overcharges or extra charges beyond the initial estimate, often because the shop claimed the problem was more involved, the job took longer than expected, or the shop never gave the initial lower quote; or once the company had the victim's money, it didn't do the work.
- A car was held for payment when the victim disputed a charge or overcharge, resulting in the victim usually being helpless to do anything but pay to get the car. While some victims were able

to negotiate the owner down, many others agreed to pay the full amount, as they needed their only car, and any rental fees while disputing the charge could prove excessive.

- The shop took no responsibility for stolen property, even when the theft was likely to have been committed by the company's employees, manager, or owner, since it occurred while the car was under the sole care of the company. While the company might have claimed it had no responsibility for anything left in the car and even pointed to signs claiming no responsibility, victims may still have felt scammed when their property got stolen and the company did nothing to help them.

Thus, apart from some clear-cut scams by unscrupulous repair shops that car owners are frequently warned about, many of these "scams" are less clear-cut, because it can be hard to measure poor work, inappropriate or unauthorized charges, what mistakes lead to damages, and how far a shop's responsibility should extend when subsequent problems develop after a repair. In the cases described by the victims in the preceding examples, it would seem that the owners and managers did take advantage of them, and used the ultimate threat—holding their car until they paid—to get them to pay. But in general, most of these claims would not hold up in court because of the lack of proof for verbal promises and the lack of certainty about the quality of the work performed or the shop's responsibility for problems that developed after the car left the shop, even if they occurred within a few hours or days of the customer taking the car. Thus, most victims did end up paying. They shared their complaint that they had been the victim of a scam, even though they might not have had the clear-cut evidence required by a court. And certainly the vast majority of these cases would be civil ones, unlike many other scams, such as the credit card and phony check scams by con artists whose only purpose is to get money from the victim.

In many of these auto repair cases, the problem seems to develop when something goes wrong with the service provided, so there is a poor repair, further damage, unexpected extra charges, unmet promises, extensive delays, poor communication, and the like, leaving the individual who agreed to the repair with high expectations that weren't fulfilled. Certainly, if numerous complaints are made against a particular company, that shows a clear pattern of taking advantage of vulnerable customers. But often, only one or a few individuals report being scammed by a particular company for individual reasons, rather than the dozens or hundreds of victims reporting complaints in the credit card and phony check scams. In some cases, individuals checking on a repair shop after the fact do discover previous complaints against that company on the scam report sites or complaints made to the local Better Business Bureau, but not always.

Avoiding being victimized by these auto repair scams involves being prepared for a number of different scenarios under which these problems can occur, as discussed in the final section of what to do.

Protecting Yourself from Auto Repair Scams

Because there are so many different types of repair scams, and they often occur at established businesses, it can be difficult to tell that you are being drawn into a scam. You may actually need certain repairs, and you may only be victimized if there are problems in performing the work and the company seeks to evade responsibility. Or there may be lies and misrepresentations about what the company can do, what the charges will be, the timing of the repair, and more.

However, here are some general guidelines about what to do so you are less likely to be scammed. In some cases, you may have little choice about where to go because of an emergency breakdown, so you can't pick and choose which company to use, but you can take steps to protect yourself from a repair shop trying to take advantage of your difficult situation. Use the following general guidelines where you can:

- Look for recommendations from friends and associates who have had a good experience with a company.
- Ideally, go to a company in your area with an established reputation.
- Be cautious when responding to advertising promotions or coupon offers of big discounts and free services, since they are often a come-on to get you to buy more products and services. Be careful of upsells and get only what you need.

- Ask for all estimates, quotes, and descriptions of work done to be in writing; if you are given a recommendation over the phone for additional work, ask for that to be in writing too.
- Besides the paperwork from the company, keep your own record of agreements, promises, meetings, and conversations about your repair.
- Limit your advance deposit as much as possible, and don't pay for the whole job in advance if you can avoid it. In some shops, you don't pay until the job is completed; you sign your approval for an estimate given to you when you drop off the car, and then you pay at the end.
- Learn what you can about your car so you will be more knowledgeable about what the auto repair shop is offering to do. You will be less likely to be victimized by unnecessary repairs or poor work.
- If the company claims to have replaced any parts, ask them to give you the old parts they have replaced. This will help you know that they really replaced them; you can always throw out these old parts later.
- Avoid leaving personal property in your car in plain view to reduce the chance of it being stolen by a passing thief or someone in the company. If you put anything in the trunk, take a photo of it and show it to the service manager. Indicate that you are taking a photo for the record. You can indicate that this is just for insurance purposes, so you don't appear to be suspicious of the shop.
- Be aware of your manufacturer's guidelines for what services are recommended at different mileages or months of owning the car. This way you can better know if you need such services as an engine flush, auto-transmission flush, or new air filter, since these are common upsells to get you to buy unneeded parts or services.
- Ideally, get a second or third opinion from different shops in the case of more expensive repair jobs. Be willing to spend a small diagnosis fee (i.e., about $35 to $50) to learn what is wrong with the car. Then you can independently judge the company based on its cost and reputation, not because it offers to fold the diagnosis fee into your costs if you get a repair.
- Before getting an expensive repair, check out the company through friends and associates, the local Better Business Bureau,

and the major scam sites. If the company gets good recommendations and ratings, great; if there is just one report, consider that this complaint could be based on misunderstandings and unrealistic expectations and that there could be two sides of the story. But if there is a pattern of complaints, take this as a warning to stay away.

Make it clear up front that the shop should only do what you authorize in writing. While you may owe for the initial quote and the labor to investigate any issues noted in this investigation, tell the shop it cannot do work without your written authorization and it cannot hold your car as collateral to get paid. Should the shop refuse to return your car, call the local police. Many car owners are scared they will lose their vehicles if they don't pay, but you should make it clear that you won't pay for what you did not authorize in writing, and you consider it fraud if the shop won't release your car after doing unauthorized work.

Use your owners' manual as a guide for what services to expect to do when, and keep track of when you completed your oil changes and at what mileage, as well as noting any other work you have done. Also, write down reminders for other service work you can expect to do, such as tire rotations or transmission flushes. This recordkeeping can help you spot when you are offered upsells of services and products you don't need, because the service has recently been done or isn't due for some time.

Be wary of falling for five common upsells:

- a flat tire replacement instead of a patch
- a radiator coolant replacement, unless your coolant is contaminated or hasn't been replace for 100,000 miles
- a preventive oil replacement, since it is unnecessary to change your oil prematurely
- an unnecessary air filter replacement, unless the mechanic can show you that your filter is actually clogged with dust and grime
- overpriced replacement parts; ask how much the labor and parts cost separately, and compare the prices with those at a local auto parts stores so you don't get gouged—or obtain the parts yourself to reduce their cost

If you believe you have been the victim of a scam, file a complaint with your state attorney general's office, local consumer protection agency, and the Better Business Bureau—or threaten to do so, which might get you a reduced bill.

Ultimately, your best protection is to go to trusted local shop owners who are active in a local Chamber of Commerce, have good Better Business Bureau ratings—if they are rated—have gotten favorable reviews on consumer review sites, such as on Yelp or Angie's List, and even better, have testimonials for great work from neighbors, family, friends, and business associates. In fact, you might be able to find a local online group through an organization like Next Door, where you can ask for a recommendation for an auto repair shop, and besides getting some recommendations for good shops, you may get some negative reviews of places to avoid. (And if you have a good experience, post a good review yourself.)

Notes

1   "Auto Repair Fraud," MyAutoRepairAdvice.com, http://www.myautorepairadvice.com/car_repair_fraud.html

2   "Car Repair Scams," FraudGuides.com, http://www.fraudguides.com/cars/car-repair-scams

3   "Top Auto Repair Shop Scams to Avoid," AutoBlog, July 31, 2013. http://www.autoblog.com/photos/repair-shop-scams

4   Ibid.

5   Ibid.

6   Doug Bonderud, "Beware of These 3 Common Car Repair Scams," Angie's List, August 21, 2014. http://www.angieslist.com/articles/beware-these-3-common-car-repair-scams.htm

7   Ibid.

8   Ibid.

9   "Are You Falling Victim to These Common Auto Repair Scams?" ASP Staff, October 10, 2014. https://www.asapwarranty.com/blog/2014/falling-victim-common-auto-repair-scams/

10 "Don't Fall for These Auto Repair Tricks," AutoBlog.com, May 19, 2014. http://www.autoblog.com/2014/05/19/car-repair-tricks-scams-upsells

11 Jim Wang, "Car Repair Scams to Watch Out For," *Reader's Digest,* http://www.rd.com/slideshows/car-repair-scams

12 Ken Amaro, "Ken's Top 10: Auto Repair Scams to Avoid," WTLV-12-25, March 2, 2011. http://www.firstcoastnews.com/news/article/193896/343/Kens-Top-10-Auto-Repair-Scams-to-Avoid

13 Ibid.

14 Jim Wang, "Car Repair Scams to Watch Out For," *Reader's Digest,* http://www.rd.com/slideshows/car-repair-scams

15 Aaron Crowe, "9 Common Auto Repair Scams to Avoid," *Cheap Car Insurance,* May 5, 2014. http://www.cheapcarinsurance.net/9-common-auto-repair-scams-to-avoid

16 Jim Wang, "Car Repair Scams to Watch Out For," *Reader's Digest,* http://www.rd.com/slideshows/car-repair-scams

17 Ibid.

18 "Don't Fall for These Auto Repair Tricks," AutoBlog.com, May 19, 2014. http://www.autoblog.com/2014/05/19/car-repair-tricks-scams-upsells

19 Doug Bonderud, "Beware of These 3 Common Car Repair Scams," Angie's List, August 21, 2014. http://www.angieslist.com/articles/beware-these-3-common-car-repair-scams.htm

20 ASAP Staff, "Are You Falling Victim to These Common Auto Repair Scams?" ASAP Warrant.com, October 10, 2014. https://www.asapwarranty.com/blog/2014/falling-victim-common-auto-repair-scams

21 Ibid.

22 Ibid.

23 Ken Amaro, "Ken's Top 10: Auto Repair Scams to Avoid," WTLV12-25, March 2, 2011. http://www.firstcoastnews.com/news/article/193896/343/Kens-Top-10-Auto-Repair-Scams-to-Avoid

24 Ibid.

25 "Auto Repair Scams," Coalition Against Fraud, http://www.insurancefraud.org/scam-alerts-auto-repair.htm#.VT11oCFVhBc

26 "Auto Repair Scams," Auto Repair by City, http://www.autorepairbycity.com/wordpress/info-on-repair/auto-repair-scams

27 Ibid.

CHAPTER 5:

SEND MONEY

The "Send Money" scam is one of the pernicious scams, usually perpetrated by scammers overseas who have a variety of schemes for getting victims to send them money. To do so, they prey on some of the most basic emotions—fear, love, and greed—to get people to send off money to a stranger who gives them a story that convinces them to act quickly and send off the money before having a chance to assess the truth of the story or discover he or she is another victim. Sometimes this is known as the "advance fee scam" or the "Four-One-Nine" scam, which is the Nigerian law for fraud, since a majority of these kinds of messages originally came from Africa, and especially Nigeria, though now they come from all over the world.

The losses from these scams are enormous. According to a Truth or Fiction report, the US Secret Service reports that thousands of people have lost hundreds of millions of dollars on these schemes. Back in 2001, 2,600 Americans reported being scammed, and sixteen of them lost more than $300,000, while many who have lost money don't report it. Fifteen years later, these same scams are continuing.[1]

There are a number of different forms of the scam, which generally come in the form of an email, fax, or phone call giving you a story about what you need to respond to quickly. These are some forms the scam takes:

- You are a winner or beneficiary of something, and now you need to send money to cover the fees, such as for taxation, shipping, or documents, so you can receive your big earnings. (Greed)
- Your help is needed to receive or transfer funds out of the country into a secure location for some reason (the sender has inherited a big fortune and has to transfer the funds to avoid a huge tax bill; the sender's wealthy family is fleeing from a corrupt government that is seeking to take its money, and so on), and you will receive a substantial payment or commission (typically about 15 percent) for your help, but you have to put up some money to show you are worthy and can be trusted or to pay for advance transfer fees. (Greed/Altruism)
- Some authority, such as the IRS, requires an immediate payment from you for some reason, such as back taxes or the failure to pay a fine. If you don't pay immediately, you risk various calamities, including going to jail, losing your house or car for nonpayment, and having your fines and penalties greatly increased. (Fear)
- A friend, family member, relative, or close business associate needs help and is turning to you as their last hope. The various reasons for needing help might range from that person losing a wallet and credit cards in a foreign country to being in a serious accident to being kidnapped, and your help is needed to come to the rescue. (Fear/Love)
- And still other stories about why you need to send money to help a loved one who is in trouble, make money yourself, avoid a penalty if you don't send it, or otherwise gain some benefit by sending the money. You generally need to act quickly and keep the matter secret, based on a variety of different explanations for why the matter is urgent and confidential and why you should respond to this person who is either pretending to be someone you know or a stranger you should believe. They make you trust that they have selected you for some special reason, such as being a good person who will do good works or a likely business partner interested in this great opportunity.

These requests for funds, should you fall for them, are clearly fraudulent and are created for the sole purpose of getting you to send money. Once you do, there can be little recourse since you have typically sent the money via some untraceable means, such as Western Union or MoneyGram, or have sent a money order or cashier's check to a party, often using a false name, in another country.

They depend on your trust or belief, evoked from the story you are told. Sometimes the revelations can be particularly devastating. Apart from discovering you were taken in by a story that wasn't true and have lost money as a result, you may experience other consequences and responses. For example, thinking you are a beneficiary, you may make other purchases and take on other debts. If you send money to help a friend in need, you may experience relief to discover the person is actually home and well. Sometimes you may be further victimized by being asked to come to the country to help with the money transfer or to assist your friend, only to be personally threatened or kidnapped until you come up with more money. And then there is the utter embarrassment of falling for the false story.

What follows is an overview of how some of these send-money scams work and the effect they have had on some victims.

The You-Are-a-Winner-or-Beneficiary Scam

It can feel great to be a big winner of something or to discover you have suddenly inherited or gained an unexpected windfall. You feel like celebrating, and if the winnings are large enough, you can have visions of changing your life and even adopting a whole new lifestyle.

That's the kind of desire that the lottery winner or beneficiary scam seeks to take advantage of, so that individuals who think they are winners or beneficiaries will be willing to send them the much smaller amount they are requesting in advance for taxes or transfer fees. Of course, after they do, the scammers disappear. The victims suddenly find they can't contact the scammers and learn too cruelly that not only are their hopes dashed for the future funds they dreamed of getting, but they have also lost whatever money they have sent the scammers. For in these cases, the scammers are usually far away, often in another country, and have used fake names, addresses, emails, phone numbers, even websites. So after the scam unravels, there is usually no way of contacting them or getting back any money.

Certainly, many recipients of the initial emails, letters, and phone calls are immediately wise to them and know it's a scam. In fact, unlike many other scams, where victims report the scam after the fact, many of the individuals reporting these scams have been immediately suspicious when they first were contacted. But many other victims are taken in—which is why the scammers keep using this approach. It's so inexpensive to set up fake personal contact information and send out thousands, if not millions, of emails and get at least some victims sending them money.

Here's how these scams work.

You Won the Lottery Scam

Often these lottery scam letters are not very elaborate, and usually they come from an official for the lottery advising you that you have won some money. Now you just have to send in a payment for the taxes, transfer fees, administrative charges, or the like so the funds can be released and sent to you. Of course, there are no funds. In some cases, the scammers use the names of real lotteries; in other cases, these are made-up names or names that are close enough to the real names to look official. At one time, these letters used to come by mail or phone and cost consumers about $120 million a year. Now, with email, the potential for loss is even greater (www.consumer.ftc.gov/articles/0086-international-lottery-scams).

I got one of these letters in May while writing this book, presumably from the FBI, saying I was selected as the winner of a huge lottery sum. Letters from the FBI and other official agencies, such as the IRS, are often used in scams because the people who receive them fear that they could be subject to prosecution for an offense unless they immediately respond to demands for money or identity information. However, while the website of the FBI was real, the purported division within the FBI— the "Anti-Terrorist and Monetary Crimes Division"—was not, nor was the signer, James Comey, correctly identified, since he was listed as the director of the Office of Public Affairs, though he is currently the director of the FBI.

In any case, the letter went on to say that after an investigation, it was discovered that my email address had been selected by an online banking system, so I had won the princely sum of $50 million from a lottery company outside the United States, and now all I needed to do was send $540 for the deposit with the IMF (presumably the International Monetary Fund), which could not be deducted from the winnings, and for shipping the cashier's check to my home address. All I had to do was contact the agent in charge of the transaction, along with my name and contact information, so I could send the money by Western Union or MoneyGram. Then he would send me my $50 million prize. Here's a copy of the letter I received, which—apart from the amazing, huge prize amount—includes many tip-offs of this being a scam, such as the use of Western Union and MoneyGram, the misspellings, the free Gmail account, and the signature with the reference to including a photo of the director and the homepage—obviously meant to be included but left off of the letter.

Anti-Terrorist And Monetary Crimes Division FBI Headquarter, Washington, D.C. Federal Bureau Of Investigation,Washington, D.C. J.Edgar Hoover Building 935 Pennsylvania Avenue, Nw Washington, D.C. 20535-0001 www.fbi.gov ATTENTION: BENEFICIARY
This e-mail has been issued to you in order to Officially inform you that we have completed an investigation on an International Payment in which was issued to you by an International Lottery Company. With the help of our newly developed technology (International Monitoring Network System) we discovered that your e-mail address was automatically selected by an Online Balloting System, this has legally won you the sum of $50 million United State Dollars USD from a Lottery Company outside the United States of America. During our investigation we discovered that your e-mail won the money from an Online Balloting System and we have authorized this winning to be paid to you via INTERNATIONAL CERTIFIED BANK DRAFT.

Normally, it will take up to 5 business days for an INTERNATIONAL CERTIFIED BANK DRAFT by your local bank. We have successfully notified this company on your behalf that funds are to be drawn from a registered bank within the worldwinde, so as to enable you cash the check instantly without any delay, henceforth the stated amount of $50 million United State Dollars USD has been deposited with IMF.We have completed this investigation and you are hereby approved to receive the winning prize as we have verified the entire transaction to be Safe and 100% risk free, due to the fact that the funds have been deposited with IMF you will be required to settle the following bills directly to the Lottery Agent in-charge of this transaction whom is located in USA, UNITED STATE OF AMERICA. According to our discoveries, you were required to pay for the following,

(1) Deposit Fee's (IMF INTERNATIONAL CLEARANCE CERTIFICATE)

(2) Shipping Fee's (This is the charge for shipping the Cashier's Check to your home address)

The total amount for everything is $540.00 We have tried our possible best to indicate that this $540.00 should be deducted from your winning prize but we found out that the funds have already been deposited IMF and cannot be accessed by anyone apart from you the winner, therefore you will be required to pay the required fee's to the Agent in-charge of this transaction In order to proceed with this transaction, you will be required to contact the agent in-charge (Mr Wilson Jenkins) via e-mail. Kindly look below to find appropriate contact information:
CONTACT AGENT NAME: Mr Wilson Jenkins
        E-MAIL: info.fbiagent12@gmail.com

You will be required to e-mail him with the following information:

FULL NAME:
ADDRESS:
CITY:
STATE:
ZIP CODE:
DIRECT CONTACT NUMBER:
OCCUPATION:
You will also be required to request Western Union or Money Gram details on how to send the required $540.00 in order to immediately ship your prize of $50 million USD via INTERNATIONAL CERTIFIED BANK DRAFT from IMF, also include the following transaction code

in order for him to immediately identify this transaction : EA2948-910.
This letter will serve as proof that the Federal Bureau Of Investigation
is authorizing you to pay the required $540.00 ONLY to Mr David Dye
via information in which he shall send to you,
Mr.James Comey
Director Office of Public Affairs
Federal Bureau of Investigation F B I
Yours in Service,Photograph of Director
Homepage

In this case, even the FBI is aware of the scam, and in a press release over five
years ago they warn about a spam email claiming to be an "official order"
from the FBI's non-existent Anti-Terrorist and Monetary Crimes Division, as
well as other government offices informing recipients they have been named
a beneficiary of millions of dollars. Or they may use these official names to
claim that individuals face some kind of penalty or prosecution unless they
refund money or pay a penalty. But individuals shouldn't respond to any of
these emails or click on embedded links, which may contain viruses or malware, and they should not provide any personal information (or personally
identifiable information—PII in government lingo) that might compromise
their identity or subject them to identity theft (www.fbi.gov/news/pressrel/
press-releases/e-mail-scammers-continue-to-send-fake-fbi-messages).

Even with this warning, the scam continues to be alive and well,
though there are many variations, such as one warning posted by the
law firm of Whitehouse and Cooper. The firm received a similar letter
to mine, supposedly from the FBI, though indicating that the award
was only for $3.5 million and the amount to send was only $380, and
now the FBI was working in cooperation with the UN to provide this
money to the rightful beneficiaries (www.whitehouse-cooper.com/
scam-alert-fbi-isnt-sending-3-500000000-million-usa-dollars).

However, while some of lottery scams appear to come from government agencies, many others appear to come from officials of the lotteries
themselves, stating that you have won a prize—even though you may
have never heard of this lottery and did not enter it. You just have to contact someone who claims to be an official of the lottery company and then
send in some money to receive your winnings. Typically the rationale for

paying these fees is that they are for insurance costs, government taxes, bank fees, or courier charges. And usually you have to respond quickly as well as keep your good fortune a secret—although typically, lottery winnings are announced through the media and entrants have to come forward to get their prize after they learn they have a winning number—and they definitely don't have to pay any money up front to obtain their winnings. While these supposed lotteries occur in many countries, Spanish, Canadian, and Australian lotteries are among the most common (www.actionfraud.police.uk/fraud_protection/lottery_fraud).

Sometimes if you check, you will find that the scammers have used the name of a legitimate overseas lottery, such as the Loteria Primitiva or El Gordo in Spain. But if you haven't actually entered that lottery by buying a ticket from an authorized distributor in that country, you can't win. Moreover, a reason that the scammers want you to "respond quickly or risk missing out" is they don't want you thinking about or checking up on this seemingly great news if you start to wonder if this could be a scam (www.scamwatch.gov.au/content/index.phtml/tag/lotterysweepstakescams). Another trick that these scammers sometimes use is stalling the payment of your winnings by asking for more fees to release the money if they haven't already disappeared after you send the first payment.

In some cases, beyond asking for money, the scammers may ask you to provide personal information to prove you are the winner as well as bank account information so they can directly deposit the money into your account. But in that case, the scammer will not only collect money from you but will also use your personal information for identity theft and take money out of your account, not put money in it. If the scammers do send you a check for part or all of your winnings, it will ultimately bounce and you will be out that and any bounced check fees too.

Here are some examples of individuals who received these lottery letters and reported the scam on one of the scam report sites, the Ripoff Report (www.ripoffreport.com). With a few exceptions, they recognized the attempt to scam them.

For example, Karen from Tomball, Texas (July 15, 2011), reported:

Received a letter in the mail with a check for $3,500. Claims I won a lottery for $50,500 and wants $2,500 to pay the IRS for taxes. When the check is scanned the "VOID" shows up and the $3,500 check is invalid. They want you to send them the $2,500 for the IRS taxes but it goes directly to them. You call a number to verify your winnings and name and they tell you where to send the $2,500 to an agent with payment of the IRS taxes. They ask you if you want the balance of your money in a cashier's check, money order, or direct deposit. They are just trying to get your bank account number.

Joanne from Randolph, Massachusetts (April 30, 2009), had this to say:

> Received letter stating winner of De-Lotto North American Sweepstakes Lottery on Shoppers Promotions . . . They sent a check for $4,875 and wanted $2,875 sent back for paying of taxes.
>
> This is a scam, check is not good. Check written on Wells Fargo Bank. Bank states check is fraudulent.
>
> Worst thing, they are using several high name company sponsors at the end of the notification. I check with several of the sponsors to ask them if they allowed their names to be used. I received an answer from Home Depot and Wal-Mart. They were both concerned and informed me what I should do.

A big scam tip-off, of course, is being notified that one has won a lottery one hasn't entered, as Marie in Lithonia, Georgia (December 28, 2008), reported.

> Received a letter stating that I have somehow won a Canadian Lottery that I did not enter, was send check for 5,985 dollars to then wire transfer 4980 dollars to someone else but this was supposed to be part of my winnings form the lottery that I somehow won. And I have to call a Mr. Howard Power who is the claims agent.

However, should you mention your suspicions, the scammers will typically hang up, as Walt from Greenville, Ohio, reported.

> Got letter in the mail saying we won 125,000 dollars they sent a check for 4,875 and said we had to call this number before cashing check. I asked

them about it being a scam. They hung up on me. Watch out for these people. As soon as you mention scam or fraud, they hang up on you.

And those who check often find that the account for the check does not exist or the addresses or numbers are phony or in another country, as Donna from Elizabeth, Pennsylvania (June 25, 2008), reported.

> I got a letter today with a check from the bank of Hawii for $3900. The letter told me to call the 1-905-598-3712 and Mike Ronald or Marta Gibbs would tell me what to do next. I called the number and got a voice mail. I looked up the number. It is an Ontario number and I called the Bank of Hawii to find out if the check is real and the account does not exist.

But while most of those reporting the scam weren't fooled, one man was and lost about $4,000 as a result, as Ron from Salyer, California (November 1, 2008), reported:

> Td Financial Inc. Melissa King Michael Heim said i won lottery. . . . Received letter with check amont 3,995 saying I won lottery prize of 75,000 and need to moneygram 2,985 to said people for taxes and after that a check would come in 48hrs by fedx. no check and my bank said that the one i cashed was no good so iam out about 4,000 dollars, thanks (to) Td Financial. Inc.

In sum, these lottery scams, which have been around for over five years, take various forms and use different covers, ranging from letters from government agencies to letters from lottery officials or agents. But whatever the form these take, as in many other scams, the tip-off is asking you to send money up front to claim your winnings for some reason, such as to pay taxes on the winnings or to pay for administrative or transfer fees. And very often you are advised that you've won a lottery you didn't enter, though a variation is claiming your email was selected in a random drawing. Another tip-off is when the notice comes from a free email address, such as Gmail or Yahoo, and there may be many typos and grammatical mistakes in the letter.

The best approach is to never reply to the email or text message, even to unsubscribe. Don't call a phone number in the email. Don't click on any links, which could be a source of spyware or malware, and don't open any attached file. Moreover, don't provide your credit card or bank account information. And don't send any money or personal details, which can open you up to identity theft. Help others avoid the scam by reporting it to the various scam report websites, family and friends, and government officials that monitor scams.

You Are a Beneficiary

The beneficiary scam may share characteristics with the lottery winner scam in that you are a winner of something, but it can be more complicated to provide a credible reason why you have suddenly been named as a beneficiary, which scammers need to achieve their goal—getting you to send some money in advance for assorted fees needed to collect your benefits, and in many cases getting identity and bank information data to access your accounts and pretend to be you. So there can be extensive emails back and forth, as the scammers build their story and overcome any doubts you may have that this is real. They must get you to believe and act to send them money, as well as provide them with the personal information they need from you. These email exchanges can help you to further bond with the person you believe the scammer is, so you come to trust the scammer and believe his story, even though it's an unusual one.

There are a number of common story lines. Specific details differ, and typically the person who contacts you is either the person who has decided to gift you for your good works or some person who is a lawyer or a representative of an organization or government agency that has been assigned to contact you to give you money. This is usually because you are the next of kin or someone has left money to you. They may claim an authority for giving the funds or obtaining the funds from one or more real organizations or government institutions, or they may claim a sponsorship or relationship with these well-known companies—but, in fact, any link between them is false. They are simply scammers, using these mainstream, highly regarded organizations and institutions for a cover to make their claims seem more believable. But if you do some checking, you are likely to find out that the organizations named are unknown or that the scammer is unknown to the legitimate organizations and government agencies.

For example, I got one such letter, allegedly from the "President of the European Union Commission," informing me that they wanted to help me get paid money that was owed to me from a contract or inheritance worth $15 million. Supposedly they already had a payment approval in my name and just needed to hear from me in order to release these funds. As is common in these pitches, the letter came from out of the blue about an agreement or inheritance I had never heard of. These letters tend to be long and full of details, sometimes referring to real organizations that the scammer claims to be affiliated with but isn't. They often cite all kinds of legal and banking jargon—which may make the letter sound learned and legitimate but often is wrong and confusing. It is used to explain how the scammer happens to be contacting you. Also, in some of these letters, the scammers stress the need for an urgent response, lest the funds be returned to the bank or someone else claim the funds that are supposed to be meant for you. Then, if you do respond, the scammers may request additional identifying information, supposedly needed for documents to release the funds to the correct person or fees to cover things like insurance and taxes. But if you further respond and send money or provide information, any money you send is gone, the scammer uses any personal information to use your identity or drain your bank account, and if you try to contact the scammer he or she is long, long gone. Also, as is characteristic of these letters, mine was full of grammatical mistakes.

Here are some excerpts from this letter, which arrived as I was writing up this section:

From President of the European Union Commission
200 Wetstraat / Rue DE la Loi
1000 Brussels Belgium
Attn; Sir/madam

Sir,

It has come to our notice after the European Union Meeting on unpaid contract/Inheritance fund originated from Africa,Europe and ASIA Etc.I deemed responsibility of this after the meeting to contact you my self after your file and other files got to me. We understood you have not being paid your contract fund/Inheritance worth fifteen million, five hundred thousand united states dollars only ($15,500,000,00), since you personally executed the contract awarded to you under category "A" Through the Africa/Europe/Asia community Inheritance act. Sir,based on this,we have signaled the head of the central banks Governors in Africa,Europe,Asia the presidents, accountant generals concerning this matter. As it stands right now, we have secured a payment approval order/voucher in your name a bank have been appointed to take care of the payment which we shall monitor until the said amount is confirmed into your bank account.

Sir to oursuprise this Morning,someone brought this account details instructed us that he is your next of kind that we should wire the approved fund into his bank account bellow

First Niagara Bank
Account: 8210087485
Routing: 222370440
FNFG US 31
New York
Name; Peter Clarke

Furthermore,i would like you to be kind enough to reply my mail, to enable me to send you more details for us to continue with this process. We are aware also after the investigation that you have spent a huge lot of money trying to get your impending fund we say to you sir/madam, that we are sorry for all you have being through we intervened because of people like you. Meanwhile, i shall be waiting for your prompt reply and confirmation.Note sir, that this process will be carried out immediately you reply us with your details. We shall be behind you to monitor and to give you guide line thank you

Yours Truly,

Mr.Jean-Claude Juncker

What's unusual about this particular pitch letter is it suggests that I have already entered into some agreement to get these funds that are due to me, and I have to act quickly before some pretender to these funds gets in before me, even though I actually have never even heard of this agreement. Presumably, the appeal to greed may overcome someone's lack of knowledge of any of this to convince them to respond to get these funds now in their name before someone else claims them.

More commonly, these beneficiary/inheritance scams, which are reported on various scam sites, take one of the following forms.

In one case, a dying person, usually a woman, has found your name and wants to leave her inheritance to you because she feels you will do good humanitarian works. As the story goes, she has sought you out as a beneficiary because she has no living relatives left; in fact, in some versions of the story, her husband has just died, usually in a tragic accident, leaving her with these funds she wants to give away.

In another scenario, a lawyer, bank representative, government official, or estate executor has gained access to or control over these funds and is seeking out the next of kin. In some cases, you have been selected because your name is similar to that of the person who has died; in other cases, the holder of these funds has simply found your name for some other reason, and now he wants to release these funds before a certain time limit, when the funds will revert back to the bank or other government entity. Sometimes this offer to make you the next of kin is presented as a business proposition, which might seem to be illegal or unethical, but the person contacted shouldn't be concerned about this because the banking system works this way, or because he or she will be protected by the official sending the letter from being revealed as not really next of kin to the person who has died. He or she just has to say he or she is on certain documents, and then the bank will release the funds to him, while the official arranging this will be taking a percentage of these funds—typically 30 to 50 percent—for making these arrangements.

And in some cases, you are simply getting a cash award as a matter of luck from an official organization.

Typically, the alleged funds in question are substantial—a million dollars up to about $10 to $20 million—but regardless of the arrangements offered and the amounts of the inheritance, there is no money.

In fact, the common ploy if you respond, as in any of these beneficiary scams, is to get you to send your own money to pay to get these funds, as well as to provide personal and bank information. So whether the scammer seeks to hook you by altruism (doing good for humanity) or greed (even if you really aren't the beneficiary, this can be arranged and you will get a big share of the proceeds), the outcome is the same. You lose money—and maybe your identity, too.

For instance, here are some examples of the dying woman scam. Note the use of a Gmail, Yahoo, or Hotmail address, commonly the sign of a scammer using a free, easy-to-set-up account using any name one chooses. I have edited them slightly with punctuation to make them more easily readable, though I have left most of the grammatical errors. Both are from the SpamEmailReport (http://spamemailreport.com/tag/beneficiary-scam).

From: Mrs Margret Sauer lisa4102@hotmail.fr via yahoo.fr
Reply to: margretsauer@yahoo.com

From Mrs Margret Sauer
Beloved,
Compliments of the day to you! My name is Mrs Margret Sauer, I'm 57yrs old.I am a nationality Deutsch. I'm married to Deutsch (a German) Mr. Wolfgang Sauer who worked with ELF OIL COMPANY for thirty years before he died in the plane crash on 25th of July 2000 with other passengers aboard
Immediately after the death of my husband, who has left me everything he worked for and because the doctors told me I will not live longer than some weeks because of my health, I decided to WILL/donate the sum of $2,400,000 (Two million four hundred thousand dollars) to you for the good work of humanity, and also to help the motherless and less privilege and also for the assistance of the widows.
I wish you all the best and may the good Lord bless you abundantly, and please use the funds well and always extend the good work to others. I will appreciate your utmost confidentiality in this matter until the task is accomplished as I don't want anything that will jeopardize my last wish. Pls: kindly get back to me so that we can discuss more.

Thank You and Bless You richly!
Yours Sincerely
Mrs Margret Sauer

Similarly, Mrs. Ann Johnson wants to donate the $10.5 million left by her husband after his death, though she is going to have a cancer operation and is still hoping she might survive. But no matter, she has decided to donate the money to you anyway to do the good work of the Lord and help with the less privileged and motherless. In this case, her reason for picking a stranger is that she doesn't want her ungodly relatives to benefit from this money should she die, and she has sent previous letters with no response, so she is trying again. Her letter echoes much of what was in the letter from Mrs. Margaret Sauer, as if they were adapted from a template for scammers to use in doing email blasts to potential victims. Here's her letter:

From: Mrs.Ann Johnson <mrsann_johson@outlook.com>
Reply to: mrsannjohnson2@gmail.com

Hello Friend,

I have sent you several letter since the past 2 weeks without reply from you hope you get this. My name is Mrs.Ann Johnson.I am a dying woman who had decided to donate what I have to you. I am 59 years old and was diagnosed for cancer about 2 years ago,immediately after the death of my husband, who had left me with every thing he worked for.I have been touched by God to donate from what I have inherited from my late husband to you for the good work of God,rather than allow my relatives to use my husband's hard earned funds ungodly.

I will be going in for an operation,and i pray that i survive the operation. I have decided to WILL/donate the sum of $10,500,000(Ten million five hundred thousand dollars) to you for the good work of the lord,and to help the motherless,less privileged and also for the assistance of the widows.Upon receipt of your email and your full contact details,i will instruct my bank to send the funds to you via western union to avoid any cost from your end.

Thank you and God bless you.

In other cases, the "dying" woman is motivated as a new Christian convert or as a believer in doing the Lord's work to make a donation to someone who will do God's work, and she wants to change her will accordingly with the help of her attorney, sometimes because she doesn't want the money to fall into the hands of her greedy relatives. Moreover, the victim is supposed to keep the whole matter secret, presumably to make sure that her will is carried out (and no doubt to keep the victim from contacting law enforcement about the scam). The references to Christ or citations from the Bible are designed to make the victim think this is a truly religious person, when the use of religion is used to further the scam. Here are two examples of this approach from the Ripoff Report (www.ripoffreport.com), both contributed by Helene from Elgin, Illinois (January 26, 2009).

> From: "Mrs Augusta A Madu"
> To: undisclosed-recipients
> Dear Beloved Friend,
> Greetings in the name of Lord Jesus Christ, I am Mrs. Augusta Madu, a new Christian convert suffering from long time cancer of the breast and have only six months, presently I am in a Hospital in London taken my treatment. I decided to divide $10 million wealth to churches in Africa, America, Asia and Europe and for humanity in general.
> So please confirm these items as below if you are interested to assist:
>
> 1, your full name
> 2, your mailing address
> 3, your telephone and fax numbers.
>
> On receipt of the confirmed items, I will forward it to my Attorney so that some necessary changes will be made on the documents to enable you have claim to the Consignment/Donation, but note that until this Donation of $10 million is delivered to you, I will strongly insist that this transaction most be keep a top secret, as I wait your gentle and kind response to this mail

God bless you and your family.
Mrs. Augusta Madu

From: "Prapaporn Suprasert"
To: undisclosed-recipients

My name is Mrs.Prapaporn Suprasert Janeth; I got your information while browsing through internet in search of a reliable person who could be of help. I am 61 years old and was diagnosed for cancer about 2 years ago, after the death of my husband who had left me with everything he worked for. I have been touched by the Lord to donate from what I have inherited from my late husband to charity for the good work of humanity, rather than allow my greedy relatives to use my husband's hard earned funds inappropriately.

I will be going in for an operation tomorrow morning and I have decided to will/donate the sum of $2,500,000 (Two million five hundred thousand dollars) to you/Organization for the good work of the God also for the assistance of the widows according to (JAMES 1:27). At the moment I cannot take any telephone calls due to the fact that my relatives are around me and my health status. I have adjusted my WILL and my Executor is aware I have changed my will; you and him will arrange the transfer of the funds from the bank wherethis funds is deposited to your humble self. I wish you all the best and may the good Lord bless you abundantly, and please use the funds well and always extend the good work to others.

Contact my Executor: Mr Cheung Klint With this specified Email: cheung502@live.com.

Do enclose along with your full names contact telephone/fax number and your full address and tell him that I have willed ($ 2,500,000.00) to you and I have also notified him that I am WILL-IN that amount to you for a specific and good work. Thanks and God bless. NB: I will appreciate your utmost confidentiality in this matter until the task is accomplished as I do not want anything that will jeopardize my will. And also I will be contact with you by email as I don't want my relation or anybody to know because they are always around me.

Thank You,
Mrs.Prapaporn Suprasert Janeth.

In the case of the representative of the available funds to a beneficiary, one claim is that the names are similar, so that is why this person is contacting you. Alternatively, the representative is looking for a "reputable" person to act as the next of kin, and the rep's law firm will portray you as the next of kin in return for a percentage of the proceeds—anywhere from 30 to 50 percent. Supposedly the plan might be perceived as illegal, which is why there is a need for secrecy, but if you go along with the scheme, you stand to get millions in the inheritance. In other words, they are appealing to your sense of larceny, though if you succumb and are willing to push the boundaries for what's legal in these claimed next-of-kin cases, you are the one who will become the victim, since to get this bounty you have to supply assorted personal information, as well as some payment up front for the tax, transfer, and other costs involved with creating these fake kinship papers and legal fees. In effect, the scammers are appealing to someone who is willing to be dishonest to get the money, and then, in a kind of turnaround, they are the ones who get scammed.

Here are some examples of these next-of-kin letters.

This next one is presumably from the attorney of a man who died suddenly, leaving a large amount of money in a tax-free island used by rich people to hide funds. So now, since the decedent has no known relative, the bank is looking for a relative to claim the funds, or the government will claim them. Thus, the attorneys are looking for a "reputable" person to act as the next of kin, and they will claim that person is directly related to and from the same country as the deceased to claim these funds. Sure, it's all a lie, and no really reputable person would go along with it, but if you have a bit of larceny in your soul and believe that the government would otherwise get the funds, the scammers might just suck you in to going along with the scam. Here's a copy of the letter, reported by Joe of Houston, Texas, to the Ripoff Report in January 22, 2009.

Hello,

I will like to seek your help in a business proposal, which although is sensitive by nature and not what I should discuss with someone I don't know and have not met using a medium such as this but I do not have a choice.

I am Mr. David Walker, personal attorney to late Dr. Edward, who died of a cardiac arrest a few years ago leaving behind a large sum of money with a commercial bank in the Island of Seychelles which is a tax free zone, a place where plenty of rich people tend to hide away funds not ready to be used or invested. I will not mention the amount of money which runs into several millions in United States Dollars and name of bank presently until we have agreed to deal. I trust you will understand the need for such precautions.

So far, valuable efforts has been made to get to his people but to no avail, as he had no known relatives more because he left his next of kin column in his account opening forms blank and he has no known relative. Due to this development the bank has come forward to ask us as his personal attorneys to bring forward a close relative to claim the funds otherwise as the Seychelles national laws would have it, any dormant account for five years will be declared unclaimed and then paid into the government purse.

To avert this negative development my colleagues and I have decided to look for a reputable person to act as the next of kin to late Dr. Edward so that the funds could be processed and released into his account, which is where you come in. my law firm will also act as your personal attorneys since we will be portraying you as being directly related to our late client being from the same country.

All legal documents to aid your claim for this fund and to prove your relationship with the deceased will be provided by us. Your help will be appreciated with 30% of the total sum which I would disclose in my next email Please accept my apologies, keep my confidence and disregard this letter if you do not appreciate this proposition I have offered you.
I wait anxiously for your response.
Yours Faithfully,
David Walker

Here's another one where a banker, presenting a business proposal, is seeking someone to pose as the next of kin. Presumably the banker has not been able to locate real relatives of this American who died in a plane crash on Alaska Airlines, so now there is an abandoned sum of $10.5 million. The banker is proposing to split this sum sixty-forty and is making this proposition because the prospective partner is an American—presumably any American will do—and there is a need to act quickly, because he has only five days to complete this transaction. As Shanette of Surry, Virginia, reports on the Ripoff Report (October 16, 2006), here's a copy of this letter, which isn't even addressed to a particular person, comes from a free email account (netscape.net), and is sprinkled with a number of grammatical and spelling mistakes, which should be a tip-off that this is a scam. Supposedly the prospect's name came from a reliable—but unnamed— source in England.

ATTENTION,

    With due respect, please pardon me for contacting you. This is a genuine matter of utmost importance and immense mutual benefit which must be kept highly confidential. It is with genuine interest and trust that I have contacted you. I am Dr.David Bersson Lawrence, From Harlsden, North West London, here in England. I am in search for a credible person or company overseas for joint business venture.

I work for Natwest Bank London. I am writing following an opportunity in my office that will be of an imense benefit to both of us. In my department we discovered an abandoned sum of $10.5million USA Dollars (Ten million five hundred thousand Usa Dollars) in an account that belongs to one of our foreign customers Late Mr. Morris Thompson an American who unfortunately lost his life in the plane crash of Alaska Airlines Flight 261 which crashed on January 31 2000, including his wife and only daughter. The choice of contacting you is aroused from the geograpgical nature of where you live, particularly due to the sensivity of the transaction and the confidentiality herein.

Now our bank has been waiting for any of the relatives to come-up for the claim but nobody has done that. I personally has been unsuccessful in locating the relatives for six (6) years now, I seek your consent to present you as the next of kin / Will Beneficiary to the deceased so that the proceeds of this account valued at 10.5Million Dollars can be paid to you. This will be disbursed or shared in these percentages, 60% to me and 40% to you.

I have secured all necessary legal documents that can be used to back up this claim we are making. All i need is to fill in your names to the ducuments and legalise it in the court here to prove you as the legitimate beneficiary then you can make contacts with the secuirty company where the fund is presently deposited as a diplomatic Consignment.

while we have made arrangements with Diplomatic Envoy in service to move the money through diplomatic process to your country with all the necessary papers to enhace depositing the money into a bank in your country.

All I require now is your honest Co-operation, Confidentiality and Trust to enable us see this transaction through. I guarantee you that this will be executed under a legitimate arrangement that will protect you from any breach of the law. Please, provide me the following: as we have 5 days to run it through. this is very very URGENT PLEASE.

Contact me via my alternative and private eamil:berssondr@netscape.net

1. Full Name
2. Your Telephone Number
3. Your Contact Address.

Your urgent response will be highly anticipated and appreciated.

Best regards,
Dr.David B.Lawrence
Please Endeavour to get back to me via this email: berssondr@netscape.net

Still others go into extensive detail to try to explain why they are contacting you, have this high position with access to a large amount of money, want to make it available to you, and it is okay to do what may seem like an unethical practice because that is how the banking world operates. For example, here's a letter from the Spam Email Report, supposedly from Soo Won on March 13, 2013, though I received much the same letter, with almost exactly some of the same paragraphs, on May 11, 2015, making it look as if the scammers are adapting letters from a basic template. Some of these letters are extremely long, about eight to ten pages, as if the extensive detail will help to show this is a sincere letter, though I have only included some excerpts.

From: Soo Won <soo_won@yahoo.com>
Reply to: soo_wonn@yahoo.com.co

Dear Friend,

. . . I am a, staff of Private Banking Services at the Bank of China (BOC). I am contacting you concerning our customer and, an investment placed under our banks management 7 years ago. I would respectfully request that you keep the contents of this mail confidential and respect the integrity of the information you come by as a result of this mail. I contacted you independently of our investigation and no one is informed of this communication. I would like to intimate you with certain facts that I believe would be of interest to you.

In February 2006, the subject matter; ref: bb/boc/bank/0012 came to our bank to engage in business discussions with our Private Banking Services Department. He informed us that he had a financial portfolio of 8.370 million United States Dollars, which he wished to have us turn over (invest) on his behalf. I was the officer assigned to his case; I made numerous suggestions in line with my duties as the de-facto chief operations officer of the Private Banking Services Department, especially given the volume of funds he wished to put into our bank. We met on numerous occasions prior to any investments being placed. I encouraged him to consider various growth funds with prime ratings. . . .

In mid 2006, he asked that the money be liquidated because he needed to make an urgent investment requiring cash payments in Europe. He directed that I liquidate the funds and had it deposited with a firm. . . . I undertook all the processes and made sure I followed his precise instructions to the letter and had the funds deposited in a security consultancy firm, the firm is a specialist private firm that accepts deposits from high net worth individuals and blue chip corporations that handle valuable products or undertake transactions that need immediate access to cash . . . In January last year, we got a call from the security firm informing us that the inactivity of that particular portfolio. . . .

A person who suited his description was declared dead of a heart attack in Alabama U.S.A. We were soon enough able to identify the body and cause of death was confirmed. The bank immediately launched an investigation into possible surviving next of kin to alert about the situation and also to come forward to claim his estate. . . .

In line with our internal processes for account holders who have passed away, we instituted our own investigations in good faith to determine who should have right to claim the estate. This investigation has for the past months been unfruitful. . . . My official capacity dictates that I am the only party to supervise the investigation and the only party to receive the results of the investigation. . . . According to practice, the firm will by the end of this financial year broadcast a request for statements of claim to BOC, failing to receive viable claims they will most probably revert the deposit back to BOC. This will result in the money entering the BOC accounting system and the portfolio will be out of my hands and out of the Private Banking Services Department. This will not happen if I have my way.

What I wish to relate to you will smack of unethical practice but I want you to understand something. It is only an outsider to the banking world who finds the internal politics of the banking world aberrational. The world of private banking especially is fraught with huge rewards for those who occupy certain offices and oversee certain portfolios. . . . You should have begun by now to put together the general direction of what I propose. There is US$ 8,370,000.00 deposited, I alone have the deposit details and they will release the deposit to no one unless I instruct them to do so. . . .

My proposal; I am prepared to place you in a position to give instruction for the release of the deposit to you as the closest surviving relation. Upon receipt of the deposit, I am prepared to share the money with you in half. That is: I will simply nominate you as the next of kin and have them release the deposit to you. We share the proceeds 50/50. . . . I assure you that I could have the deposit released to you within a few days. I will simply inform the bank of the final closing of the file relating to the customer I will then officially communicate with firm and instruct them to release the deposit to you. . . .

I am aware of the consequences of this proposal. I ask that if you find no interest in this project that you should discard this mail. I ask that you do not be vindictive and destructive. If my offer is of no appeal to you, delete this message and forget I ever contacted you. Do not destroy my career because you do not approve of my proposal. You may not know this but people like myself who have made tidy sums out of comparable situations run the whole private banking sector. I am not a criminal and what I do not find against good conscience, this may be hard for you to understand, but the dynamics of my industry dictates that I make this move. Such opportunities only come ones' way once in a lifetime. I cannot let this chance pass me by, for once I find myself in total control of my destiny. These chances won't pass me by. I ask that you do not destroy my chance, if you will not work with me let me know and let me move on with my life but do not destroy me.

I am a family man and this is an opportunity to provide them with new opportunities. There is a reward for this project and it is a task well worth undertaking. I have evaluated the risks and the only risk I have here is from you refusing to work with me and alerting my bank. I am the only one who knows of this situation, good fortune has blessed you with a name that has planted you into the center of relevance in my life. Let's share the blessing.

If you find yourself able to work with me, contact me immediately so we can initiate this process towards a conclusion. I wish to inform you that should you contact me via official channels; I will deny knowing you and about this project. I repeat, I do not want you contacting me through my official phone lines nor do I want you contacting me through my official email account. Contact me only through this email address. I do not want any direct link between you and me. My official lines are not secure lines as they are periodically monitored to assess our level of customer care in line with our Total Quality Management Policy. Please observe this instruction religiously. Please, again, note I am a family man; I have a wife and a Daughter. I send you this mail not without a measure of fear as to what the consequences, but I know within me that nothing ventured is nothing gained and that success and riches never come easy or on a platter of gold. . . .

I await your response.
Mr. Soo Won,

In other cases, the request may come from a person outside of the country who is unable to claim the inheritance and needs some help from someone in that city, such as this one reported by Daniel from San Jose, Alabama, to the Ripoff Report (January 15, 2015):

Thanks for your mail, i want to really ask you for a favor but then i do want to be sure if i could count on you and trust you because its just something i have thought for a while before deciding to let you in on this, after our lil conversation together , i recently found out i had an inheritance my mom have deposited in your city and i would really love to claim it, tho i was told during my investigation the trying to claim it must require going through someone that has lived in your city for 4 months or is a residence of your city. Costa Rica

However, i do not know anyone rather than you i started talking to, and since you live in the same place i decided to let you know. I am prepared to give you 20% of the total sum, but please i do not want to be cheated. The amount i am talking about here is $13,000,000.00, $13million US Dollars . . .

I am looking to set up something, say like restaurant business, or maybe something more like real estate,just to take care of me and my younger ones, but then like i said if i can trust you and you can help i would do my part

I hope you would also advice me on what to invest both in your city that might yield be great profit. . . . Well i am here just looking out the window, cant sleep, so bothered, because i do have limited time to get this money . . .

Hoping to hear from you soon.

Ash

In the event you don't respond to one email, they will often try again to make sure you realize you really are a beneficiary of this inheritance. Here is an email reported to the Ripoff Report by cry caddy of Reno, Nevada (June 23, 2010).

On behalf of the Trustees and Executor of the estate of Late Engr. Luis Eduardo,I once again try to notify you as my earlier letter returned unde-livered. I hereby attempt to reach you again by this same email address on the WILL.

I wish to notify you that Late Engr. Luis Eduardo made you a ben-eficiary to his WILL.He left the sum of Twenty two million five hundred thousand United States Dollars ($22,500.000.00USD)to you in the codi-cil and last testament to his WILL.

This may sound strange and unbelievable to you, but it is real and true. Being a widely travelled man, he must have been in contact with you in the past or simply you were recommended to him by one of his numerous friends abroad who wished you good.Late Engr. Luis Eduardo died on the 12th day of March,2008,at the age of 80 years, and his WILL is now ready for execution.

According to him this money is to support your humanitarian activities and to help the poor and the needy in our society. Please if I reach you this time as I am hopeful, endeavor to get back to me as soon as possible to enable me conclude my job. I hope to hear from you in no distant time through the email address or phone number below.

Email:
Phone: +34 688 292 754
Yours in Service,
Emiliana Abella(Mrs)
Secretary To-Barr. Fernando G. Luna

In short, these inheritance beneficiary scams may take various forms, but basically they provide an elaborate story about why the person has access to a large inheritance—either as a person who is dying, a relative of that person, or an official in a bank or other high position—and then why they have chosen you to be the favored recipient. It may be because you are thought to do good works, live in the same country or city, or may be open to a business proposition whereby you claim to be the next of kin, even though you really aren't. But then there is a justification for doing what may seem to be an illegal or unethical act, in that the money will just go back to the bank or government, and there is no risk to you. You do have to keep the deal secret, because it is not officially authorized.

In some cases, they may pretend to be from a commercial company, insurance agency, or government agency, and they may typically provide accurate information about that company. The trick is that they are trying to make you believe they really do represent or work for that company.[2]

Should you respond to this initial come-on, you will be asked to send an advance fee to pay for legal fee, bribes, or other expenses in what is sometimes called an "advance fee" scam. Once you do, you may either never hear from them again, or they may ask for even more money. In some scenarios, they may then seek to get personal information, including your ID and bank account information, which they can use to access your account and for other identity fraud schemes.[3]

While it may seem unlikely, many people do fall for these schemes, such as one woman who reportedly put $50,000 on her credit cards after being contacted by a "barrister" for Jurgen "Hans" Kruger who died December 13, 2004, before the scammers asked her for another $10,000, and the FBI stepped in while she was trying to gain access to her $30 million inheritance, supposedly left to her by Mr. Kruger because he "believed she was a good person to give money to because she would help others in need."[4] While the part about the man's death was probably true, the rest about the person being his barrister certainly wasn't. That's one of the techniques the scammers use—taking some of what is true and using it to advance their own believability in order to convince victims to send them money and give out personal information.

Help Me Transfer Funds from My Country

The "help me transfer funds from my country" scams are much like the beneficiary scams, except the story is different. Instead of being a direct beneficiary, you benefit by helping someone in another country who has access to a large sum of money for some reason get the funds to a safe place in your country. You will receive a hefty percentage—typically a 10 to 25 percent commission—for your efforts. But first, as in the beneficiary scam, you have to put up some money to cover costs such as for legal documents or to show good faith.

In some cases, you could be asked to transfer actual money, but then you will commonly be involved in laundering money, which is done illegally by putting the money in a series of bank accounts to hide its original—and usually illegal—source, according to a ScamWatch Report. In that case, the money is likely to come from organized crime or the proceeds of other scams, such as Internet banking. Eventually, the authorities might trace the illicit funds to your account.

In another scenario, the scammers may actually allow you to keep a small percentage of the total transferred. In some cases, though, the scammer will ask you why you did not transfer some of the money you did not receive and then may "pressure you to make up for the 'missing payment' out of your own pocket."[5]

But more generally, the scammer is simply out to get you to pay some upfront money or get your bank account and ID information to use for other purposes.

Some Authority Requires You to Pay Money

In this scam, commonly done by phone, you are contacted by someone posing as a government official or law enforcement officer who claims you owe money for something, and you need to pay right away in order to avoid being arrested or going to jail. The idea of the scam is the person will be so afraid of the consequences that he or she will give requested personal information—for example, to verify the information on the ticket, warrant, or other legal document—or will quickly provide credit card information to pay the fine. The IRS tax scam is one of the most popular versions of this scam, and it is especially prevalent around tax time in March and April, when people are most worried about getting their tax returns to the IRS.

One of the reasons these scams work so well is the scam's "bold simplicity" in which the victim is suddenly facing the unexpected threat of arrest. So they are "caught off guard and may be quick to part with some information to defuse the situation." The scammer gets the victim scared and then offers a quick fix—such as a fine payable by credit card to resolve the problem.[6] Or they ask for identifying situations that might show it isn't you who is in trouble.

In the jury duty scam, according to an FBI warning, the caller claims to be an officer of the court, and since you failed to report to jury duty, a warrant has been issue for your arrest. Generally, you will respond that "I never received a notice," so then the caller will ask you for some information for "verification purposes" to make sure you are the right person. And typically this will be your birth date, social security number, and perhaps even a credit card number so you can quickly pay the fine and clear up the whole matter. This is just another way of stealing your identity and running up bogus charges on your account—or they might sell your credit card information to someone else to use.

One tip-off that this is a scam is that court workers will never contact you to tell you that you missed jury duty and will hardly ever try to call you by phone.[7] Rather, almost all jury notices come by regular mail. Moreover, court workers will never call to ask for private information.

The traffic ticket scam takes the form of an online notice or phone call advising you that you have a traffic ticket from a particular jurisdiction and have to pay a fine, sometimes because you already missed a court date. In some cases it can be very clear this is a scam, such as if the traffic ticket was issued in a city or state where you have never been. But in other cases the scammer may target victims in a certain area. On a phone call, the scammer may claim to be a law enforcement official[8] and will generally ask you to pay the fine, usually by providing your credit card information. Then the scammer might use your card to obtain even more money.[9] However, if you get the notice about the ticket by email, commonly you are asked to click a link or download an attachment, which could be a way to put a Trojan horse on your computer to attack your Windows system or put more malicious files on your computer.[10]

Finally, there is the IRS scam, which has been described as "the largest and most pervasive impersonation scam in the history of the IRS," according to an *NBC News* article published on—when else—Tax Day, April 15.[11] The way it works is that scammers call Americans all over the United States and pose as IRS agents who are claiming they owe back taxes. If they don't pay immediately, they face arrest. In some cases, they threaten deportation.

The number of these calls is in the millions, resulting in thousands of victims. According to the FTC, nearly 55,000 people called to complain in 2014, twenty-five times the 2,185 complaints received in 2013. This was the single largest complaint the FTC received in 2014. A number of these complainants and others, totaling over 400,000 people, have filed complaints with the US Treasury Department since 2013, and more than 3,000 people were cheated out of over $15 million. Many victims are seniors because they are often at home, answer the phone, and have the money to pay their supposed debt.

A key reason the scam works so well is the use of fear tactics: a law enforcement official calls and threatens to arrest you if you don't pay immediately. Many people are so scared that they will pay, even if they don't feel they owe the money, because of the fear that something very bad will happen if they don't.

For example, one of the calls received by Doug Shadel, a fraud prevention expert working with AARP's fraud network, went like this:[12]

Hi, this is Officer John White. We are calling you from criminal investigation department of IRS. The reason you are getting a phone call from the department is to inform you that IRS has got the arrest warrant out for you and your physical address is under federal investigation. So call me back on my department number to get the detailed information about your case. My call back number is . . . I repeat, it is . . . very important to hear from you today.

When Shadel called the number to see what "Officer White" would say, he said that Shadel "owed $2,700 in back taxes, that his call was being monitored and recorded by Homeland Security, and that if he didn't agree to pay immediately, a warrant for his arrest would be signed."[13]

So if Shadel didn't already know it was a scam, he would likely have been terrified and made arrangements to pay if he could.

But even if it is clear this is a scam, it is difficult for the IRS or anyone in law enforcement to crack down because many of the scammers are outside the United States. Also, they typically call using blocked calls, private numbers, untraceable numbers, or spoofed caller ID.[14] Consumer education is generally the best way to stop this scam—and if anyone tries to call you claiming to be from the IRS, unless you have previously gotten an official notice in the mail, it's likely to be a scam. Not thinking you owe anything is usually a good sign that you are speaking to a scammer, since the IRS will first notify anyone of any debts in arrears by letter. No real IRS agent will call you to demand you pay your taxes owed unless you first get a prior official notice. Moreover no one will ask for your credit or debit card number over the phone. And no one will threaten to involve the local police or other law enforcement officials to arrest you because you haven't paid.[15] Another sign of a scam is the threat that you will lose your driver's license or that you will be deported. Also, don't think the caller really is from the IRS just because they give a badge number, which could be phony; because they know your Social Security number or the last four numbers, since they could have found or stolen this; or because the "IRS" shows up on your call ID, because they can fake it, according to the Federal Trade Commission.[16] Should you get such a call, it's best to simply hang up, and whatever you do, don't send them any money or give them any credit or debit card money, because once they have your money, it's gone.

Someone You Know Needs Help

Still another scam to get you to send money—and sometimes give out your personal identity and credit card information—is the call to help out someone you know. It can be particularly persuasive when the call comes from a family member, relative, or close friend via email, phone, or even a private message on Facebook. This scam is sometimes called the "grandparent" scam, because one approach, usually by phone, is to call the grandparent to help a grandchild who desperately needs help.

Common explanations for needing the money are that the person has lost their passport, documents, and money in a foreign country; the person got robbed while traveling and now needs the money to continue traveling and get back to the United States; and, in a most pernicious approach, the individual has been kidnapped while abroad, and now either the "victim" or the scammer is asking you to come up with the funds needed. In all of these cases, nothing has happened to the person who is traveling or supposedly kidnapped; instead the scammers are reaching out to people who might pay money to help if they believe the story told to them is true. The goal is to get you to quickly wire or send the money by Western Union or MoneyGram to them before you discover this really isn't true. If you check, you will discover the person who supposedly is in trouble knows nothing about the request for money.

In one typical scenario, you will get an email from a friend or relative who is overseas and has been robbed of all their money and credit cards. They haven't been able to get help quickly enough from their embassy or they have been stranded somewhere and haven't been able to get to a major city for help. So they are asking you for a short-term loan and will pay you back as soon as they get back. You just need to wire them the money.

Often the request will seem believable, because the scammers have hacked the email account of a person you know and have actually sent the message to everyone in that person's email account. Or they may have cloned the account and changed the address just slightly, such as changing an *n* to an *m* in the email: johnjohnson@yahoo.com to johnjohnsom@

yahoo.com, hoping you won't notice the difference. When you hit reply, the message will go to the scammer's fake account.[17]

In another scenario, you may get a private message in your Facebook inbox from a former or current associate or friend on your friends list who is on vacation. They have lost their purse or wallet or it has been stolen. They still have their phone, so they can send out messages through Facebook, and they just want to get a small loan and will pay you back on their return. In this case, the scammers may have actually created a fake version of the account of your associate or friend, so it looks like the real thing: all the better to fool you.

In still another variation, often done by phone, the target is usually an elderly person, which is where the "grandparent" scam name comes from. There is a desperate plea to help out a family member. Often the call comes from another country where the relative of the victim is in desperate straits and needs some money to help him out.

For example, in one scenario described on WAScam.net, a man receives a call from a doctor treating the nephew of his wife, and now the nephew needs $16,000 for a medical treatment or he could die. The victim might even have a chance to talk briefly to the nephew, who sounds different from usual, which is because he is very ill. Should the victim have questions to ask via email or on the phone, the scammers are prepped to answer, since they have used social media to get information about the family. The caller can seem very real, while the made-up medical emergency scenario requires the victim to act quickly to send off the money before he or she can start thinking whether the information is really correct.[18] In fact, the victim might feel pressure to respond without seeming overly skeptical because, as a good family member, he or she feels a need to respond quickly to help a relative out.

Sometimes these scammers can hit real pay dirt and con individual victims out of thousands of dollars, sent to help a supposed relative in peril.

For example, one grandmother from the Chicago area was bilked out of $35,000 before the scam was discovered, as reported in a Target 5 Investigation.[19] The scam began when the scammers targeted Alice Solinski, a grandmother to eleven grandchildren and thirteen great-grandchildren.

It started when Solinski got a phone call from a young girl who sounded upset. She said, "Grandma, can you help me?" and when Solinski asked, "Who are you?" the caller finally said, "I'm your oldest granddaughter," to which Solinski said, "Kim," to which the scammer quickly agreed. Now she had a name she could use to help demonstrate the scam was really real. As scam expert Jason Echols—a consumer protection specialist with Age Options of Oak Park, an agency that serves seniors—points out, a common way to initiate the scam is to start with "Grandma?" or "Grandpa?" and let the victim fill in the blanks.

In Solinski's case, once she provided the name and asked, "What do you need?" the scammers continued to the next phase of the scam—sharing their fake story to show how much her long-lost relative needed the money and how she could best obtain the money to send it.

So then the "granddaughter" tearfully explained what had happened. As she told Solinski: "I'm in California . . . I'm at a girlfriend's wedding. We've had an accident." When Solinski wanted to know what happened and why she sounded so funny, the granddaughter gave an explanation for that too. "I hit my [face] and I broke my [nose] . . . I need some money to get out of jail."

Then she described she couldn't pay for lawyers, "so they gave me a court-appointed lawyer," though she couldn't remember her name, and now claimed, "We need $15,000 for bond money, and we need you to send it this address and this account."[20]

Though most law enforcement agencies consider the request to wire money a big red flag of a scam, Solinski went to the bank twice, once to procure the needed $15,000 bail money, and then another $20,000 to pay the supposed private lawyer, since her "granddaughter" wanted a better lawyer than the public defender.

Even then, she still might have escaped, since a bank manager tried to warn her against sending a wire with this money. But Solinski was determined, "feeling she needed to help her granddaughter." In effect, the scammers were using emotional blackmail to get her to feel she had to act quickly save her granddaughter, who allegedly had no one else to turn to.

Ultimately she lost $35,000 simply because she believed the scammer's claims and felt she had to act quickly, as the scammers wanted, to get the money to them. Only later did she discover it was all a lie, because her real granddaughter, Kim Finely, was very much alive and well. She felt horrible that her grandmother was pulled into the scheme by thinking Kim was hurt or in trouble.[21]

Unfortunately, Solinski didn't know enough to question the story in the first place. This can include trying to contact the person who is supposed to be in trouble to see if the story is really true or asking some personal questions to make sure the person calling really is one's loved one. The request to wire money is another warning sign, as is the call to act urgently. Another way to check on a scam is by calling the local police.

By contrast, one couple was able to avoid a scam where they could have lost several thousand dollars. As described in a CBN News story, Leon and Nina Merrick, who later reported their near-scam experience to the Montgomery County Consumer Protection Agency in Maryland, got a phone call purportedly from their grandson while they were sitting at their kitchen table. First the caller said, "Hi, Grandma, how are you doing?" but when Nina asked, "Who is this?" the supposed grandson's answer suggested that this could be a scam, since he responded, "It's your grandson, Joshua." Nina replied to him, "Joshua never calls me Grandma. He calls me Safta," which means grandma in Hebrew.[22]

Then came the story meant to arouse the Merricks' sympathy and get them to help out. In this case, the caller claimed to be out of the country in Greece to attend a friend's wedding. But now he was in jail due to a wrecking a rental car in a car accident and needed $3,500 to pay for the damages in order to leave the country. The Merricks were to keep the call secret to avoid angering his parents about what happened. As he stated on the phone:

> "I am in big trouble. Promise you are not going to tell my parents. I am in big trouble. They would not let me go and get out of the country until I pay the damages."

In response to Nina's question about the size of the damages, the caller replied, "$3,500."

The caller's pretense quickly fell apart when Nina handed the phone to Leon and he pushed the caller to give him a number so he could call back, and when he wondered why the caller's voice did not sound like his grandson's. The caller had a ready answer for the question about his voice: he claimed that his voice sounded different because he had split his lip in the car accident. But when Leon pressed for a phone number, the grandson tried to slip away by explaining, "I can't give you the number. I am going to pay you back every penny, don't worry, don't worry. If you are not going to give me the money they are not going to let me leave the country."

When Leon continued to insist he have the phone number and finally told the caller, "That's it. No money," the phone call was disconnected, presumably because the caller hung up. Leon quickly hung up the phone and called his grandson, who was "safe at home in Israel."[23]

So they escaped becoming victims by following the key tips from the FBI to avoid being scammed by the grandparent scam, which include the following:

- Resist the pressure to act quickly.
- Try to contact your grandchild or another family member to determine whether the call is legitimate.
- Never wire money based on a request made over the phone or in an email, especially overseas. Wiring money is like giving cash—once you send it, you can't get it back.[24]

A seventy-nine-year-old woman from Madison, Wisconsin, wasn't so lucky when a man called claiming to be her twenty-seven-year-old grandson, according to a Madison.com story. The man said he had been a passenger in a car in which drugs were found and now he was in a jail cell in Des Moines, Iowa. He said he was embarrassed about being arrested and did not want her to tell anyone he was calling for bail money. Eventually his story convinced her. So she went to the grocery store and used her credit card to put $3,000 on a Reloadit card, after which another caller claiming to be "Officer Walton" from the 16th Precinct called her to provide the identification numbers on the Reloadit card. But after she had sent the $3,000, he told her additional bail money was needed because there had been a mistake. So now, suspicious, she called her grandson's home, where his wife answered and assured her he was at work, not in jail. Later it turned out the scammer had called her from a number in Quebec, Canada—not Des Moines, Iowa. It was too late to get back her $3,000, but at least she didn't lose any more.[25]

While these examples have featured the classic grandparent victim, the "help me" scam targets multiple people who are asked to help someone they know who is in some kind of trouble, which could be a friend, relative, neighbor, business associate, or just about anyone. And then there is some kind of story that explains why the person is in trouble and is asking for your help, whether by email, through personal message on Facebook or other social media, or by phone. After that, there is an explanation of how much the person needs to get out of trouble and why (such as to get out of jail, pay off men who are threatening him because of a debt, pay a hospital bill, or whatever). And then there is a request to send the money by using a credit card or via Western Union or MoneyGram.

But whatever the story, the key to not being a victim is checking out the story with the real person, asking personal questions of someone who is asking for help to determine if he or she can accurately answer them like the real person, asking for a number to call them back rather than having them only call you, and refusing to use a credit card or send a Western Union or MoneyGram. And then, of course, if you suspect a scam you can always hang up and report your suspicions to the appropriate law enforcement agencies that handle that kind of crime in your area or nationally, such as the FBI or the Internet Crime Complaint Center.

Notes

1   "Run Money Through Your Account for a Foreigner and Get Millions of Dollars—Fiction!" Money/Financial, March 17, 2015. http://www. truthorfiction.com/nigeriascams.

2   "The Email Beneficiary Scam," *Home Income Opportunities*. http://www. home-income-opportunities.com/email-beneficiary-scam.html.

3   Aaron Larson, "False Promises of Inheritance—Spam Email Fraud, *Expert Law*, January 2011. www.expert.aw.com/library/consumer/spam_email_ fraud3.html.

4   "Jurgen Kruger Inheritance," Reported by Robin of Globe, Arizona to the Ripoff Report, February 16, 2009.

5   "Transferring Money for Someone Else," *Scam Watch*. http://www.scam-watch.gov.au/content/index.phtml/tag/TransferringMoneyForSomeoneEls e?pageDefinitionItemId=685565.

6   "The Verdict: Hang Up: Don't Fall for Jury Duty Scam," *FBI,* June 2, 2006. http://www.fbi.gov/news/stories/2006/june/jury_scam060206.

7   "Scam Alert: Jury Duty Identity Theft," *Lawyers.com*. http://consumer-law.lawyers.com/consumer-fraud/scam-alert-jury-duty-identity-theft.html.

8   "Scam Alert: Paying for traffic violations over the phone" Call for Action. http://callforaction.org/scam-alert-paying-for-traffic-violations-over-the-phone.

9   Anthony J. Mallo, "Beware Traffic Ticket Scams," Traffic Ticket Office: A Law Firm, August 8, 2014. http://www.trafficticketoffice.com/traffic-tickets/beware-traffic-ticket-scams.

10 Matt Liebowitz, "Motorists Beware Fake Traffic Ticket Email Scam," *Security on NBC News.Com.* http://www.nbcnews.com/id/44181400/ns/technology_and_science-security/t/motorists-beware-fake-traffic-ticket-email-scam#.VVPIzvlVhBc.

11 Herb Weisbaum, "'Imposter' Tax Scam Worse Than Ever, Congress Holds Hearing," NBC News. http://www.nbcnews.com/business/taxes/tax-impostor-scam-worse-ever-congress-holds-hearing-n341906.

12 Ibid.

13 Ibid.

14 Michael Zakkour, "I.R.S. Tax Phone Scam Claims More Victims Ever as 2015 Tax Day Arrives," *Forbes*, April 14, 2015. http://www.forbes.com/sites/michaelzakkour/2015/04/14/i-r-s-tax-phone-scam-claims-more-victims-than-ever-as-2015-tax-day-arrives.

15 Ibid.

16 Amy Herbert, "Another Tax Scam: IRS Imposters," *Federal Trade Commission Consumer Information*, January 29, 2015. https://www.consumer.ftc.gov/blog/another-tax-scam-irs-imposters.

17 "Help Me Scam—Also Called the 'Grandparent' Scam," WA Scamnet. http://www.scamnet.wa.gov.au/scamnet/Types_Scams-Social_networking_scams-Help_me_scams.htm.

18 Ibid.

19 Lisa Parker and Robin Green, "Scam Bilks Grandmother Out of $35,000," Target5, July 13, 2013. http://www.nbcchicago.com/investigations/target-5-lisa-parker-grandparents-scam-1880000771.html.

20 Ibid.

21 Ibid.

22 Efram Graham, "Help Me, Grandma! Wait, This Is a Scam," CBN News, December 25, 2012. http://www.cbn.com/cbnnews/us/2012/June/Help-Me-Grandma-Wait-This-Is-a-Scam.

23 Ibid.

24 Ibid.

25 Bill Novak, "Madison Woman, 79, Loses $3000 in 'I'm in jail,
    Grandma' Scam," Madison.com. http://host.madison.com/news/local/
    crime_and_courts/madison-woman-loses-in-i-m-in-jail-grandma-scam/
    article_08c83bfd-e7f9-55bf-a255-7197010902c1.html.

CHAPTER 6

THE GREAT MANY SCAMS AND WHAT YOU CAN DO

The previous chapters have highlighted some of the most common and pervasive scams. A comprehensive compendium of all scams would be like an encyclopedia since there are so many different scams. Most are variations on the main approaches already outlined—to get you to cash an overpayment and send the balance in the phony job and roommate schemes, to send money to help someone or gain a benefit for oneself, to provide credit card information to get a product or service, or to reveal personal data and provide access to one's bank account. What differs are the particular stories and strategies adapted to different fields and different audiences.

The scams continue to work because they appeal to powerful emotions, such as fear, love, and greed. You want to help and protect someone. You fear the consequences of something happening unless you act now. You are attracted by the appeal of a breakthrough drug or beauty treatment, and feel there is low risk for a free, short-term trial. You are attracted by the opportunity to get some money, even if it might seem strange to suddenly discover you are the beneficiary of a will from someone you never met or heard of. Even if the person proposing the scheme is suggesting that it might seem unethical or illegal to claim a kinship you don't really have, for a small amount from you up front, you could make millions.

The scams described here are just the tip of the scamberg. There are many more. Just about any product or service, any company or organization, any government agency, will find it is variously involved in scams. Scammers create counterfeit products and use a pretext to claim an affiliation with a company, organization, government agency, or law enforcement to get someone to do something because they believe the claims about the product, service, or affiliation. It is as if once a product, service, company, or institution becomes well known, there is the potential for scammers to swoop in to create a scam to gain money from the unsuspecting by using that product, service, or name in some way. When one scam is shut down, the scammers, unless arrested, convicted, and jailed for a previous scam—though often they escape law enforcement efforts since they are out of the country or have well-concealed tracks—come up with still another scheme.

In effect, just as technology evolves and spawns new technological breakthroughs, so scams evolve, taking advantage of the latest in technology and new products, services, companies, and organizations to develop and implement their scams. For example, just as the Greeks used their Trojan horse to enter the city of Troy to win the war and traders traveled around the US selling phony medical nostrums from their horse-drawn carts in the 1880s, today's con artists use the Internet to hack into and invade personal and corporate computers to sell all kinds of counterfeit products and services or trick victims into revealing personal and bank information. The technology and techniques are more sophisticated, but the scam lives on, in a different form.

The Many Other Scams

Here are just some of the more recent scams that have received widespread press coverage. Undoubtedly you can think of many more, suggesting that the best way to avoid being scammed is to follow some general rules, since it can often be difficult to tell the scam from the real thing.

Bank Scams

These typically come in the form of emails from your bank inviting you to engage in certain actions to gain rewards or keep your account current. You may be asked to participate in an online survey that offers money or prizes, update your account details, activate your bank or credit card, verify unusual transactions, or provide account information to qualify for fee refunds. Sometimes you may get an email that your account will be frozen or suspended due to suspicious activity unless you take certain steps, such as clicking a link or providing certain personal information. Here the scammers want access to your computer or your identity, so the key to avoid being scammed is to not follow any of the links because you can end up with unwanted downloads to your computer. Also, do not give out your personal banking details, since reputable companies and banks will never ask for this information online. And if in doubt, call your bank.

Online Sales Scams

Here sellers are typically advertising nonexistent goods of all types, hoping you will pay. You will never get the goods or they will be shoddy or defective, not the ones advertised. In some cases, a scammer may take over someone else's advertisements so you think they are a legitimate seller, as in the case of scammers pretending to be a landlord and getting money for a rental, using the real landlord's ad as a come-on. Even paying on a secure payment system might be a scam, since you are referred to a copy-cat site. Conversely, sellers have been scammed in selling to strangers who have given them fake checks or money orders or have used stolen credit cards. While there is some risk for buying anything online, this is reduced when you buy from established online merchants who have extensive websites that are difficult to spoof. If you do buy through an online auction or commercial website, check their section on fraud prevention for tips on how to protect yourself. Use a service like PayPal that lists verified merchants or keep a low balance on your credit card, so you only transfer the funds you need to pay for current purchases, and as possible, don't give out your credit or bank account information to a new site. And never wire transfer or send money to people you don't know using a wire transfer or Western Union, because such transfers are almost impossible to track.

Charity Scams

In this scam, you get a phone call or email about someone claiming to represent a charity, such as the fight against breast cancer, or a police group, like the Police Athletic League who claim to help underprivileged kids in a sports program. The scammers may even set up a phony website that looks like the one created by the real charity. Sometimes these scams pop up after a real disaster, and they claim to be offering disaster relief to those injured or to the families of those who have been killed. The best approach here is to deal only with official charities, and ideally initiate the approach yourself. Be cautious when you get emails, text messages, or phone calls, and ask for identifying information that you can check out yourself before you donate. Be especially wary if you are asked to wire transfer a donation, since those are untraceable.

Your-Computer-Is-at-Risk Scams

In this scam, you are commonly contacted by phone or email by someone who is purportedly from one of the major computer or software companies, such as Microsoft, to tell you about a special update to protect your computer. You think it is coming from that company. Then you are supposed to click a link to protect yourself; sometimes you are even supposed to download software. That click or download puts malware on your computer or searches for identity and password information. The ideal approach here is to not click or download anything until you have verified that the contact did, in fact, come from the real company. Also pay attention to news on technology developments, since sometimes, as more and more people are scammed in this way, the company will put out an alert about the scam—and sometimes the scam protection software from vendors like McAfee and Norton will recognize this scam and block future emails. But initially just be cautious.

Sometimes this scam is difficult to identify because often when you buy new software you will get emails about updates you can buy and download. Or after you make a purchase, to verify that you made the purchase and activate the software, you may get an email requesting that you click a link if you ordered the software. If such an email follows soon after a purchase, it is generally valid, and after you click the link, you will get confirmation that your software is not activated. However, if the email seems to come out of the blue, asking you to verify something you got some time ago, it is best to check it out to see if the email you just got really did come from the company. Then the company can verify whether it was sending out such emails or not.

The Home-Repair Rip-Off

This scam with a long history seems quaintly old-fashioned, since it doesn't involve any of the latest technology or emails. Rather, it is based on a one-on-one personal contact that targets homeowners. In this scam, one or two con artists come to your door; commonly they arrive in a pick-up truck or van and may have some leave-behind literature, or often not.

The basic scam is that they are offering to do some home repairs, including painting walls or exteriors or roofing, and in some cases, they—or someone they hire—actually goes around your house breaking things so they can later fix them. Or later, after they get a deposit on the work, they disappear, leaving you and many neighbors with a worthless contract you can't enforce, since the con artists are gone.

The Psychic's Vision

In this scam, a person claiming to be a psychic will offer a series of visions about your coming good fortune, if only you act on it. Usually he or she contacts you by email and has hints about what you might gain, should you want to buy one of the talismans or charms on offer that will bring you wealth, such as you might get if you play the lottery or bet on horses. According to ScamNet, these scam artists commonly obtain your name and email from a mailing list or from your response to an ad, such as to get a free horoscope, which is a ploy some con artists use to get personal information about you. Then they "prey on people's vulnerabilities by promising to change their lives through luck charms or winning lottery numbers."[1] However, these so-called psychics often do not exist. Rather, they are "fictional characters created by mailing companies to fleece you of your number" and they use photos from commercial photo libraries.

For example, I once responded to an ad, and since then I have gotten an email every day or two from two psychics with the same message that I can expect great fortune in the future, that a certain day is my lucky day, that if I am feeling "deceived . . . frustrated . . . scared . . . I want to help you find the answers and peace you are seeking." All I need to do is sign up for their service for $2 a month for the "guidance and help you'll need to overcome anything!" Another psychic advised me, after I hadn't responded to these mailings for over two months, that she was still holding "the solid sterling-silver Cross of a Thousand Miracles," which would be the answer to my prayers.

Tech Support Scams

These scammers, who typically operate from India and Pakistan, offer technical support to fix a damaged computer, although it is rare that any technician from a PC manufacturer or tech support company would call a nonclient computer owner to claim there is an immediate threat to that person's computer and the company needs to gain remote access to fix the problem. Supposedly, the computer has been affected or is about to become affected by malware that could damage its operating system or lead to identity theft, but they can fix it. However, once you give them remote access to troubleshoot and fix the problem, the scammers can actually infect the system with malware or cause other damage, or they might send you to a third-party website that can damage your computer. Basically, the scam is like the old home-repair scam, where the con artists claim you have different kinds of damage or they actually cause it and then fix it. Similarly, these con artists do much the same in accessing your computer so they can cause errors and then charge you for unnecessary repair services. Plus they can gain your identity data, since they usually ask you to pay by credit card. The best response here is to not give anyone remote access to your computer unless you know who this person is, such as if you are working with a local computer guru. Rather, it's best to hire a local computer repair service, and they can check out any warnings you get, too.

Fake and Counterfeit Merchandise Sites[2]

The big problem with these sites is that it can be hard to tell the phonies from the legitimate sites that are selling real and often specialty merchandise. As reported by ScamGuard, many of these sites operate primarily out of China, and these sites "sell name brand items or mimic the websites of big name brand companies," but they aren't selling the real products. Instead, they are selling fake or counterfeit products at much-reduced prices, and sometimes you may actually get the merchandise, which ships from international locations, so you may not be aware of the scam for weeks. But whether the merchandise arrives or not, the goal of these scammers is to get the credit card numbers of victims and then use those numbers to make purchases themselves or even sell that information on the black market.

The strategy to avoid being scammed by these sites is to contact the phone number of the company that really has that brand, as well as check on the website of the major scam sites to see if the website for a company is legitimate.

Pets-for-Sale Scams

This scam is similar to the other fake website scams for counterfeit products, but in this case the site owners claim the site is associated with pet adoption or animal nurseries, and you can choose from a wide variety of pets at far below the prices others charge for them. The victim not only doesn't get the pet, but they are also asked to pay the insurance, shipping, and other service to deliver the pet, and typically has to pay with wire transfers, Western Union, and MoneyGram payments, which goes to a foreign bank. To avoid this scam, simply don't pay for any pet with any cash transfer method, and go to local pet adoption, pet stores, rescue services, or breeders to get your pets.

Collection Agency Scams

It can be bad enough if you actually owe money and get contacted by a collection agency. But in this case, whether you owe money or not, a fake collection agency might contact you, with India and Pakistan being major sources of these scams. These scams are a little like the IRS scams, where fake law enforcement officials threaten you with arrest or jail if you don't pay the amount you supposedly owe, except here the claim is for other kinds of debts. These scammers call victims, claim to represent a collection agency, even the US Attorney General's Office, and commonly ask the victim to start making payments or threaten that they will begin litigation or may embarrass the victim at work. In some cases, they actually have gotten information about the amount of money that is owed, which can be available from various services. For instance, before or after filing for bankruptcy, individuals may get many notices from companies offering to help consolidate their debts or pay them off—so these fake collection agencies can similarly get this information.

Reportedly, this scam can go on for months, with the scammers making repeated calls for payments until the victims pay. And sometimes the scammers will repeat the demand for even more money to pay off debts from the same victim or they will sell or share this information with other scammers who similarly harass the victim.

Unless you really do owe money to a collection agency that is representing a debtor or has purchased a debt, don't respond to any collection calls, and if possible block them. You might also report the callers for these fake collection agencies to law enforcement and the agency that regulates collection agencies in your state.

Grant and Payday Loan Scams

These scammers take advantage of people who are seeking financial help. One approach is to obtain information from websites or ad agencies that invite consumers with bad debts to apply for payday loans. The information is then sold to companies that offer the loans. While many of the companies that purchase this data are legitimate, scammers can also gain access to this information by posing as a legitimate company.

Then the scammers advise individuals seeking a payday loan that they can qualify for low-interest loans by paying a processing or security-related fee, to show that the victims will have the ability to repay the loan when it comes due. Then the scam operates much like other send-money scams in that the scammers ask the victim to pay this fee through a wire transfer or cash sent via a Western Union payment. In addition, some scammers will ask for bank account information so they can directly deposit the payday loan once approved, but later they use that information to take money from those accounts or sell the account information to those who will do this.

Similarly, scammers can contact individuals seeking grants, though they tell them a somewhat different story. For example, they claim they represent the US government and can help victims access grant money if they pay a processing fee, using the same kinds of wire transfer or cash transfer payments that are not traceable. Plus, they can use the individual's banking information just as in the payday loan scam.

Work-from-Home Scams

Still another scam reported on the ScamGuard's top ten list is the scam where one can work from home. One just has to pay some upfront fees to secure the position or the training required. One type of work is inspecting and shipping merchandise, where the scammers are commonly located in Russia, the Ukraine, and Eastern Europe. In this scam, the scammers set up attractive websites, which are supposedly owned by companies involved in shipping. Or the scammers might set up sites that claim to offer work-at-home opportunities because they represent US companies that don't have international shipping services. Then they use ads on job search websites to appeal to victims or they contact victims through their job board profiles, and appear to go through an interview process using email or messenger applications. Everyone interviewed gets offered a job. Then the scammers use stolen credit cards to buy the merchandise they ship to the victims, with instructions on how to open the packages, inspect the merchandise, and reship it to another location.

In some cases, the scammers simply end all contact with their new employees or they further victimize them with phony paychecks with larger amounts than due for the time worked, as in the other phony job scams, like the mystery shopper previously described. Then the victim is supposed to deposit the check and pay out the overpayment via bank transfer to one or more people who weren't previously paid for their work, which may be identified as something like verifying documents or buying office supplies. When the check bounces, it turns out the victim not only worked for free but paid their own money to the scammers.

The best approach to avoid being a victim of this scam is to simply not sign up for a job of receiving and shipping packages. Plus, as in any of these check overpayment scams, don't refund any money from a check. Instead, ScamGuard recommends asking the company to reissue the check for the correct amount. It is likely that the scammer will either insist that you send out the overpayment as instructed or cut his losses, so you will never hear from the scammer again.

Dating and Relationship Scams

This is one of the cruelest scams, since the scammers are playing on the victim's search for a love relationship, so the victim not only feels betrayed in love but loses money. In the typical approach, which begins on one of the dating sites or in the relationships section of an online classified site like Craigslist, the scammer responds to your ad—or maybe you respond to the scammer's ad. In either case, the scammer provides a cover story along with some photos, which can readily be obtained online to convey the image the scammer wants to present.

One way to expose a potential scammer early on is to check out where the scammer is from and avoid long-distance relationships, since scammers don't care how far away you are. In fact, the farther away the better, since you are less likely to be able to meet, which makes it easier to hide the truth. Another way to check out the scammer's story is to ask questions about the place the scammer claims to be from, where they go to school, where they work, and what they do. You may discover contradictions or errors should you do some research online about their location or profession. Ask to see current photos, or even ask them to take and send you a photo on the spot from their phone or webcam. Or if they claim that isn't possible, ask them to send a photo of them holding a paper with a message to you or write their username on their hand, so you know you have a photo of the person you are communicating with in real time. If you can't get such a photo, it's a sign this is likely a scam. But often victims don't do these checks, so they get increasingly drawn into thinking they have a real love relationship, when it's all part of the build-up for the scam.

Another sign of a scammer is someone who comes on too quickly after you have just met online. They may talk about how perfect you seem for each other, how you were brought together by fate or God, and may even mention marriage. Another warning sign, according to ScamGuard, is they may "say they feel depressed when they don't talk to you." The idea of this kind of talk about how close you are is to "manipulate your emotions," so you feel invested in the relationship.[3]

The final stage of the scam, after having built up these feelings of love and maybe marriage in the future, is to ask you for money because of some emergency. For example, your newfound love is suddenly struck by a serious illness, is involved in a car accident, needs a medical treatment for cancer, or whatever. The bottom line is that he or she now needs cash. Or maybe he or she is very eager to meet you and wants money in order to come visit. As soon as the request for money comes, you can be fairly sure it's a scam. It's time to end the relationship and move on.

Otherwise you could become the victim of a scam, such as reported by Murraya, who recognized the scam once her romantic partner began asking for money, and Sheila, who was tricked into sending money; the man disappeared once she questioned him about some contradictions.

As Murraya, who felt betrayed by love, reported:

Unfortunately, I was romance scammed on Match.com. I was romanced, sweet talked, sent flowers, teddy bear, and told that I was his so-called destiny. He was extremely clever, intelligent, and his profile and pictures were quite believable. Except now, he is in Ghana on business. He has called me numerous times and the country code does match. However, the last communication was he was robbed and everything he had was taken. Can I send money to help. Of course I refused, he did not get upset and said he understood. Have not heard from him for two days.

Usually, he would call, text several times a day. Probably, he moved on because I refused to help. Tried several websites to detect him but neither his name or e-mail register. Ladies beware! Be very careful, people are our to break our hearts and destroy our lives. It is not our fault, they are trained to do these horrible things. I only wish I could get him incarcerated!

For Sheila, the betrayal was doubly painful because the scammer took her money as well as her love. As she described it:

I met Hassan Muhammad (an arab man) at Shaadi (martimonial) website. I was romanced with his sweet talk, sent me many beautiful viber messages & i totally fall in love with him. Saw him twice on skype and he was based in UK. After 2 weeks he claimed that he have a project in Miri Sarawak and after he finish his project he will come visit me in Singapore. When he arrived (in) Miri, he ask me to transfer 4k as he claimed that he did not bring enough money to pay the workers there. I was trick to believe him and did a transfer of 7 times to a malaysian bank account totaling to 6k from dec'13 to Mar'14.

Till today he did not visit me and stop calling me cause i confronted him on viber why is one of the account number name is complained at scamguard website. I went mentally sick and was so afraid to even tell my friends and family.

But eventually i managed to gather my strength to report him to police in malaysia. However with very little details about him, i doubt it the police can do anything. Hard lesson learned after my first time going online to get a boyfriend. Hope this scammer will be caught soon. Such a heartless bastard ever been born in this world cheating woman's money.

Phony Ads for Cars and Other Products and Services

Aside from the scammers selling counterfeit products or just trying to get your credit card or bank account information online, there are the even more dangerous ads where the ads are a come-on for a personal meeting that turns into a robbery, or worse. From time to time these stories surface in the paper, where someone responds to an ad to buy a car, laptop, or other product and goes to meet the seller, only to find there is nothing to buy. Instead, the ad was designed to lure the victim to a house or isolated location where the seller and an associate or two can rob the victim of the money brought for the purchase, as well as other money he or she might have, and sometimes the robbers will take credit cards, watches, or other valuables. In some cases, the victims not only lose their money, but can end up dead.

The opposite scenario is where the victim places the ad and the criminal responds as if he or she is a real buyer. But at the meeting, instead of bringing money, the "buyer" pulls out a gun and may take the product for sale as well as any money the victim has on hand. And here, too, the victim might end up being killed, especially if he or she resists the robber or robbers.

In this case, the best approach, if one does place or answer these ads, is to carefully screen all the callers to get identifying information and even call them back. It's best to first meet the other person at a public location, such as a coffee shop, where there are other people, even if you are the one placing the ad. If you feel comfortable with the person you have met, you can show a small product where you are or walk together to the location of the car or other product.

Investment Scams

There are also all kinds of investment schemes, which could fill a book of their own. As one might expect, this is a fertile field for frauds since this is where the money is, so scammers of all stripes come up with a wide variety of approaches. They can readily find victims, since many investors have limited knowledge about how the many different mechanisms for earning money work, making them vulnerable to apparently knowledgeable financial professionals advising them.

Here are just some of the major investment scams, as described by the New York State Attorney General Eric T. Schneiderman:[4]

- Promissory notes may offer investors the promise of high returns of 15 percent or more but little or no risk, typically with a maturity of nine months, and they are often sold by independent insurance agents. But often the notes are short-term debt instruments issued for a fraudulent institution or companies that don't exist.

- Prime bank schemes claim to offer triple-digit returns due to access to the investment portfolios of the world's elite banks, so the investor can gain access to the "secret" investments of the wealthiest people in the world like the Rothschilds. In reality, the "prime bank" term usually refers to the top fifty or so banks in the world that trade in high-quality and low-risk instruments, such as Federal Reserve notes and International Monetary Funds bonds. Con artists often use this term to claim they are using investor funds to purchase and trade the instruments of these banks for big gains, but often these instruments don't exist, so people lose all their money, as pointed out by an Investopedia article.[5]

- In Ponzi schemes, the initial investors get a high rate of return from the money from later investors, who lose it all when the scheme collapses. The emphasis is on bringing in new investors rather than selling a product or service. Some common signs of a scheme include an invitation from someone you know to go to an opportunity meeting, a powerful presentation that offers you a quick means to wealth, big commissions for products, courses, or recruiting others, and an emphasis on bringing in others so the pyramid keeps growing.

- Boiler room operations start with cold callers who call about a new business. While some of these new businesses may be legitimate, the signs one isn't include strangers calling from another state trying to sell you an unfamiliar investment, vague responses to your questions, an unwillingness to disclose the actual street address of the office rather than its drop box number, and high-pressure sales methods to get you to invest now or lose the opportunity.

- Coin swindles offer an opportunity to invest in rare coins that will increase in value over the years. Often this expected increase in value is not true.

- Precious metal schemes are run by con artists who claim to be offering gold, silver, platinum, or other precious metals direct from the mines using a new technology to recover trace amounts that other companies haven't been able to obtain.

- Gold bullion scams feature con artists who don't really deliver the gold bars, but claim they are storing them in vaults. But in one such scheme, the scammers never even bought any gold; they just took the millions from investors for themselves.
- Pump-and-dump stock schemes are those in which con artists push a stock, usually a low-cost stock for $5 or less, which a small group of insiders have bought. The scammers claim that the stock will greatly increase in value, perhaps because of a big business deal or breakthrough technology about to be announced. But then after the price is pumped up, the scammers quickly make a big profit by selling their stock, after which the price plummets, and the remaining shares sold to unwary investors can become worthless. There may not even be a business deal or breakthrough technology in the first place.
- Phony international investments are schemes in which scammers offer high returns on certificates of deposits or other investments through a bank that only exists on paper. Even legitimate foreign investments can be risky because of "loose or nonexistent investor protection regulation, currency fluctuations, limited opportunities to pursue grievances, and political instability in some nations."
- In phony franchise and business opportunities, potential business owners are given inaccurate information about the real worth of the business. Often investors may be misled because the ad for the business opportunity appears in a newspaper, magazine, or TV program with a good reputation. But these outlets commonly don't screen ads. And some pitches for start-ups promising high returns for those on the ground floor are designed to just bring in money for the con artists, and the business never starts up.

Still other saving and investment scams may be offered by free financial seminars, where the presenters promote products and services that are for sale. While some are legitimate offerings, others are scams. Another type of scam offers investors the opportunities to buy pre-IPO shares of popular companies, such as a Facebook or Twitter, using a variety of promotions on the social media, Internet sites, phone, email, or in-person pitches.[6]

Finally, some additional investment cons described by Financial Mentor include these:[7]

- Penny stocks, which are ripe for investment fraud because many of these stocks fall below the minimum asset and shareholder requirements for SEC reporting and there is rarely any legitimate coverage by analysts or the press, so scam artists can easily evade scrutiny. Then, too, because of their low prices, small daily volume, and small number of stocks issued, con artists can readily control the stock and artificially manipulate prices, such as in a pump-and-dump scheme. And then because there is limited volume, it can be difficult to sell off a large number of shares without pushing down the price.
- Affinity groups, in which con artists recruit a trusted, leading member of the group, who commonly doesn't know much about investments, into pitching the fraud to others in the group. A common ploy is to claim that the group, such as a church or professional organization, will benefit the group as well as the investor. The fraud works well because it places a trusted individual in the role of the sales person, which overrides "the natural distrust we have for schemes promoted by strangers."[8]
- Bogus business offerings that promise low-risk, easy money investments, particularly when these are certain types of businesses. Among these are oil and gas scams, where you are offered a "working interest" in "proven oil and gas wells," but in fact end up investing in fake drilling equipment on worthless land or vacant wells that haven't produced anything for a very long time. Another area ripe for fraud is new technologies where people are asking for investments in a new patent or invention that will make you wealthy. Because there are many legitimate franchises, it can be easy to be taken in by a bogus franchise where scammers use over-inflated store results and phony testimonials to get large upfront franchise fees for services, supplies, and goods that they have represented to be worth much more than they are.[9]

Publishing Scams

Finally, since I'm involved personally in the publishing industry, I want to mention the widespread scams in the industry, since there are thousands of prospective victims who are trying to get into a highly competitive industry, and most have little knowledge about how the industry works. As Dave Bricker reports in "Publishing Scams and How They Work" on theworldsgreatestbook.com, "a huge industry has arisen to prey on writers who are unsure of this path." One type of scam is the self-publishing rip-off where the writer is overcharged generally about $1,000 to $2,000 to get a book into production, with inflated charges for editorial and design services. Even when the writer is promised a high royalty, sales are minimal, so the writer loses almost everything invested in producing the book.[10] It may get onto Amazon and Kindle, but it has almost no sales, since the publisher does almost nothing for distribution and promotion.

In addition, there is the agent scam, where the agent charges up-front money to review, edit, or revise a book or proposal, and then the agent doesn't sell the book. It can be perfectly fine for a writer to hire a ghost-writer or editor to handle editorial improvements. But there is a conflict of interest when an agent who is getting 15 to 20 percent to sell the book to a publisher also does that. In many cases, the agent is largely making money from the editorial services, but is getting to do them because the writer thinks the agent will be representing him or her once these editorial changes are made. The agent may do little to actually pitch the book; essentially the agent has become an editor-ghostwriter posing as an agent.

Avoiding the Many Scams That Are Out There

Given the vast number of scams that victimize many millions of people each year, what can one do? It would seem like there is a scam for every possible industry and taking advantage of virtually every technology. It is as if as soon as there is a new industry, a new technology, a new product or service, some scammers are out there thinking of how they create a new type of scam, which in turn is a way to outwit the reports of the scam, because it is too new. Just as a new legitimate company takes time to promote its products or services and build up its clientele, so does it take time for potential victims and scam watchers to know there is a new scam out there and so beware.

While some of the scams described in the book can be obvious give-aways, like the scams to get credit card and bank information or get victims to deposit a check and send the scammers cash, others can be uncertain when you don't have enough knowledge to know if something is true or not, such as when an auto mechanic tells you that you need certain repairs when you don't. This lack of knowledge and belief by victims is the major card that scammers play in order to appeal to and take advantage of victims. They are like good liars and sociopaths who conceal their schemes in a veneer of "truth-telling" and charm.

Thus, ultimately, it can be difficult to evade all scams since they pop up everywhere, and as society and technology evolve and change, so do the scams. But by taking into account certain basic principles and strate-gies, one can reduce the likelihood one will become a victim, and one can also report the scam to various agencies and scam report organizations to alert other prospective victims so they avoid becoming victimized, too—and at some point, there may be enough law enforcement interest that the scammers get arrested and convicted, too.

Where possible, deal with local and trusted knowledgeable individuals and reputable companies.

Even when dealing with those you know and trust, if possible, check out what they tell you by doing things like asking questions to get more information about their source, because sometimes they can be misled, too.

Never ever deposit an advance-payment check or money order, even if it looks real, and then pay someone the difference between the total and what they were supposed to pay you; ask them to reissue the check or advise them you will need to wait about three weeks until you know the check has cleared; at this point, scammers will generally disappear. You can also ask your banker to look at the check, since many will recognize a fraudulent check; not all do, though the bank's back office will know, which is the reason for the three-week time for fully clearing any check.

Don't give your credit card information for your regular card to unknown individuals and companies in buying products, subscriptions, and services over the Internet, especially if you are offered a free trial or special low-price introductory offer, which might be a come-on to get your card and then charge additional amounts that you don't realize you have authorized. One strategy to avoid such unauthorized charges is to transfer funds as needed onto special credit cards that normally have a low or no balance until you put in these funds, so individuals and companies can't put through additional charges without coming back to you for authorization, which you can turn down. Additionally, you might carefully read any terms and conditions agreements, which most people don't read or find, to see what you are actually agreeing to. You might find that the agreement is setting up the unsuspecting for a rip-off, because it indicates that the person has agreed to future charges unless he or she cancels the subscription or additional shipments of a product.

Closely monitor your bank and credit card accounts, perhaps through online banking, so you can quickly see if unauthorized charges come through. If so, you can quickly notify the company to refund these charges. If they don't, you can complain to your credit card company or file an affidavit of fraud with your bank, and commonly the card company or bank will refund these charges.

Don't give out your personal identity or bank account information to individuals or companies you don't know after an initial contact or when you first get approached about a job opportunity, since this is often a fishing expedition by the scammers to get this information.

Recognize that sometimes the website or contact information for legitimate companies is spoofed when you get an email for an offer from that company, so when you email or call, put the real company's name or website in a search engine or browser, which will be likely to take you to the company's real site, and use that information.

Don't let high-pressure salespersons pressure you into making a quick decision, especially when a purchase or investment of several hundred dollars more is involved. Take some time to think about the offer, and if you have to decide right away, say no, because this is likely to be a scam. If it's not, the salesperson should be willing to give you at least a day or two to consider.

Ask questions to get specific details, and don't be satisfied with vague answers. Also, any specific details should match up with what you already know, such as the name of a place or person or any facts you can research online. Should there be a mismatch, be suspicious, though you might ask the individual to give you an explanation. If you find their response suspect, walk away.

In the case of investments, get specific printed information about the business, stock, or other investment opportunity, and don't invest more than you can afford to lose.

Recognize that any opportunity meetings or free seminars and workshops are free for a reason—to get prospects to buy or invest in something. Look for specific information about what you are getting and resist the urge to get caught up in the excitement that a good salesperson can raise at these events. Evaluate the offering as you would any offer to purchase or invest based on what you see in writing, not just what the salesperson tells you at the workshop or seminar.

Notice any discrepancies in an offering of a franchise or business opportunity based on an established reputable company, since this could suggest a hoax, leading you to think that the real company is behind this.

Be suspicious of any requests for money that come from the Internet or social media claiming to be from a friend, relative, or business associate, whether they are requests for help while in a foreign country or for any other reason, since this could come from a hacked account. If you are tempted to help, check out the request by trying to contact the friend, relative, or business associate by phone or contact their close family members to see if they could really be where they say or are actually at home.

Check out any suspicious product, service, or investment offerings you are considering on various scam websites, such as Ripoff Report, Scamwatch, and SpamGuard.

Pay attention to reports of scams and hoaxes that appear in the newspapers and on the Internet news from time to time. Then, steer clear of them.

If you become aware of or are the victim of a scam, report your experience to the appropriate law enforcement officials, such as the local police or sheriff if this is a scam in your area, or to the appropriate FBI office (www.fbi.gov/contact-us), or to the Internet Crimes Complaint Center (www.ic3.gov/default.aspx).

In sum, be aware—be very aware—because especially in these days of the Internet and all kinds of new technologies, there are an increasing number of scams taking advantages of these technologies. It is also easier to create false identities on the Internet and gain information about others who could be prospective scam victims. At the same time, while the lack of privacy controls on the Internet make private information about others increasingly accessible, the scammers are able to skillfully mask who they are by creating false identities and personas and easily move around as they create new scams. So people you know and trust can easily become spoofed or victims, as well.

Thus, while there may be no foolproof way to avoid being scammed, you can at least reduce the likelihood that you will fall for a scam or reduce your potential losses.

Notes

1   "Psychics, Clairvoyants and Other Lucky Charms," *Types of Scams,* WA Scamnet, http://www.scamnet.wa.gov.au/scamnet/Types_Of_Scams-Psychics_clairvoyants_and_other_lucky_charms.htm

2   "Top Scams of 2015," Scam Guard, https://www.scamguard.com/list-of-scams

3   https://www.scamguard.com/how-to-avoid-dating-scams

4   "Common Investment Scams," Attorney General Eric T. Schneiderman, http://www.ag.ny.gov/investor-protection/common-investment-scams

5   "Investment Scams: Different Types of Scams," Investopedia Staff, http://www.investopedia.com/university/scams/scams1.asp

6   "Saving and Investing Scams," *Investor Scam Alert: Avoiding Investment Scams,* http://www.usa.gov/topics/consumer/scams-fraud/money/investment-fraud.shtml

7   "16 Investment Frauds You Must Avoid," Financial Mentor.com, http://financialmentor.com/free-articles/investment-advice/investment-fraud/16-investment-frauds-you-must-avoid

8   Ibid.

9   Ibid.

10 Dave Bricker, "Publishing Scams and How They Work," *WGB,* April 15, 2015. http://theworldsgreatestbook.com/self-publishing-scams.

Books for Future Reference

Anthony, T. (2013). *How to Avoid Work at Home Email Scams*. Thomas Anthony Publisher.

Dupree, S. (2013). *How to Spot and Avoid a SCAM: Protect Your Money*. Amazon Digital Services.

Elliott, C. (2011). *Scammed: How to Save Your Money and Find Better Service in a World of Schemes, Swindles and Shady Deals*. Wiley.

Felix, M. (2014). *Internet Scam for Beginners*. Amazon Digital Services.

Gilbert, D. (2012). *Scam Proof Your Online Shopping—Safety Tips for Shopping Online*. Donald Gilbert Publisher.

Johnson, S. (2009). *Scams, Schemes, and Fraud: How Not to Become a Victim*. Milligan Books.

Kirchheimer, S. (2007). *Scam-Proof Your Life: 377 Smart Ways to Protect You & Your Family from Ripoffs, Bogus Deals & Other Consumer Headaches*. Sterling.

Kiyosaki, R. T. (2013). *Rich Dad Scams*. Plata Publishing.

Koukouvitis, T. (2013). *Scam Detection Kit: Scientific Tools to Demolish Hoaxes, Scams, Frauds and Everything In-Between*. Thodore Koukouvitis Publisher.

Leamy, E. (2004). *The Savvy Consumer: How to Avoid Scams and Ripoffs that Cost You Time and Money*. Capital Ideas.

Munton, J. (2011). *The Con: How Scams Work, Why You're Vulnerable, and How to Protect Yourself*. Rowan & Littlefield Publishers.

Murray, P. M. (2010). *Consumer Fraud & Financial Scams Exposed: The Lowdown on 18 Scams You Should Never Fall For*. Amazon Digital Services.

Reeves, H. (2013). *Scams, Frauds, and Hoaxes.* Amazon Digital Services.

Ricker, B. (2012). *Scam Faces and Deception.* Amazon Digital Services.

Shadel, D. (2012). *Outsmarting the Scam Artists: How to Protect Yourself from the Most Clever Cons.* Wiley.

Stevenson, R. J. (2000). *The Boiler Room and Other Telephone Sales Scams.* University of Illinois Press.

Weisman, S. (2008). *The Truth about Avoiding Scams.* FT Press.

Wright, S. (2006). *Don't Get Burned on EBay: How to Avoid Scams and Escape Bad Deals.* O'Reilly Media.

Appendix

Following are examples of the Beau Derma/Revita Eye ads.

BEAUDERMA

HOME

Beau Derma Skin Care Solution

A Simple Solution Better than Botox

Many results have shown that you will be able to reduce all the signs of aging, including wrinkles, bags, age spots, crow's feet and many other benefits in your skin you will see with our new amazing skin care formula. If you have tried various methods to look wrinkles and look younger, but nothing seems to be working for you? When people start thinking about reducing wrinkles they think about all the ways you can do it, the most popular ways are Botox injection, Laser surgery and even cosmetic surgery but these solutions are not the way you should be using.

>>Click Here to claim your trial bottle of Beau Derma while supplies last!<<

These solutions are not the most natural and won't always help your skin the way you want. We...

>>Click Here to claim your trial bottle of Beau Derma while supplies last!<<

These solutions are not the most natural and won't always help your skin the way you want. We have formulated a serum that will help you reduce all signs of aging, reduction of wrinkles without having to have needles in your skin, or any doctor visits. Our formula Beau Derma will help you at the most cellular levels and will equally start from the outside in instead of the inside out. This helps you look and then your cells.

Benefits of Using Beau Derma

We have seen clinically results when people have used Beau Derma an clock wrinkle reductions formula. In fact, we have seen more than 57% of the people have used this formula twice a day for 10 days have seen more than 74% wrinkles reduction. Apply this formula to your outer skin face and all areas you wish to heal, this cream will then absorb into your skin starting at the top layer of your skin. At the formula almost into your skin, it will touch every layer of skin heading its way into the cells of our skin repairing damaged skin, reviving the dead skin and keeping your skin and healthy.

- Healthier skin
- Wrinkle reduction
- Increase collagen production
- Reduce signs of aging

This formula was made from the most natural and amazing ingredients you will find in a skin care formula. Anyone can use this formula to have the amazing skin, they are looking for, this means both men and women of all ages. This serum will work on your skin no matter your skin type ruff or soft...

- Healthier skin
- Wrinkle reduction
- Increase collagen production
- Reduce signs of aging

This formula was made from the most natural and amazing ingredients you will find in a skin care formula. Anyone can use this formula to have the amazing skin, they are looking for, this means both men and women of all ages. This serum will work on your skin no matter your skin type ruff or soft; you will have the most amazing skin you have ever had. If you are ready to have truly amazing skin, then you will need to get started today with the most natural and advanced skin care formula around.

Smoother, More Amazing Skin With Beau Derma

There are many amazing results you will see while using this simple and easy to use formula to reduce all signs of aging. To learn more how this formula will work on your skin or to order your bottle of Beau Derma now, click on the order button below.

Recent Studies have shown that you will be able to reduce signs of aging much faster if you combine these our two step program below.

Step 1: order Beau Derma

Step 2: Order Revita

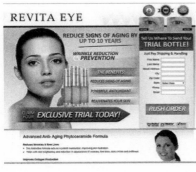
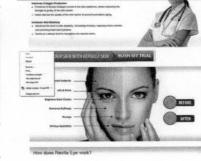
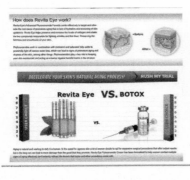

Index

Books from Allworth Press

Allworth Press is an imprint of Skyhorse Publishing, Inc. Selected titles are listed below.

Feng Shui and Money
by Eric Shaffert (6 x 9, 256 pages, paperback, $16.95)

How to Plan and Settle Estates
by Edmund Fleming (6 x 9, 288 pages, paperback, $16.95)

Internet Book Piracy
by Gini Graham Scott (6 x 9, 322 pages, paperback, $24.99)

Legal Forms for Everyone, Fifth Edition
by Carl Battle (8 ½ x 11, 240 pages, paperback, $24.95)

Legal Guide to Social Media
by Kimberly A. Houser (6 x 9, 208 pages, paperback, $19.95)

Living Trusts for Everyone
by Ronald Farrington Sharp (5 ½ x 8 ½, 160 pages, paperback, $14.95)

Millenial Rules
by T. Scott Gross (6 x 9, 176 pages, paperback, $16.95)

The Pocket Small Business Owner's Guide to Working with the Government
by Marc Lamer (5 ¼ x 8 ¼, 248 pages, paperback, $14.95)

The Smart Consumer's Guide to Good Credit
by John Ulzheimer (5 ¼ x 8 ¼, 216 pages, paperback, $14.95)

Your Living Trust & Estate Plan, Fifth Edition
by Harvey J. Platt (6 x 9, 352 pages, paperback, $16.95)

To see our complete catalog or to order online, please visit *www.allworth.com.*